FOLLOWING GOD'S PEDAGOGY

Principles for Children's Catechesis

Sister Mary Michael Fox, OP

LTP

LITURGY
TRAINING
PUBLICATIONS

Nihil Obstat
Deacon David Keene, PHD
Chancellor
Archdiocese of Chicago
October 12, 2022

Imprimatur
Most Rev. Robert G. Casey
Vicar General
Archdiocese of Chicago
October 12, 2022

FOLLOWING GOD'S PEDAGOGY: PRINCIPLES FOR CHILDREN'S CATECHESIS © 2023 Archdiocese of Chicago: Liturgy Training Publications, 3949 South Racine Avenue, Chicago, IL 60609; 800-933-1800; fax: 800-933-7094; email: orders@ltp.org; website: www.LTP.org. All rights reserved.

This book was edited by Michaela I. Tudela. Michael A. Dodd was the production editor, and Juan Alberto Castillo was the designer and production artist.

Cover image by Sabena Jane Blackbird, Alamy stock photo.

27 26 25 24 23   1 2 3 4 5

Printed in the United States of America

Library of Congress Control Number: 2022950057

ISBN: 978-1-61671-720-9

FGP

CONTENTS

FOREWORD

For many years the Church has sought to strengthen the work of catechesis, the direct teaching of the faith, because catechesis has an indispensable role in helping the Church respond to the call of the last three pontificates for a New Evangelization. The 2020 *Directory for Catechesis* represents the Church's newest efforts to clarify the particular nature of catechesis by situating it firmly within the evangelizing work of the Church.

In *Evangelii nuntiandi*, Pope Paul VI reminds us that the Church "exists in order to evangelize" (EN, 14). Indeed, everything we do in the Church must have a missionary aspect. At the heart of evangelization is catechesis. Catechesis is at the service of the new evangelization; the two are so interrelated and interdependent. Evangelization and catechesis are not the same thing: evangelization is the broader work of the Church; catechesis is a critical moment in that work.

The *Directory* highlights the centrality of the *kerygma*, the Good News of salvation in Jesus Christ, in catechesis. It points out that catechesis must be enlivened by the *kerygma* at all stages. This is because catechesis is never just talking about a set of facts, but always about introducing people to a Person—the Person of Jesus Christ. Catechesis is always, like everything in the Church, about bringing people into a deeper relationship with the Trinity through Jesus in the Holy Spirit. Thus, the purpose of catechesis is to seek and form disciples who have encountered Jesus Christ, who have surrendered their lives to him, and who will in turn become missionaries themselves. If we lose this understanding of catechesis, then we are simply just teaching facts and will never make true missionary disciples.

Thus, the Church today is calling for a renewal in catechesis that is an *evangelizing catechesis*, one in which the *kerygma* remains the constant proclamation even while a systematic exposition of the faith is given. On this point the 2020 *Directory* gives important guidance:

> We must not think that in catechesis the *kerygma* gives way to a supposedly more "solid" formation. Nothing is more solid, profound, secure, meaningful, and wisdom-filled than the initial proclamation. All Christian formation consists of entering more deeply into the *kerygma*, which is reflected in and constantly illumines, the work of

catechesis, thereby enabling us to understand more fully the significance of every subject which the latter treats. It is the message capable of responding to the desire for the infinite which abides in every human heart. (preface, 5–6)

Disciples are those who know the Lord personally. They have encountered his saving love and, like St. Paul, they have been seized by Christ, making him the center of their hearts. The temptation has been to consign this moment of conversion strictly to the initial stage of evangelization, yet we know that conversion to Christ is ongoing, and for this reason there can be no *systematic* catechesis without a simultaneous *evangelizing* catechesis. How does one go about offering an *evangelizing catechetical education*? Sr. Mary Michael Fox offers us a very good place to start.

First, Sister's historical review of the modern catechetical project corrects any naïve notion that the problems we face in catechesis are new or consigned to the post–Vatican II period. The Church has struggled for a very long time to recapture the dynamic catechesis experienced in the first centuries of Christianity. With the publication of the 2020 *Directory* and the Holy Father's institution of the lay ministry of catechists (*Antiquum mysterium*), we are in a position to return to the freshness of the first centuries of our faith.

Second, Sister's examination of what it truly means to be educated in the faith (DC, 31) moves the discussion of renewal beyond longstanding polemic positions that juxtapose those who favor a robust doctrinal or notional approach and those who favor an affective or experiential approach to catechesis. Catechesis must be both. It must proclaim Jesus in such a manner that he is *known* and *experienced* (DC, 2). As Sister so carefully explains, our catechesis must strive simultaneously to appeal to the person's intellect, will, and emotions.

Finally, Sister Mary Michael initiates a new conversation regarding the nature of catechetical content as it relates to the nature of the child. Drawing from her doctoral research of the unique approach to children's catechesis known as the Catechesis of the Good Shepherd, Sister helps us to see that the particular doctrine we teach to children must be communicated in a manner that they can receive and in a manner that stimulates a response of faith. Her insights into what she calls the *perichoretic* nature of catechesis offers a compelling argument for a catechetical pedagogy that integrates the theological, methodological, and anthropological dimensions of catechesis (DC, 179).

Sister helps us to recognize that *God* is the protagonist in all catechesis. As catechists, we have an indispensable role; yet it is *God* who enlightens the mind and moves the heart. He does so in a gradual, progressive, personal, incarnational, and beautiful manner. Through his deeds and words, God makes known to us his Plan of Salvation and invites us to participate in that Plan. His words are simple—poetic at times—evoking a sense of wonder that stimulates the mind and penetrates the heart. His actions are instructive—didactic at times—revealing the mystery of his love and his mercy. His invitation to follow him is clearly intentional, even while leaving us to respond in freedom. Our catechetical pedagogy must do no less.

Following God's Pedagogy: Principles for Children's Catechesis is a welcome and needed contribution to the Church's current efforts to renew her catechetical mission. Bishops, pastors, diocesan directors, and catechists will find Sister Mary Michael's work informative and compelling. The Church needs an authentic *ressourcement* in catechesis—a return to its original source and dynamism (DC, preface). This book is an inspiring place to begin.

— Andrew Cozzens
Bishop of the Diocese of Crookston, Minnesota
Chairman of the USCCB's Committee on
Evangelization and Catechesis

LIST OF ABBREVIATIONS

Documents of the Second Vatican Council

DV   *Dei Verbum*

GME   *Gaudet Mater Ecclesia*

GS   *Gaudium et spes*

SC   *Sacrasanctum concilium*

Other Abbreviations

AN   *Acerbo nimis* (Pius X)

CT   *Catechesi tradendae* (John Paul II)

CCC   *Catechism of the Catholic Church*

DCE   *Deus caritas est*

EG   *Evangelii gaudium* (Francis)

EN   *Evangelii nuntiandi*

FR   *Fides et ratio* (John Paul II)

LE   *Laborum exercens* (John Paul II)

DC   2020 *Directory for Catechesis*

GDC   1997 *General Directory for Catechesis*

GCD   1971 *General Catechetical Directory*

PDG   *Pascendi Dominici gregis*

INTRODUCTION

This book is the culmination of over ten years of academic research on the nature of catechesis. As important, it is the fruit of over fifty years of lived research. As a matter of academia, my research began in my postgraduate studies in catechetics. As a matter of lived research, it began in the 1960s when my mother first introduced me to God. She, God rest her soul, was my first and best catechist. How fitting for me that the new 2020 *Directory for Catechesis* was published on her birthday, March 23, the feast of St. Turibius of Mogrovejo.

Isabelle Margaret Lennon Fox was a woman who possessed a living faith. My earliest memories of self involve watching her pray and praying along with her. Long before she ever began to teach me about the True Presence of Jesus Christ in the Eucharist, I observed her receiving Jesus Christ in the Eucharist and, from her posture, I knew intuitively that something holy was happening inside her.

Mom had a way of bringing the faith alive through a variety of experiences. The year was marked by the liturgical seasons with regular celebrations of the saints; devotions to the Blessed Mother that included praying the Rosary in May and October and a very prominent altar to Mary; and during the Holy Triduum, participating in all of the sacred liturgies. My childhood was filled with daily Mass, weekly novenas, frequent confession, First Friday adoration, and donuts from the local bakery on Sunday. Week after week, I accompanied my mother to confession until I myself could celebrate this great sacrament of mercy. My mother didn't just tell me about Jesus, Mary, the sacraments, and the saints: she witnessed to me a life that was influenced by their reality.

My mother was not perfect. She had a real Irish temper and struggled against Jansenist tendencies inherited from her own catechesis; yet she wanted to ensure that my catechetical formation was marked by joy and sincerity, by love and truth. She wanted to instill in me an understanding that these components of faith are not incompatible. I have always known that Jesus, Mary, and the saints are *real persons*, indeed my closest companions. I loved them, and I knew that they loved me. I could also list the Commandments, the works of mercy, the holydays of obligation, and a whole host of other doctrines. I had my own copy of *The New Saint Joseph Baltimore Catechism*. What is more—*I loved it.* I am not claiming that my faith formation was perfect; I certainly would not dare to suggest that I was! But my catechetical formation, at least as a child, was always simultaneously one of the head and the heart, the body and the soul, knowledge of Christ and experience of his love. Over the years, I have come to recognize that my faith formation was quite the anomaly especially for its time because my mother offered me both a rich liturgical experience of God *and* a systematic intellectual study of the Church's teachings.

In postgraduate school, I studied the Church's catechetical texts with great interest and, at times, consternation. For many years, the Church has been exhorting catechists to examine their practice in light of the "divine pedagogy" and to authentically integrate content and method, doctrine and life, head and heart. I was particularly intrigued by a passage in *Catechesi tradendae* that reads: "There can be no opposition between *orthodoxy* and *orthopraxis*" (doctrine and life). . . . Christianity is inseparably both" (CT, 22). Perplexed, I questioned the matter, "Why and how would anyone seek to separate the two? After all, God wants us to *know* and to *love* him."

My question sparked a research investigation into the history of modern catechesis. There I discovered the roots of the polemical debates between two schools of catechists: one favoring a more "cognitive" approach to catechesis and the other favoring a more "existential-affective" approach. Again, the bifurcation between head and heart was bewildering.

Not long after I began my investigations, I was exposed to the Catechesis of the Good Shepherd (CGS), an approach to faith formation for children based upon Maria Montessori's work. Truth be told, I was there to "check it out," to see if it was faithful to all those catechetical documents I had recently studied. As I watched various "lessons" (which I now know are called *presentations*) unfold, I immediately recognized that something about this approach was different from the kind of catechetical instruction that I was using and had seen modeled by nearly every catechist I knew. The exchange between the catechist and the children was so conversational and yet with clear intent. The doctrines spoken were so simple and yet so profound. The materials were so beautiful and theological. I was deeply moved by the whole experience. It reminded me of my mom and how she introduced me to God.

I began to wonder: Could this be the approach to catechesis that the Church has been seeking in her documents? Could this approach bring together doctrine and life, content and method, the head and the heart?

Could it reconcile the polemic between religious knowledge and religious experience that continues to have a negative impact on catechesis? My doctoral research on the pedagogy of the Catechesis of the Good Shepherd approach sought to answer these questions. Colleagues in the field of catechesis and friends in the United States Association of the CGS with whom I have shared my research persisted in asking that my findings be published. That is why I wrote this book.

The goal of this book is to demonstrate to you that the CGS approach does indeed form the mind and the heart of the child. It does indeed reconcile religious knowledge and religious experience and it does indeed align with the Church's catechetical documents—so much so, in fact, that after reading the new 2020 *Directory for Catechesis*, I wondered which CGS catechists served on its committee!

Why the Church Needs This Book

For the past one hundred years, catechists have been trying to improve catechetical practice. One generation (1900–1940) thought the problem was methodological and tried to resolve the matter by finding better ways to teach the catechism. The next generation (1940–1970) thought the problem was theological and proposed doctrine in a different form other than the catechism. A third generation (1970–2000) saw the problem as anthropological: catechesis gave answers to questions people were no longer asking. The remedy, it was thought, would be to give greater attention to the person and his or her questions and experiences of God. Each of the catechetical phases had something to offer, but the emphasis on one component over and against the other left catechesis in a state of crisis that exists even to this day. This is because, according to the 2020 *Directory for Catechesis* (DC), catechesis requires an integrated approach; one that brings together in symphonic fashion its methodological, theological, and anthropological components (DC, 179).

The 2020 *Directory* recognizes that catechesis needs an authentic *ressourcement*—a return to its "original existence" (DC, preface). Just as there was a way of *being* a disciple of Christ (see Acts 2:42), there is a way of *forming* others to be disciples today—an intentional way. God has shown us this way. It's called his divine pedagogy (DC, 166). Even in the face of dynamic historical and cultural changes among God's people, the catechetical process must always remain inspired by *God's way*—his *original pedagogy of faith* (CT, 58). This is the hope and the plan for authentic catechetical renewal that the Church sets forth in the new 2020 *Directory for Catechesis*.

The divine pedagogy is a biblical concept that refers to God's way of revealing himself and his message of salvation (see DV, 15; DC, 13). It refers to the manner in which God called forth a people (see Isaiah 41:4); how he guided them along the path of righteousness (see Psalm 23:3); how he fashioned them into his Church (see 1 Peter 2:9). *Pedagogy* is also an educational term, understood as the art or science of teaching. It comprises two words: *paidos*, which means "child," and *agogos*, which means "to lead." A conceptual definition of *pedagogy*, then, would be "to lead the child." The image of the divine pedagogy as God leading the child is quite evocative, reminding us that God is the *true* teacher; we are but mere servants. Conversion, faith, transformation of heart and soul are all *God's doing*. And yet in drawing attention to the divine pedagogy, the Church is clear that catechesis is an *educational* activity and catechists do have an essential task of teaching the faith (DC, 180)—and in a particular manner (DC, 2).

What kind of educational experience does the Church want? Given all the other aspects of catechesis emphasized in the 2020 *Directory*, we know that it is not a matter of mere transfer of information. Rather, inspired by God's own pedagogy, catechesis is a "dynamic and complex reality" (DC, 8) that strives through a variety of ways to proclaim the truth of Jesus Christ as a living reality to be encountered and by which to be transformed.

In making the appeal to the divine pedagogy, the Church draws from a rich understanding of the ancient Jewish and Greek word *paideia*, which was much more than a specific content or even a specific method. No, the word *paideia* was an all-encompassing intellectual, physical, moral, and cultural transformation of the child into a faithful Hebrew or a true citizen of Athens. Thus, God's pedagogy draws together all the elements of catechesis necessary to bring a baptized Christian to full maturity in the faith as a committed disciple of the Lord (see DC, 165).

Yet the questions linger: What do the principles of God's pedagogy look like in catechetical practice? How does one proclaim Jesus such that he is known *and* experienced (DC, 2)? How does one accompany another in fidelity to Jesus and his Church along their journey of faith (DC, 8)? How does one create an appropriate spiritual, psychological, and physical space in which God can do *his* work of transformation (DC, 221)? How does one teach while allowing the other freedom of response (DC, 53)? How does one *"evangelize by educating and educate by evangelizing"* (DC, 179; original emphasis)? I am convinced that the Catechesis of the Good Shepherd approach is a critical place to begin finding the answers to these practical and existential questions.

Even though CGS is an approach to children's catechesis, its pedagogical principles can be, and in a few isolated places in the United States are being, used for adult faith formation.[1] The Church needs this book to demonstrate what the unique pedagogy of God can actually look like in catechesis. I have examined the unique pedagogy of the Catechesis of the Good Shepherd approach in light of the pedagogy of God and against the backdrop of the various efforts to renew catechesis. Specifically, this book answers the following questions:

1. *What are the theological standings of CGS? What is its content?*

2. *What are its anthropological standings? How does it understand the child?*

3. *What are its methodological standings? In what way is it able to communicate the content of catechesis in a manner that the child can receive?*

4. *What are the critical elements of the CGS pedagogy? What makes for a specific, authentic, and unique catechetical education?*

The reconciliation to the catechetical crisis, which I have determined to be a wedge between a cognitive approach to catechesis and an existential-affective approach (head vs. heart), is not found in the isolated attention given to any one of the components listed above, but only in the interdependent —*interpenetrating*—relationship of all three components.

By way of analogy, the interdependent relationship among content, method, and the child is similar to the interdependent unity that exists between God the Father, God the Son, and God the Holy Spirit, a theological concept artistically depicted as three intersecting ovals, as in the Celtic Knot. St. John Damascene used the Greek word *perichoresis* to describe the inner life of the Blessed Trinity as something of an *interpenetrating dance* among the three Divine Persons.[2] While each Divine Person remains distinct, God is *one*. It is not possible to adequately consider God the Father except in relation to God the Son. Nor can we adequately consider God the Son except in relation to God the Father. Likewise, the Holy Spirit cannot stand alone, for he *is* the loving relation that exists between God the Father and God the Son.

---

1. Patricia Coulter's 1992 dissertation demonstrates the impact that CGS training can have on the faith formation of participating adults. For many years, CGS Membership Coordinator Mary Heinrich offered presentations to RCIA groups and other adults at her parish in Urbandale, Iowa. In 2009, the General Chapter of the Missionaries of Charity Sisters voted to insert the CGS formation courses into their formation *ratio*.

2. John of Damascus, *An Exact Exposition of the Orthodox Faith*.

Such understanding of the inner life of the Trinity helps us to recognize that the nature of catechesis must also possess a *perichoretic* relationship between its theological, methodological, and anthropological components.

There is still no universal agreement among catechetical leaders and theorists as to the best catechetical approach, but the new 2020 *Directory* provides clear and hopeful direction. I have been relieved and encouraged to find that so much of what the *Directory* proposes is already embodied in the Catechesis of the Good Shepherd approach. More importantly, everything that I find in the CGS approach is confirmed by the 2020 *Directory*. If we want catechesis to reach its intended goal of making disciples through an authentic education in the faith, as we are inspired by the 2020 *Directory* to do so, our choice of catechetical *content* must be informed by the particular nature of the *person*. Simultaneously, our choice of *methodology* must be informed by *both* the nature of the content *and* the nature of the person. In other words, we utilize *this* content in *this* manner because of *this* person.

Why You Need This Book

In 1954, two Italian women began an experiment in catechetical education that paralleled the Church's most intensive examination of the nature and goal of catechesis. Sofia Cavalletti was a Scripture scholar and theologian schooled by Eugenio Zolli at the prestigious La Sapienza in Rome. Gianna Gobbi was a master educator schooled in the philosophy and methodology of Dr. Maria Montessori. These two women brought to catechetical education what had not yet been discovered—namely, that there is a unique manner *in which* God reveals himself to the child and *by which* the child receives him.

Cavalletti and Gobbi posed a question that has global repercussions: "If catechesis is to put the child 'not only in touch but in communion, in intimacy with Jesus Christ' (CT, 5), what method helps us to do this?"[3] It is a question that all catechists should ask themselves. In an unrelenting quest to find the best answer to that question, the theologian and the educator embarked on a fifty-year catechetical *adventure* in children's catechesis. They referred to it as such because they did not lead the way: they followed God and the child. The result of their adventure, the Catechesis of the Good Shepherd, probes the conventional understanding of catechetical content

---

3. Sofia Cavalletti, Patricia Coulter, Gianna Gobbi, and Silvana Montanaro, *The Good Shepherd and the Child: A Joyful Journey*, ed. Patricia Coulter (Chicago: Catechesis of the Good Shepherd Publications, 1994), 38.

and reproposes it in a manner (method and language) that corresponds to the child's nature. In so doing, the CGS approach concludes a long-standing quest by catechetical theorists to reconcile religious knowledge and religious experience, doctrine and life, head and heart by bringing together in a *perichoretic* fashion the theological, methodological, and anthropological dimensions of catechesis. As a valid catechetical education in use in over sixty-five countries, the pedagogy of CGS strives to form the whole child—heart, mind, body, soul.

Regardless of the age you teach or the setting in which you work, this book will offer you a concrete application for a faithful approach to catechesis from which you can make adaptations to your own unique catechetical setting. The 1971, 1997, and 2020 catechetical directories give us the principles for catechesis. CGS shows you what those principles look like in practice. While certain aspects of the book no doubt will interest you more than others, resist the temptation to skip any of it. Encouraged in particular by the 2020 *Directory for Catechesis*, we have an opportunity to evaluate our catechetical practice and reorient our ministry in simple yet definite ways. This book offers a faithful point of reference for you to do just that. Those who are familiar with or perhaps are already using the Catechesis of the Good Shepherd approach will find in this book a clear and compelling articulation for what the approach is and what it is not.

Chapters 1–4 provide a condensed narrative of the catechetical movements throughout the twentieth and twenty-first centuries, which sought to remedy the problems in catechesis. The conversation is not merely a matter of looking at the past. Catechesis continues to be impacted negatively by various prejudices related to catechetical content, method, and the person receiving catechesis. It is my hope that these chapters will help you navigate the perennial challenge that catechists face to be both innovative and faithful. Chapter 5 provides a selected review of current attempts to renew catechesis in light of God's pedagogy. Each attempt has considerable merit and is worthy of more explanation than this book can afford. That being said, I find that the Catechesis of the Good Shepherd approach offers the fullest expression of God's pedagogy and offers all catechists specific insight into and application of the principles of that pedagogy.

Chapter 6 explores the biographical background of the main architects of the CGS approach, Sofia Cavalletti and Gianna Gobbi. Included in this chapter is also an exposition of the life and work of Dr. Maria Montessori, whose philosophy of education and anthropology of the child greatly influences the CGS approach. This chapter gives you confidence that

Cavalletti and Gobbi did not stand on their own, but in the tradition of all great Catholic thinkers, they drew from the treasury of the Church, both the old and the new (see Matthew 13:52).

Chapters 7 and 8 examine the catechetical content of CGS. The 2020 *Directory* offers a needed explication regarding catechetical content and one that the CGS approach has embraced all along: "God has shown himself. In person. And now the way to him is open. The novelty of the Christian message does not consist in an idea but in a fact: God has revealed himself" (DC, 13, quoting Pope Emeritus Benedict XVI).

Chapters 9 and 10 examine the particular qualities and needs of the child that Cavalletti and Gobbi recognized and responded to in the catechetical setting. The child has his own hungers and thirsts for God that have not historically been recognized, much less appreciated. In a profound gesture of humility, the scholar of theology (Cavalletti) and the master educator (Gobbi) chose to follow the child rather than impose preconceived ideas of what a child should think, say, or feel about God. Fifty years before the 2020 *Directory* drew attention to the fact, these women recognized that children "have the capacity to pose meaningful questions relative to creation, to God's identity, to the reason for good and evil, and are capable of rejoicing before the mystery of life and love" (DC, 236).

Chapters 11 and 12 examine the nature of education and the CGS method of signs that Cavalletti and Gobbi recognized as the best way of communicating to the child the mysteries of the Catholic faith. Through a method of signs and typology, the child comes to receive the deposit of faith all while leaving open for the child those "pathways of discovery" and "existential doorways" to his inexhaustible mystery (DC, 2).

Chapter 13 serves as a synthesis of the various elements related to content, the child, and methodology that converge to form a cohesive pedagogical approach. I have titled this chapter "Pedagogical Principles" to draw attention to this convergence. It bears repeating: the CGS approach does not work because it has figured out the right catechetical content or the right method or even because it has recognized the needs of the child; it works as an effective approach because all three of these elements come together in a *perichoretic* fashion that patterns itself on the pedagogy of God.

Finally, chapter 14 is the story of two catechists who experienced a "Copernican" turn in their approach to children's catechesis from their experience of being with children in the CGS atrium. As one formation leader shared with me, "It is often too hard to explain to others the beauty of the CGS approach. They have to see it for themselves." It is my hope that these compelling stories serve as a final inspiring argument that the pedagogical principles of the CGS achieve their intended purpose: to help the child know, experience, and respond to God's personal and inexhaustible love.

Is this book biased? I don't think so. I began with a serious academic investigation, and I do not gloss over a few points of disagreement with Cavalletti. Still, over the course of my thirty years as a catechist and instructor in catechesis, I have observed several catechetical approaches. I know of no other catechetical approach that embodies God's pedagogy to the same degree as the Catechesis of the Good Shepherd. I know of no other approach that possesses such a faithful and rich understanding of the content of catechesis. I know of no other approach that truly understands the unique needs of the child's mind, heart, and body. I know of no other approach that uses a method that fits both the content and the child in the way that the CGS approach does. Its pedagogical principles are unsurpassed and are validated, paragraph after paragraph, in the 2020 *Directory for Catechesis*.

In 1954, Sofia Cavalletti and Gianna Gobbi embarked on a catechetical adventure, but they did not go on a proverbial wild-goose chase. They were guided by critical guard rails: the Catholic Church, educational and theological experts, and the children. To me, it is clear that they were also guided by the Holy Spirit. Cavalletti and Gobbi were women of prayer, deeply steeped in the liturgical life of the Catholic Church and its doctrines. This is why they were able to create a catechetical approach that provides both a true knowledge of God *and* an authentic experience of him. God has always had a way to be with his people; to speak to them; to form them; to bring them into his eternal exchange of love (see CCC, 21). The Catechesis of the Good Shepherd knows this way—knows the pedagogy of Jesus the Good Shepherd. It's time for all of us to know it as well.

PART I

History of Modern Catechesis

Chapter 1
Critical Historical Background

Introduction

The purpose of this book is to show how the Catechesis of the Good Shepherd (CGS) approach to catechesis brings together, in a symphonic manner, the theological, methodological, and anthropological components of catechesis. This book is the fruit of many years of study and personal experience with the CGS approach. Though it is tempting to launch directly into my findings, it is necessary to examine first the history of modern catechesis, and I will point to 1905, the year that Pope Pius X promulgated *Acerbo nimis*, as the beginning of modern catechesis. It was not until I gave a thorough examination to the modern catechetical project—that intentional effort on the part of the Church and catechetical theorists to improve the practice of catechesis—that I came to fully appreciate the unique nature of the CGS approach, which stands out among all other approaches. My research has also enabled me to recognize how the CGS approach settles a long-standing conundrum in the field of catechetics that has set religious knowledge against religious experience in the minds of many catechists. I would like very much for everyone engaged in the work of catechesis to recognize the reasons for this conundrum in hopes that a new generation of catechists can form disciples of the Lord who *know* and *love* him.

The Church continues to experience a catechetical crisis. Millions of adults acknowledge having been baptized in a Christian denomination, but they no longer believe that Jesus Christ is the Son of God—much less do they affiliate themselves with any church. The reasons for this crisis vary, and it is not my intention to explore them here. I would like, however, to clarify a pervasive misconception promoted by many catechists and catechetical leaders, who cast blame for the crisis on a post–Vatican II "content-less catechesis" (see 1997 GDC, 30) or on a pre–Vatican II method of memoriz-ing the *Baltimore Catechism*. Both styles of catechesis have proved to be problematic, as you will come to see in this book.

In the field of catechesis, there exists two schools of thought that seem to be irreconcilable. One side argues for a more rigorous doctrinal approach, while the other argues for a more personal-experiential approach. More than once have I heard, "It's not about the doctrine, Sister. People need to fall in love with God." Equally as many times, I have heard, "The problem with catechesis is that it lacks rigor. We need to teach more doctrine." These two positions reveal a great misunderstanding and caricature on both sides of a polemical argument that pits religious knowledge against religious experience.

As I see it, the challenge facing catechesis today is in helping each side to recognize the importance of the other and to embrace both innovation *and* tradition. Catholicism has always been a religion of the *both/and*. God is *both* three *and* one. Christ is *both* true God *and* true man. The Church is *both* divine *and* human. In like manner, catechesis must strive to form *both* the mind *and* the heart to offer *both* a knowledge of God *and* an experience of him. What is needed to solve the catechetical conundrum is an approach that recognizes the importance of sound doctrine *and* the personal encoun-ter with God. We need an approach that engages the head and the heart—indeed, the whole person, body *and* soul.

The various attempts to improve catechesis have focused on one or the other of its primary components. In the course of the modern catechet-ical project, catechists have tried either to improve its method of delivery or the nature of its content. When neither of these attempts achieved the desired goal, others took a totally subjective turn, focusing exclusively on the person receiving catechesis to the detriment of offering a systematic and objective body of doctrine. Yet to be effective in making lifelong disciples of the Lord, catechesis requires an approach that understands the dynamic relationship between content, method, and the person—an approach that integrates, in a *perichoretic* manner, the theological, methodological, and anthropological components of catechesis. I am convinced that the Catechesis of the Good Shepherd approach does this, as I will illustrate through the course of this book.

You might be asking, "If we have an approach that works, then why study past mistakes in catechesis?" One reason is to avoid repeating those mistakes. By studying the recent history of catechetics, we can resist the temptation of being unfairly suspicious of innovation or being unfairly suspicious of tradition. Another reason is that the CGS approach is not immune to deviations and has to some degree already suffered from unfaithful improvisation that compromises its *perichoretic* genius.

Before moving ahead with our historical overview, allow me to stress once again the importance of integrating the three components of catechesis: theology, methodology, and anthropology; or in catechetical terms, content, method, and the person (see GDC, 149). As we will see in this chapter, an overemphasis on one or the other has created an imbalance in catechetical practice. This chapter serves as a backdrop against which we will examine the components of the Catechesis of the Good Shepherd approach, highlighting how it provides a beautiful, interdependent relationship among content, method, and the child. Why look back to the past? Because it is impossible to reconcile the current polemics in catechesis without understanding their root cause.

Modern Catechesis in Crisis

For the greater part of the twentieth century, catechetical practice underwent a series of radical transformations. During this time, catechetical theorists benefited and suffered from the influence of explorations in biblical theology, psychology, and educational theory. New ideas about the nature of divine revelation sparked theological debate regarding the nature of doctrine. New ideas about the human person championed a subjectivism and an individualism. New ideas regarding educational pedagogy rejected the deeper truths of the human nature and the nature of knowledge. All of this triggered, if not a real, at least a conceptual rupture between religious knowledge and religious experience in catechetical practice. While one generation of catechists emphasized the importance of knowing doctrine, a subsequent generation placed greater emphasis on fostering an experience of God.

Those familiar with the history of religion would agree that the tension between religious knowledge and religious experience is long-standing. Some critics, including Sofia Cavalletti, blame the scholastics (1300–1500) for a style of teaching theology that over-rationalized God. Others blame Martin Luther (1483–1546), who challenged the Church's authority to teach objective doctrine, championing instead a subjective interpretation of Scripture. Still others blame the Church's response to Luther that emphasized the objective nature of doctrine. In truth, the wedge between religious knowledge and religious experience began with philosophical ideas regarding the nature of *knowledge* and *reality* that influenced theological positions regarding the relationship between *faith* and *reason*.

Congruent with the challenges made against religious faith and religious knowledge were those put forward by philosophers against the very notion of objective reality and the mind's ability to know anything real or otherwise. Philosophers whose names are familiar—Hobbes, Descartes, Spinoza, Locke, Hume, Kant, Lessing, Schleiermacher, and Hegel—all left their influence on the way we think about reality and religion and ultimately on the way we conduct catechesis. A systematic examination of their influence is not possible here, but I want to focus specifically on two persons who bear immediately on our consideration of the wedge between religious knowledge and religious experience in catechesis: Gotthold Lessing (1729–1781) and Friedrich Schleiermacher (1768–1834).

Gotthold Lessing was a German philosopher and playwright. Lessing defended the Christian's right for freedom of thought over and against external religious authority. He was caught up in the philosophical arguments about the nature of knowledge that raged across Europe during the Enlightenment period (1715–1789). Though a baptized Christian, Lessing struggled with accepting as true anything of a miraculous nature contained in the Scriptures, due to the lack of rational proof for miracles. Faith in such irrational events was, for him, too much to embrace, referring to it as "the ugly, broad ditch" that he could not seem to cross no matter how hard he tried.[1] The saying "You just have to make a leap of faith" is something of a response to Lessing's ditch.

The German Protestant theologian Friedrich Schleiermacher likewise engaged the philosophical arguments regarding reason and faith, but from a different angle. Schleiermacher was greatly influenced by Immanuel Kant, whose revolutionary epistemology denied that experience could give us any knowledge of things as they are in themselves. Following the Kantian school of thought that knowledge remains in the realm of the subjective, Schleiermacher tried to leap over Lessing's Ugly Ditch by way of a personal (subjective) religious experience. According to Schleiermacher, the only way a person can gain confidence in the reality of Jesus is through a personal experience of him. He writes, "The piety that constitutes the basis of all ecclesial communities regarded purely in and of itself, is neither a knowing nor a doing but a distinct formation of feeling, or of immediate

---

1. Gotthold Lessing, "On the Proof of the Spirit and of Power" *Philosophical and Theological Writings*, trans. H.B. Nisbet (Cambridge University Press, 2005), 87.

self-consciousness."[2] For Schleirmacher, it is an experience of God that gives faith, not creeds or doctrines created by a church or through rational understanding.

For most of the sixteenth and seventeenth centuries, the philosophical debates surrounding faith and reason were limited to the secular academic world or within the Protestant churches. The Catholic Church held fast to the teachings of St. Thomas Aquinas. Little by little, however, the philosophy of the Enlightenment seeped into the minds of Catholic clergy, most notably Alfred Loisy (1857–1940) and George Tyrell (1861–1909). Loisy and Tyrell rejected several Church teachings and even the Church's authority to make dogmatic proclamations. Their emphasis on religious experience over and against religious knowledge remains a hallmark for the Modernist heresy. Certainly it is only by the gift of faith that we are able to believe anything contained in the Scriptures, but faith is not, and never can be, opposed to reason as St. Pope John Paul II so eloquently expresses in his encyclical *Fides et ratio*: "Faith and reason are like two wings upon which the human spirit rises to the contemplation of truth" (FR, 1).

The Modernist Heresy and Catechesis

The Modernist heresy that raged throughout the eighteenth and nineteenth centuries is almost too complex to define. Pope Pius X referred to it as "the most pernicious of all the adversaries of the Church" (*Pascendi Dominici gregis*, 3). Such condemnation by a pope sounds foreign to our twenty-first century ears, but we cannot begin to imagine the effects that the various Modernist doctrines were having on the faith of the people in the late 1800s. Thus, it would not be fair to judge the Holy Father's words as an overreaction by our standards.

One of the more damaging doctrines promoted by the Modernists was the theory of *evolution of dogmas*. A similar theory, known as *on-going revelation*, has been championed by the very influential catechist Gabriel Moran (1935–). The theory of *evolution of dogmas* suggests that God continues to give new revelation and, as such, doctrines that held true for one generation could completely change in a subsequent generation. The theories of *evolution of dogmas* and *on-going revelation* reject the notion of objective

---

2. Freidrich Schleirmacher, *Christian Faith: A New Translation and Critical Edition*, trans. Terrance Tice, Catherine Kelsey and Edwina Lawler; ed. Catherine Kelsey and Terrence Tice (Louisville, KY: Westminster John Knox Press, 2016), 8, https://onlinelibrary.wiley.com/doi/full/10.1111/moth.12363.

doctrine, suggesting instead that a person's understanding or experience of God can contradict the teachings of the Church.[3] This is not true.

The challenge to Tradition levied by the Modernist heresy precipitated the Church's fierce and necessary battle to guard the deposit of faith (see 1 Timothy 6:14–20).[4] In the wake of the Modernist crisis, Church theology (and thus catechetics) became entrenched in positions regarding religious experience and religious knowledge. The language of experience became suspect, while the object of the faith was reduced to faith in immutable propositional statements. The result in catechetical practice was that catechetical content became restricted to the catechism and catechetical method to its mere memorization. This is not to say that catechesis in the eighteenth and nineteenth centuries was a complete failure as evidenced by the number of saints during this time. Yet a closer examination of their lives suggests that more credit should be given to the faith formation they received in their home than to the instruction received in catechism class.

Attempts to Improve Catechesis

When we study the history of modern catechesis, we notice various phases of catechetical emphasis during which time catechists sought to remedy an observed problem in catechetical practice. These phases can be grouped as follows:[5]

- Phase I: Focus on Methodology (1900–1940): with the understanding that catechesis is more than mere memorization of doctrinal statements, such as those found in *The Baltimore Catechism*, catechetical renewal turned its attention to improving methodology.

- Phase II: Focus on Content (1940–1970): when efforts to renew catechetical methodology proved unsuccessful, attention was directed to revising catechetical content. The theological, biblical, and liturgical *ressourcement* awakened a discussion regarding the nature of divine revelation—and its sources. During this phase,

---

3. John T. McNeill, "Catholic Modernism and Catholic Dogma," *The Biblical World* (The University of Chicago Press) 53, no. 5 (September 1919): 507–514, https://www.jstor.org/stable/3136260.

4. Pius IX's condemnation of Modernism *Dei Filius* (1870) was followed by Pius X's *Acerbo nimis: De Christiana doctrina tradenda* (1905).

5. At the time of my research in 2011, I was alone in grouping these phases accordingly. I have since been relieved to find that a colleague in the field, Brian Pedraza, has also noticed a similar grouping pattern. See *Catechesis for the New Evangelization: Vatican II, John Paul II, and the Unity of Revelation and Experience* (CUA Press: Washington, 2020).

catechesis shifted the primary source of content from a catechism to Scripture and the liturgy.

- Phase III: Focus on the Person (1970–2000): In tandem with a cultural shift both within the Church and in the world, catechetical practice took on a more existential and phenomenological approach. For example, now during the catechetical session, greater emphasis was given to the sharing of ideas or experiences of God, rather than direct instruction in doctrine.

There is a fourth phase which has only begun to take shape wherein catechetical theorists are turning to God's pedagogy as the inspiring principle for catechetical content and method. We see in the Scriptures that God has a unique way of fashioning a people unto himself, an "original pedagogy of faith" (CT, 58). Though the 1977 Synod on Catechesis drew attention to God's pedagogy, it was another twenty years before the Church offered some guidelines for God's pedagogy in the *General Directory for Catechesis* (GDC, 139–142). Though more specific guidance is found in the 2020 *Directory for Catechesis* (DC), the practical application of God's pedagogy continues to elude most catechetical theorists, and this is unfortunate, because we have in CGS an approach that embodies God's pedagogy and in very practical and imitable ways.

Conclusion

This chapter provided you with a very brief—though critical—background to the ongoing polemic that theoretically pits religious knowledge against religious experience. In the following chapters, I will look at the various phases during the course of the twenty-first century wherein attempts were made to improve the state of catechesis. These attempts at improvement raise questions regarding the nature of catechetical content and methodology questions that I see answered in the CGS approach. Let us now turn our attention to the "methodological phase" of the twentieth century.

Chapter 2

The Search for
a Better Method

Phase I (1900–1940):
Concern for Catechetical Methodology

Warranted or not, several prominent catechetical leaders of the twentieth century, including Canon Francis Drinkwater, Maria Montessori, Josef Jungmann, Gerald Sloyan, Gabriel Moran, and Thomas Groome, hold *scholasticism* or some element of its neo-scholastic legacy accountable for the problematic separation between religious knowledge and religious experience in catechesis. Sofia Cavalletti agreed. In her seminal text, *The Religious Potential of the Child* (RPC, 1),[1] she identifies scholasticism as the reason catechesis fell into a kind of "formula-ism."[2] She notes in particular that the method of catechesis "became the transmission of propositions already solved and enunciated in synthetic form; there was nothing left for the person to do but to receive them as they were, without committing oneself on a personal level beyond the effort to memorize."[3] This approach fails to appreciate the true nature of knowledge as well as the true nature of faith. Because of the recurrent theme that cites scholasticism as the source of the bifurcation between religious knowledge and religious experience, the scholastic influence on catechesis warrants some attention.

---

1. Sofia Cavalletti, *Religious Potential of the Child: Experiencing Scripture and Liturgy with Young Children*, 3rd ed., trans. Patricia Coulter and Julie Coulter (Chicago: Catechesis of the Good Shepherd Publications, 1992).

2. Cavalletti, *Religious Potential*, 158.

3. Cavalletti, *Religious Potential*, 125.

The Scholastic Influence on Catechesis

The term *scholasticism* has been used as a catch-all phrase to describe several related characteristics of a certain type of catechesis that emphasizes intellectual formation. According to the Dominican scholar Victor White, etymologically and historically, scholasticism simply means the educational tradition of the medieval schools.[4] Scholasticism is a complex concept encompassing a vast time period (600–1400), numerous historical events, and a whole host of personages in both philosophy and theology. While there is much more to scholasticism, its defining mark was "the use of rational methods to [investigate] questions of theology"[5] and the method of teaching, organizing, and synthesizing Christian doctrine known as the *scholastic method.*[6]

The scholastic method was the rigorous application of a logical technique to the investigation of theological questions. During the scholastic period the monastic schools developed the ancient use of a three-part method of teaching: *lectio, disputatio,* and *repetitio.* The method began with a reading of the text (*lectio,* from which come the words *lecture* and *lesson*). This was followed by a period of discussion (*disputatio*) or rational argument regarding the text. Often the discussion was provoked by the master teacher's questions. Following this process of reading and discussing was a repetition (*repetitio*) of the truth exposed or concluded. During the lesson, one student was responsible for recording (*lectura* or *reportatio*) the live debate. Finally, the master teacher would dictate a finished argument known as the *expositio,* which in turn became a source text for further study.[7]

As a Dominican, I admit a certain bias in favor of the scholastics. After all, St. Dominic was inspired by God in 1206 to form the Order of Preachers specifically endowed with the charism of study and preaching. One of the mottos of the Dominican Order, *veritas,* identifies our zeal for truth; truth not in an abstract sense but in the very person of Jesus Christ who is "the way, and the truth, and the life" (John 14:6). Another Dominican motto, *contemplari et contemplata aliis tradere,* reflects the original purpose of scholastic study; namely, *to contemplate and to give to others that which is contemplated.* Contemplation of divine truth was the goal of the medieval schools. According to St. Anselm, universally regarded as the "Father of

---

4. Victor White, OP, *Scholasticism* (London: Catholic Truth Society, 1934), 7.

5. White, *Scholasticism,* 6.

6. White, *Scholasticism,* 6.

7. See Vivian Boland, *St. Thomas Aquinas* (London: Bloomsbury Library of Educational Thought, 2007), 18.

scholasticism," scholastic studies were not for the purpose of mere intellectual acumen, but for the purpose of "contemplation, understanding, and love of the supreme Good."[8]

Notwithstanding, "not all of the scholastic schoolmen had the sanity and sanctity of Anselm," White observes.[9] Enthusiasts became "intoxicated by the power of reasoning and showed a rationalizing tendency."[10] While White recognizes the good contributions of those saintly scholastic theologians, his final critique of this over-rationalization of the faith by many of the scholastic theologians is sharp: "[T]hey rationalized religion and deprived it of the element of wonderment and awe without which religion becomes a hollow mockery."[11] Lest a false caricature of scholasticism be perpetuated, I want to emphasize that the intellectual consideration of God is not the problem. The problem lies in limiting the intellect's power to only that of logic. Within the intellect are equally necessary powers of wonder and intuition by which we ponder the inexhaustible mystery of God. The unfortunate legacy of scholasticism is its overemphasis on disputation to the neglect of contemplation.

The question-answer method of disputation used in the scholastic method is easily recognized in the structure of the catechisms that began to appear around the mid-1500s. It is important to note that the Church has always had an array of sources and commentaries that contained a body of Christian data. The first-century Christians relied on the *Didache* to ensure that catechetical instruction had a certain uniformity thereby guarding the universality of the Church. St. John of Damascene (696–749) created a synthesis of doctrine entitled *De fide orthodoxa* (Of the True Faith), which influenced the Western scholastics Peter of Lombard (*Book of Sentences*) and St. Thomas Aquinas (*Summa theologiae*). Nevertheless, the catechism of the late scholastic period was of another sort insofar as it became the exclusive text for catechesis. Hence, the underlying complaint levied against "the scholastics" is often a complaint against a question-answer catechism. It is important, therefore, that we pause to consider briefly the nature of a catechism and its role in catechesis, reserving a fuller discussion of this for chapter 11, where I examine the unique methodology of the CGS approach.

---

8. White, *Scholasticism*, 13.
9. White, *Scholasticism*, 18.
10. White, *Scholasticism*, 18.
11. White, *Scholasticism*, 40.

Catechisms and Catechesis

In response to Luther's successful revolt against the Catholic Church—augmented by his own production of "The Small Catechism"—the Council of Trent (1592) obliged all bishops to provide catechesis for children on a regular basis. In the years that followed Trent, a series of catechisms emerged, and the emphasis on religious knowledge became the hallmark of catechesis. Not long after Trent, the over-correction of religious illiteracy created a crisis of another kind in that for the most part, the memorization of a catechism became the primary practice in catechesis. To be sure, memorization is not inherently problematic; in fact, memory has served as a critical component of faith since the Old Testament. The problem arises where memory becomes the storehouse for bits of information that hold no meaning for the child's head or heart.

Though I suggest a correlation between the scholastic method and the method of memorizing a catechism, it is, in fact, hard to know the *real* cause for such a method of catechesis. A parallel study of catechesis and world history would be most helpful in this regard. We know that in the mid-1500s and through the 1600s monasteries and convents in England and Germany were suppressed. France and Spain, though remaining Catholic, were at war with the Protestant countries. Poverty, plagues, and uncertainty of every kind hardly made conditions for catechesis easy. For this reason, we should look to the past with sympathy, recognizing that rote memorization of doctrine was better than no memory of doctrine.

What we do know is that in the 1700s, concern was voiced by several European bishops and catechists regarding the nature of catechetical methodology. According to Josef Jungmann, a catalyst for catechetical renewal in the 1950s, the primary concern of catechetical renewal during the 1700s was to formulate some kind of catechetical practice that would aid the transmission of doctrine in a manner "better adapted to the mental capacity of the children"[12] and "avoid the thoughtless memorization of texts which [children] did not understand."[13] Jungmann believed that the very genre of the catechism, "with its many definitions and enumerations [fostered a] certain mechanical procedure [in which] the main emphasis was on brain work and questioning."[14]

---

12. Jungmann, *Handing on the Faith: A Manual of Catechetics* (New York: Herder & Herder, 1959), 26.

13. Jungmann, *Handing on the Faith*, 31.

14. Jungmann, *Handing on the Faith*, 22.

More than merely criticize the methodological use of the catechism, the catechetical theorists during this phase offered other approaches. Jungmann identifies, among others, Father Bernhard Overberg (1754–1826), who dissociated himself from the "rationalistic spirit of his age" by presenting the faith in the form of a narrative.[15] In like fashion, the Archbishop of Salzburg, Augustin Gruber (1763–1835), resurrected St. Augustine's catechetical use of the ancient *narratio*.[16] There are others who should be added to Jungmann's list. In 1890, the Mission Helpers of the Sacred Heart (MHSH) were founded in Baltimore, Maryland, as a religious order founded for the purpose of catechizing children. In 1906, Italian educator Dr. Maria Montessori created a revolutionary way of educating children in both secular and religious studies. Beginning in the 1920s, English priest and catechetical theorist Canon Francis Drinkwater experimented with a new approach to the language of children's catechesis, relying heavily on the images that Christ used in the parables.

It is important to note that, for the most part, criticism levied against the catechism at this time in history was not initially a rejection of Church doctrine or a catechism per se. Jungmann, Montessori, and Drinkwater were all motivated by a sincere effort to find a better methodology for catechesis, one that could engage the child's heart as well as his mind. For Montessori, it was likewise critical that the child's body be engaged, recognizing the Aristotelian principle that all knowledge begins in the senses.[17] It is unfortunate that following this period of methodological experimentation, most catechists stopped using the catechism altogether, even as a reference for their own personal study.

In his assessment of twentieth-century catechesis, Cardinal Ratzinger criticized the departure from the catechism as "an initial and momentous error."[18] Likewise, Pope St. John Paul II, though himself a great proponent of finding better ways to engage the heart in catechesis, nevertheless provides a sober observation when he writes, "The blossoms, if we may call them that, cannot bloom in the desert-like places of a memory-less catechesis" (CT, 50). In chapter 11, I will examine the nature of knowledge (epistemology) and demonstrate reasons why this educational approach is insufficient for

---

15. Jungmann, *Handing on the Faith*, 29.

16. Jungmann, *Handing on the Faith*, 29–30.

17. See Maria Montessori, *The Absorbent Mind*, trans. Claude A. Claremont (Amsterdam: Montessori-Pierson Publishing Co., 2007), 167. See also Aquinas, De veritate, q. 2, a. 3, ad 19 and ST I, q. 84, a. 6.

18. Joseph Cardinal Ratzinger, "Handing on the Faith and Sources of Faith," in *Handing on the Faith in an Age of Disbelief*, trans. Michael J. Miller (San Francisco: Ignatius Press, 2006), 13–15.

gaining real knowledge of God and fostering the response of faith. Before continuing, however, I would like to reflect a little more on the concept of a catechism and why, perhaps, many catechetical theorists came to speak of it disparagingly.

Catechisms and Faith

In the years leading up to Vatican II, two schools of theology were in a fierce debate over the nature of divine revelation. One school, known as the *Thomists* or *neo-scholastics*, held the position that divine revelation referred to the communication of divine truths. The other, collectively known as the *nouvelle théologie* (new theology), held the position that divine revelation is primarily an encounter with God. There is not room in this book to discuss fully the deep philosophical and theological premises underlying the arguments.[19] The Thomistic theologians accused those of the *nouvelle theologie* of being "anti-intellectualists," possessing a Modernist "hidden agenda."[20] Conversely, those who ascribed to the *nouvelle théologie* accused the neo-scholastics of using a rationalistic theology detached from spirituality and the "dramatic world of persons."[21] We hear in these accusations the very polemic that pits knowledge against experience—head against the heart—that this book seeks to reconcile!

An inherent link exists between the arguments regarding the nature of divine revelation and those regarding the nature of faith and the role that propositional statements play in cultivating faith. What is the precise object of faith? Is our faith in propositional statements, such as those found in a catechism, or is it in God? This is a question that continues to confound many catechists.

St. Thomas Aquinas answers the question adroitly, "We do not believe in formulas, but in those realities they express, which faith allows us to touch. The believer's act [of faith] does not terminate in the propositions, but in the realities [which they express]."[22] *The Catechism of the Catholic Church* (CCC) furthers the insight of Aquinas adding, "All the same, we do approach these realities with the help of formulations of the faith which permit us to express the faith and to hand it on, to celebrate it in community, to assimilate and live on it more and more" (CCC, 170).

---

19. Several reputable authors discuss the issues fairly, namely Rene Latrouelle, Avery Dulles, Aidan Nichols, and Tracey Rowland.
20. Aidan Nichols, "Thomism and the Nouvelle Théologie," in *The Thomist* 64, no. 1 (2000): 3, 7.
21. Nichols, "Thomism," 5.
22. *ST* II-II, 1, 2, ad 2.

It is a false polemic to pit statements of faith against the act of faith. The Creed that we profess states that Jesus Christ is "true God and true man," yet we have not encountered this truth directly: it has been handed down to us from the apostles. From their encounter, we have inherited the teaching that Jesus is "God from God, Light from Light, true God from true God, . . . consubstantial with the Father, . . . who for us men and for our salvation . . . became man." By God's tender gift of faith, we are able to accept these truths with certitude, and by this same faith we are able to participate in their reality. The catechism is inextricably linked to catechesis because it articulates the faith that is common to the People of God (DC, 184). Diversity of people and plurality of liturgical expression can never replace unity of doctrine, which binds the Mystical Body of Christ in both *truth* and *charity*. That being said, whether or not the *content* of children's catechesis should be in the form of propositional statements, such as those found in a catechism, is an argued thesis in this book.

The Catechetical Response in Phase I

Despite the efforts to provide intensive catechetical instruction throughout the eighteenth and nineteenth centuries, it was apparent that religious instruction was not given expression in a rich home life and that the "de-Christianization of the masses was growing."[23] As such, the disunity grew between doctrine and life—*what a Christian professed and how he lived*. Toward the end of the nineteenth century, this bifurcation foreshadowed the challenges that would continue to impact catechetical practice throughout the twentieth century.

Pope St. Pius X, commonly known as the catechetical saint of the twentieth century due to his various catechetical initiatives, sought to increase both a knowledge of and a love for the Faith. Most notably, he lowered the age for reception of First Holy Communion, so that children of the tender age of six or seven could encounter the Lord substantially in his Eucharistic Presence. In 1905, he addressed the growing concerns regarding catechesis in his encyclical *Acerbo nimis* (AN). According to Pope St. Pius, the crisis facing the Catholic Church was due largely to the decline in religious knowledge. He writes,

> We are forced to agree with those who hold that the chief cause of the present indifference and, as it were, infirmity of soul, and the

---

23. Pius X, *Acerbo nimis* (Vatican City: Libreria Editrice Vaticana, 1905).

serious evils that result from it, is to be found above all in ignorance of things divine. . . . [T]here are large numbers of Christians in our own time who are entirely ignorant of those truths necessary for salvation. (AN, 1)

To combat this illiteracy, Pius mandated that children receive an hour of instruction from the "text of the catechism" (AN, 19).

Following the Second Vatican Council, the use of the catechism in catechesis, or its absence, was the subject of much controversy. Yet even in Pope St. Pius' time its use was met with opposition (see AN, 14). Given that *Acerbo nimis* was promulgated just two years before Pius X's condemnation of the Modernist heresy, it is likely that the opposition addressed in *Acerbo nimis* consists of any and all who placed a greater emphasis on an experience of God rather than knowledge of the Church's doctrine. Pius' *Pascendi Dominici gregis* (PDG) identifies several heretical teachings championed by the Modernists. Among them is the Modernist view that "religious sentiment" (experience) was the "origin and the nature of dogma" (PDG, 12).

It is important to recognize that already by 1905 an ideological—if not real—bifurcation existed between religious knowledge and religious experience. The Modernist heresy had tenets that were so subtle that it was easy for its opponents to fall into an *anti-experience* stance in an effort to hold fast to the teachings of the Church. Pope St. Pius X's insistence on religious knowledge, however, should not be seen as a stance against a personal experience of God. Certainly as one who would be declared a saint, St. Pius X must surely have enjoyed his own profound religious experiences. Neither should we interpret his insistence that doctrine be taught to children as reducing catechesis to mere knowledge about God. At the same time, we ought not reduce his appeal for catechetical reform to the mere increased use of the catechism. To do so is to fail to appreciate the genius of his catechetical project.

At the turn of the twentieth century, the fundamental concern regarding children's catechesis was its lack of lasting influence on their liturgical life and moral choices into adulthood. Since the standard praxis of catechesis at this time emphasized the memorization of the catechism without much, if any, attempt to help the child understand the doctrine, a number of catechists came to the conclusion that a significant contributing factor to the problem in catechesis was the misuse of the catechism and its resultant strict method of memorization. In tandem with Pope St. Pius X's call for catechetical reform, the mounting concern for children's catechesis gave birth to the *catechetical movements*, which aimed to improve methodology in order to produce a lasting effect upon the child.[24]

The Adaptive Way

Even before Pope Pius X's call for reform, a small group of religious women in Baltimore, Maryland, were already hard at work finding ways to help children learn and love the Faith. The Mission Helpers of the Sacred Heart were founded in 1890 for the purpose of catechizing the children of freed black slaves.[25] One of the founders, Mary Frances Cunningham—later Mother Demetrias—witnessed, with concern, the plight of these children who were receiving no religious instruction.[26] With the support of James Cardinal Gibbons, America's first cardinal, Mother Demetrias, along with other women of the St. Joseph's Guild, leased a house, converted it into a small convent, and used the basement of St. Martin's church to teach Sunday school.[27]

In 1930, the sisters developed a specialized method of catechesis called *The Adaptive Way*, which made use of materials such as Bible stories and pictures to encourage "active learning and help children grasp the content of the catechism."[28] They used the *Baltimore Catechism*, but did not use it in the customary manner of memorization and regurgitation.[29] Mother Demetrias believed that a more efficient way of learning Christian doctrine was to first understand the material and then commit it to memory. She proposed to do this by making catechesis a more interactive exchange between student and teacher.[30]

The Munich Method

In 1898, a German catechist named Dr. A. Weber recognized that the traditional system of catechizing children needed adaptation. Drawing from the

---

24. Jungmann, *Handing on the Faith*, pp. 33–40.

25. Mission Helpers of the Sacred Heart, "History," https://www.missionhelpers.org/community /history/.

26. Mission Helpers, "History."

27. Matthew D. Ingold, "American Initiative in the Modern Catechetical Movement: From the Release of the Baltimore Catechism in 1885 to the Publication of the General Directory in 1971" (Washington, DC: Catholic University of America, 2006), 18.

28. Ingold, "American Initiative," 19. Ingold's research includes writings only found in the archives of the Mission Helpers, specifically the work of Sr. Constance, "Historical Documentation of the Foundation, Spirit, Apostolate, and Growth of the Mission Helpers of the Sacred Heart: Book One" (1978).

29. Ingold, "American Initiative," 18.

30. Ingold, "American Initiative," 18.

psychology and educational theory of Johann Friedrich Herbart (1776–1841) and Tuiskon Ziller (1817–1882), Weber proposed an alternative method, which became known as the "Munich Method," named after the city where it was created.[31] Weber's idea is similar to *The Adaptive Way*. Before a child is asked to memorize doctrine, it must first be presented in a manner that engages her intellect and will. The approach is aptly called a method because it follows specific steps during catechetical instruction: presentation, explanation, and application.[32]

In the first step, the presentation seeks to engage the child's imagination and senses to activate her interest in learning. For example, if the doctrine under discussion is the Incarnation, the catechist might use a picture of the manger at Bethlehem and ask the child how she celebrates Christmas. The second step, explanation, seeks to engage the intellect on the level of understanding. This required catechists to break down the doctrinal truths into parts that could individually be better explained by making connections to other doctrines already studied or asking specific questions about the doctrine being presented. For example, the catechist might ask questions about the message given to the shepherds by the angels or even why angels were present at the birth of Jesus. The third step, application, seeks to engage the child's will and emotions. At this step, the catechist might ask the child how she would have responded to the angel's message or how she could imitate the shepherds who believed that the baby Jesus was the Son of God.

The Munich Method was revolutionary as a catechetical method in that it made use of the inductive process of teaching, which moves from the known to the unknown, from the concrete to the abstract. Its principles of learning, however, were already a part of the educational heritage of the Church in the epistemology of St. Thomas Aquinas. Aquinas identifies the various movements of the intellect and the will that occur during the process of knowing. His insights regarding the teaching, learning, and know-

---

31. Thomas Scannell, "Christian Doctrine," The Catholic Encyclopedia, vol. 5 (New York: Robert Appleton Company, 1909), http://www.newadvent.org/cathen/05075b.htm.
32. In 1993, the Munich Method was adapted by Msgr. Francis Kelly to include two more steps: proclamation and celebration. Known as the "Ecclesial Method," it is commonly used throughout the United States and has proven to be an effective template for the catechetical session. See Francis J. Kelly, *The Mystery We Proclaim: Catechesis for the Third Millennium* (Huntington, IN: Our Sunday Visitor, 1993).

ing process are found in a number of sources and explored further in chapter 11.[33]

The Sower Method

Canon Francis Drinkwater (1886–1982) was a priest of the diocese of Birmingham, England. Already inspired by St. Pope Pius X's call for catechetical reform, his concern about the state of catechesis was heightened after serving some time as a military chaplain during World War I. Drinkwater noticed that, though the men could not account for anything they learned in catechism class, they did remember the practices of the faith.[34] Drinkwater's experience sparked in him a life-long endeavor to seek a pedagogical praxis for children that was in "accordance with their age."[35] Drinkwater's solution was the "Sower Scheme," which came to be known as the "Sower Method."[36]

The Sower Method sought to provide a more appropriate way of teaching children according to their varied ages.[37] On this point about age appropriateness, Drinkwater anticipates the Church's directives that ask catechists to have "respect for the receptive capacity of those being catechized" (GDC, 148) and to be mindful of age-level intellectual developments (see DC, 236ff.). To promote his method and give assistance to catechists, Canon Drinkwater founded a magazine called *The Sower*. Drinkwater explained that "the aim of *The Sower* magazine was to spread the notion that religious instruction and training is not likely to have lasting effect unless it concerns itself with the heart as much as the head."[38]

The more Drinkwater considered the praxis of rote memorization, the more he became convinced of its problematic pedagogy. Addressing the 1949 international conference of catechists, Canon Drinkwater challenged the long-standing "misuse of the catechism as the material of a purely verbal memorizing." [39] Drinkwater questioned, "How did such an un-educational

---

33. *De Vertiate, Puer Jesus*, and *Summa theologiae* have been put into a summative exposition by Father Vivian Boland, OP. See Vivian Boland, OP, *St. Thomas Aquinas*, Bloomsbury Library of Educational Thought, series ed. Richard Bailey (New York: Bloomsbury, 2014).

34. Francis Drinkwater, "The Right Way of Using Catechisms," in *Educational Essays* (London: Burns & Oates, 1951), 96.

35. Drinkwater, "What the Sower Stands For," in *Educational Essays*, 72.

36. Drinkwater, "What the Sower Stands For," 72.

37. Drinkwater, "What the Sower Stands For," 69.

38. Drinkwater, "*De catechizandis parvulis*," in *Educational Essays*, 340. The catechetical mission of *The Sower* continues in *The Catechetical Review* Steubenville, OH: Franciscan University Press).

39. See Drinkwater, "The Right Way of Using Catechisms," in *Educational Essays*, 92.

custom ever become so general?"[40] Some would agree that the method of rote memorization was the result of an impoverished "general educational system put in place in the seventeenth and eighteenth centuries which relied on an exclusive pedagogy of memorization."[41] It does not seem that Drinkwater was against memorization per se, but rather its use as an "unintelligent rote-learning."[42]

Drinkwater readily admits the need for a catechism citing, "the sad results of an emotional misty vagueness in the Protestant teaching of religion."[43] Yet he is equally adamant about its proper pedagogical use:

> In religious instruction at all events, we certainly cannot do without words. The word of the Lord, the word of God—what else is the whole of our Faith but a Person and a Word? Only a word that must be made flesh, not a printed word of abstract definitions forced upon unready hearers. Nothing can be more powerful than a word, if it is the right word at the right time.[44]

Drinkwater notes that the child "needs the right sort of language: simple, concrete, the language of his own mental level. . . . [I]f the language of the Catechism is premature for the child it will remain meaningless to him however beautifully it is served up."[45]

Drinkwater specifies that the age when a catechism might be introduced is about eleven.[46] Though he does not provide reasons for settling on this age, it is commonly recognized that the intellectual horizon of the eleven-year-old child has greatly expanded and that the older child has transitioned into a "researcher" capable of gaining knowledge through the reading of texts. I know of several Level III CGS catechists who keep copies of *The Catechesis of the Catholic Church* in their atria to meet the intellectual hunger of the older child. Still, it is important to note that an eleven-year-old child who has experienced CGS Levels I and II has received significant formation in the mysteries of the faith, thereby aiding the intelligibility of the *Catechism*. Without such formation, the language of the *Catechism* would be beyond most eleven-year-old children.

---

40. Drinkwater, "The Right Way of Using Catechisms," 92.
41. Drinkwater, "The Right Way of Using Catechisms," 92.
42. Drinkwater, "The Right Way of Using Catechisms," 92.
43. Drinkwater, "What the Sower Stands For," 69.
44. Drinkwater, "Do Teaching Methods Matter?," in *Educational Essays,* 77.
45. Drinkwater, "The Right Way of Using Catechisms," 94.
46. Drinkwater, "The Right Way of Using Catechisms," 97.

As the right choice of the words remained a primary concern of Canon Drinkwater, indeed "the main thing in religious instruction," [47] he was equally concerned by experiments in catechesis that took an activities-based approach. He insists that "the activity-methods are on the wrong track if they neglect words," and "the parrot-system is mistaken because it uses the right words in the wrong ways."[48]

For Drinkwater, catechetical renewal demanded a proper integration of content-method, recognizing that a greater attention be given "to all the *activities* of religion, both to the private and personal activities, and the corporate or liturgical ones—and above all to everything connected with the Holy Eucharist and the Mass." [49] While Drinkwater is not referenced in any of Cavalletti's or Gobbi's writings, they would be in agreement that language is a critical factor in children's catechesis. In chapter 12, we will examine in some detail the importance of catechetical language.

About the same time as Drinkwater, the social sciences were breaking new ground in the fields of psychology and sociology and there was tremendous interest in applying new insights to educational theory. Catechists eager to find a way to educate children in the faith began experiments in educational pedagogy, with varying degrees of success. In his post-synodal exhortation *Catechesi tradendae* (CT), Pope St. John Paul II pointed out that

> [t]he attainments of the other sciences—biology, psychology, sociology —are providing [catechetical pedagogy] with valuable elements. The science of education and the art of teaching are continually being subjected to review, with a view to making them better adapted or more effective, with varying degrees of success. (CT, 58)

It is not in the scope of this book to examine all the experiments during this time. Only one has had direct bearing on the Catechesis of the Good Shepherd approach; namely, the work of Dr. Maria Montessori. Her specific influence on the CGS approach is further examined in chapter 6 of this book.

The Montessori Method

Dr. Maria Montessori (1870–1952) introduced a new pedagogy of catechesis in 1907 with the establishment of her *Children's House (Casa dei Bambini).* The *Casa dei Bambini* schools were established by Montessori as a place to

---

47. Drinkwater, "Do Teaching Methods Matter?," 76.
48. Drinkwater, "Do Teaching Methods Matter?," 76.
49. Drinkwater, "What the Sower Stands For," 70.

implement and evaluate her unique philosophy of education. These schools allowed Montessori the opportunity to observe children in a carefully prepared environment that aided the child's natural progress.

Although Montessori did not have the intention of officially uniting herself to the catechetical movements of the twentieth century, she joined the resounding criticism of the scholastic approach in children's education, particularly an education in the faith.[50] The magnitude of Montessori's insights is still being discovered. For example, Australian educator and international catechist formator Dr. Gerald O'Shea aligns Montessori with de Lubac's theological teaching on nature and grace, suggesting that her educational and catechetical principles serve to heal the rupture between knowledge and faith that began in scholasticism and continues in Catholic education and catechesis.[51] As a medical doctor, a voracious student of psychology, a proponent of Thomistic Realism, and a faithful Catholic, Montessori holds distinctive advantage when it comes to evaluating the effectiveness of a catechetical approach.

In her book *The Child in the Church* (first published in 1929), Montessori criticized the predominant method of memorizing the catechism, proposing instead the pedagogical method of the Church found in the liturgy.[52] Montessori sees the problem as "not so much a question of what to teach as of how and when." Her concern is the failure to recognize and respect the child as one who "has a principle within him," orientating him to truth and, more essentially, to God. [53] The Church's liturgy understands this principle and engages the child in the active learning of the faith without resorting to didactic instruction. The signs and symbols used in the Church's liturgy are in themselves instructive. "[T]he preparation of the child for his full participation in the life of the Church," she writes, "is a much wider thing than the learning by heart of certain intellectual truths. *It is life in itself.*"[54]

---

50. Maria Montessori, *The Secret of Childhood*, trans. M. Joseph Costelloe (1966; reprinted, New York: Ballantine Books, 1972), 109.

51. Gerard O'Shea, "Historical Discontinuity in Contemporary Views on Revelation," (PHD diss., John Paul II Institute for Marriage and Family, Melbourne, Australia, 2007). See especially chapter 15, "The Relationship of Knowledge and Faith," and chapter 16, "Montessori and De Lubac: A Confluence of Insights." See also *Educating in Christ: A Practical Handbook for Developing the Catholic Faith from Childhood to Adolescence* (New York: Angelico Press, 2018). Drawing upon his formation as a CGS catechist and a Catholic school teacher, O'Shea's book is an incomparable resource for all catechists.

52. Maria Montessori, *The Child and the Church*, ed. E.M. Standing (1929; reprinted, Chantilly, VA: Catechetical Guild Educational Society, 1965), 54.

53. Montessori, *Child in the Church*, 22.

54. Montessori, *Child in the Church*, 33; italics original.

In the Church's liturgy, "things [are] *done* rather than *read*." [55] These methodological considerations point to the nature of the child who particularly learns through doing and living, or better still, through "self-activity (*selbst-tatigkeit*) as Froebel called it." [56] Practical life activities, such as folding napkins, pouring water, polishing brass, and arranging flowers—hallmarks of a Montessori classroom—all serve as means of preparation for religious instruction and contemplation. [57]

Another key insight of Montessori was the recognition of the child's religious potential, which creates within her the aptitude for hearing God's voice, receiving his instruction, and entering into a deep relationship with him. [58] This is not to suggest that a systematic proclamation of the Gospel is unnecessary. Jesus clearly instructed his apostles to teach all nations (Matthew 28:19). It does recognize, however, that catechesis relies primarily upon the divine initiative, and catechetical methodology must give God primacy of place and action (GDC, 143). Young children do not require much by way of religious convincing. They already have a sense of God's reality. God is already in conversation with the child, whom he has loved into existence; *already* drawing the child to himself. Given the proper setting, the child is capable of hearing God's voice and responding with love. From this understanding of God's pedagogy, Montessori reintroduced to catechesis the importance of silence and contemplation.

Finally, Montessori recognized that the Church itself is a "specially prepared environment for drawing out and sustaining the supernatural life of man." [59] For this reason, she recovered from the early Church's catechumenate the concept of an atrium as a prepared environment for catechesis. The atrium was a special room designated for the purpose of religious instruction, usually attached to the church building to allow for easy access to the Church's liturgical life. The critical role of the *atrium* as a prepared environment for the child's faith formation is discussed in chapter 13 along with the other insights of Montessori that figure significantly in the pedagogical principles of the Catechesis of the Good Shepherd.

---

55. Montessori, *Child in the Church*, 33; italics original.
56. Montessori, *Child in the Church*, 59. For a fuller elucidation on the question of education through movement, see E. Mortimer Standing, *Maria Montessori: Her Life and Work* (1957; reprinted, New York: Plume 1998), in particular chapter 11, "The Significance of Movement in Education."
57. Montessori, *Child in the Church*. See especially chapter 3.
58. Montessori, *Child in the Church*, 22.
59. Montessori, *Child in the Church*, 32.

Conclusion

Phase I of the catechetical movement bears the hallmark of faithful innovation in catechetical methodology. All of the pivotal players at this time were animated by a genuine desire to communicate to children the message of salvation—the teachings of the Catholic Church—in a manner by which they could receive it with their mind and their heart. Many of the innovations of this time have resurfaced in our own time. The variety of activities to explain doctrine suggested by catechetical textbooks were inspired by the Adaptive Way. The Ecclesial Method that many catechists find useful originated in the Munich Method. Likewise, the CGS approach expands and deepens the Montessori Method as well as the Sower Method.

It is difficult to evaluate the influence of these early attempts at catechetical renewal. World War I and the Great Depression changed the lives of millions. People began to look more deeply into the meaning of life while theologians began to look more deeply into the meaning of faith and man's response to God. Phase II of the catechetical movement points to the desire for catechetical theorists to return to the heart of the faith by returning to the sources of faith. Mankind was in desperate need of a renewed proclamation of the Gospel and it was thought that a renewed approach to God's message of salvation might be just the way to bring about this renewal.

Chapter 3

The Search for Better Content

Phase II (1940–1970): Concern for Catechetical Content

"Beginning with the second period of catechetical movement, the realization became evermore widespread that a true catechetical renewal must also concern itself with the content of religious education."[1] So observes Josef Hofinger, noted theologian and catechetical leader of his time. Hofinger valued traditional Catholic doctrine and recognized the need for presenting Christianity as a system of truth in order to achieve a "fuller intellectual penetration of Christian doctrine."[2] Yet he also recognized that the style of systematic theology in use at his time had the tendency of becoming "theoretic and remote from life."[3] According to Hofinger, the typical presentation of the faith tradition through catechisms often created the perception that the main purpose of Christianity was "rules, restrictions, or limiting behaviors."[4] The content of catechesis needed renewal. As with the theological *ressourcement* of the 1950s, catechesis would benefit from a return to its sources, namely Scripture and the liturgy.

It does not appear that anyone has investigated the parallels between the *nouvelle théologie* and catechesis, but historically speaking, the evidence is strong that in the aftermath of the *nouvelle théologie*, catechesis experienced its greatest shift in catechetical content and methodology. Biblical

---

1. Josef Hofinger and F. J. Buckley, *Good News and Its Proclamation* (South Bend, IN: University of Notre Dame, 1968), 6.

2. Hofinger and Buckley, *Good News*, 6.

3. Josef Hofinger, *The Art of Teaching Christian Doctrine* (Notre Dame: University of Notre Dame Press, 1957), 44.

4. Hofinger, *Teaching Christian Doctrine*, 43.

scholar that she was, Sofia Cavalletti was certainly aware of the debates surrounding the nature of divine revelation and the views held by the *nouvelle
théologie* theologians. Fr. Giancarlo Panni, sj, worked with Sofia Cavalletti
from 1971 until her death in 2011 and knew her well. He explained to me
that while Cavalletti may not have personally engaged in the theological
debates of the *nouvelle théologie* theologians, she was "intellectually engaged
with their writings. . . . Their books were all in her library."[5] The names of
many of these theologians—Yves Congar, Marie Dominique Chenu, Henri
de Lubac, Henri Danielou, Tielhard de Chardin, and Karl Rahner—may be
found in the text or footnotes of Cavalletti's own books, articles, and course
notes. Clearly, their theology of revelation and history has influenced
the CGS approach and for this reason, the *nouvelle théologie* warrants our
brief examination.

La Nouvelle Théologie

La nouvelle théologie (literally, "the new theology") was a theological movement in the 1940s and 1950s that promoted a renewed approach to theology.
Those involved comprised a variety of individual theologians unaffiliated
with one particular school of theology. In addition to the names noted in
the previous paragraph other theologians include Edward Schillebeex, Hans
Küng, and Josef Ratzinger (who became Pope Benedict XVI). A primary
concern of the *nouvelle théologie* theologians was that theological investigation had become limited to the insular examination of Church teachings
already established. Often referred to as *Denzinger theology* or *conclusion
theology*, this mindset contributed to a closed system of conducting theology
that left little, if any, room for new theological insights.[6] Another concern
was that the writings of the Church Fathers had become obsolete and the
writings of St. Thomas Aquinas stagnant and even distorted.[7] The content
of the faith had become reduced to immutable propositional statements.[8]

The *ressourcement* theologians challenged the scholastic speculative
approach to theology on the grounds that it led to a sterile examination of
God as a mere object of research.[9] Jesuit theologian Jean Danielou, in

---

5. Fr. Giancarlo and I discussed this at the 2015 CGS International Conference held in Scottsdale, AZ.

6. Jürgen Mettepenningen, *Nouvelle Théologie-New Theology: Inheritor of Modernism; Precursor of Vatican II* (New York: T & T Clark, 2010), *Nouvelle Théologie*, 11–12.

7. See John Montag, "Revelation: The False Legacy of Suarez," in *Radical Orthodoxy: A New Theology*, ed. John Milbank and Catherine Pickstock (New York: Routledge, 2004), 38–63.

8. See Latourelle, "The Scholastic Renewal of the XIX Century," chap. 3 in *Theology of Revelation* (New York: Alba House, 1966).

9. Mettepenningen, *Nouvelle Théologie*, 10–11.

particular, expressed great hostility toward scholastic theology, blaming scholastic theologians as the reason "theology gradually dried up."[10] Danielou challenged his contemporary theologians to rediscover the majesty and mystery of "God as God."[11] Henri de Lubac sought to reestablish the theological method of reading the Scriptures with a full "four-fold sense" once used by the early Fathers of the Church and even the early scholastic theologians, but then fell into disuse in the later years of scholasticism.[12] De Lubac hoped that by returning to the literal, moral, allegorical, and mystical interpretation of Scripture, theologians would rekindle the spark in theology as an ever ancient, ever new contemplation of God and his self-revelation.

To a degree, the complaint of the *nouvelle théologie* was valid, but only against the scholastics of the fifteenth and sixteenth centuries. No one who has studied or prayed the mystical and poetic writings of St. Thomas and St. Bonaventure would agree that these men saw God as a mere object of research. They and others of their immediate era conducted theology on their knees. According to Dominican theologian Marie Dominique Chenu, a main catalyst of the *nouvelle théologie*, the only proper way to *study* God was in prayer and contemplation.[13]

Many of the Council Fathers at Vatican II relied on the theological insights of prominent *ressourcement* theologians who accompanied their respective bishops to the Council, serving as theological experts and giving theological advice on such important texts as *Dei Verbum*, *Sacrosanctum concilium*, and *Gaudium et spes*. Pope St. John XXIII himself appointed Cipriano Vagaggini to serve the Council Fathers as an expert in liturgical theology. Despite the tremendous positive impact of the *nouvelle théologie*, valid criticism can be made against it that the innovation of some *ressourcement* theologians inadvertently untethered theology from a universal and stable method of theological investigation that ensured its orthodoxy.

Catechetical Response in Phase II

The year 1936 is seen as a turning point in the history of catechetics due to the publication of Josef Jungmann's *The Good News and Our Proclamation*

---

10. Mettepenningen, *Nouvelle Théologie*, 90.

11. Mettepenningen, *Nouvelle Théologie*, 90.

12. Nichols, "Henri de Lubac," in *Engaging Theologians* (Milwaukee: Marquette University Press, 2013), 103–104.

13. See Fergus Kerr, "Marie-Dominique Chenu," in *Twentieth-Century Theologians Twentieth-Century Catholic Theologians* (Malden: Blackwell Publishing, 2007), 17–33:18.

of the Faith.[14] Like Drinkwater, Jungmann sought renewal in catechesis, but in keeping with the theological *ressourcement* at the time, his attention focused on the renewal of catechetical content, which in his view needed "a more relevant presentation of the very core and substance of the Christian message."[15]

Josef Jungmann (1889–1975) was a Jesuit priest and professor of liturgy and catechetics at the University of Innsbruck, Austria. Like most priests of his time, Jungmann inherited what amounts to a *manual theology.* The primary instructional tools were compendia or manuals that treated questions of theology in the scholastic fashion with innumerable distinctions and precision of expression. Jungmann was displeased with the status of seminary theology, criticizing the "neo-Scholastic vocabulary and world view."[16] In Jungmann's view, the neo-Scholastic manner of study was incapable of communicating the Gospel message in all its richness, simplicity, and directness. He writes,

> All that is genuinely Christian, the truly supernatural—the merciful
> plan of God revealed in the humanity of Christ, calling for man's
> inmost participation—all this has been largely lost from sight.[17]

Wishing to depart from the "dry formulas" [18] that were the prevailing mode of theology, Jungmann pressed his contemporaries to consider a new approach that integrated all the components of Christian formation.

While Jungmann's first concern was a matter of theological exposition, he saw the same negative influence in catechesis. In his view, the catechism was merely a diluted version of the manual theology offered in seminary formation. Catechesis had become reduced to the form of memorized answers to questions that the child might not even have posed. In contrast, Jungmann believed that the purpose of catechetical methodology was to bring "the objective Christo-centrism of Catholic doctrine to the state of vitally dynamic subjective representation."[19] He writes,

---

14. Gabriel Moran, *Catechetics of Revelation* (New York: Herder & Herder, 1966), 20.

15. Johannes Hofinger, sj, "The Place of the Good News in Modern Catechetics," in *The Good News: Yesterday and Today*, ed. Johannes Hofinger, trans. William A. Heusman, sj (New York: William H. Sadlier, 1962), 173.

16. Michael Horan, "Kerygmatic catechesis: An analysis of the writings of Jungmann and Hofinger as reflected in post-conciliar catechetical documents," (phd diss., Catholic University of America, 1989), 19.

17. Jungmann, *Good News*, 4.

18. Jungmann, *Good News*, 7.

19. Sr. Mary Johanna Paruch, "Study of the Direct Ramifications of Vatican Council II on Catechetics Including the Impact of Concilliar and Post-Concilliar Catechetical Document on the Content and Method of Catechesis," (phd diss., Maryvale Institute, England, 2007), 156.

Today religious teaching must lead the faithful to a vital understanding of the content of the faith itself, that they may interiorly grasp it, and thus grow to spiritual maturity and proper independence in religious life. It must lead in other words to the step of Christian formation.[20]

Sparked by the *nouvelle théologie*, Jungmann sought an authentic *ressourcement* in catechesis calling for a more *kerygmatic, biblical-liturgical* approach.

Kerygmatic Catechesis

The *kerygma* may be understood as the proclamation of the Gospel in its essential form. It is "simultaneously an *act of proclamation* and the *content of the proclamation* itself, which unveils the Gospel and makes it present" (DC, 58). Thus, the *kerygmatic* movement, which Jungmann began, was its own *ressourcement*, returning catechesis to the apostolic time when the pure and essential form of the Gospel was preached. Jungmann's *kerygmatic* catechesis proposed a catechetical content aimed at presenting the truths of the faith as an organic whole. "Its core [was] the good news of our redemption in Christ. Its fruit [was to] be the grateful response of our love."[21] Pope Francis, a fellow Jesuit who may have known Jungmann personally, offers a sample proclamation of the kerygma: "Jesus Christ loves you: he gave his life to save you; and now he is living at your side every day to enlighten, strengthen and free you" (*Evangelii gaudium*, 164).

From Jungmann's perspective, the good news that Jesus preached and the Good News, namely that Jesus, the Son of God, has saved us from sin, had lost its dynamic influence in the world of catechetics. Catholicism had become "a sum of obligations—an uninspiring series of 'musts' and 'don'ts'— weighting heavily on the conscience."[22] Christianity such as this, Jungmann lamented, "is not the Good News proclaimed by Christ!"[23]

Jungmann's *kerygmatic* catechesis was also inspired in part by the psychological and educational needs of the child. He challenged the conventional language of catechetical content as it was expressed at the time in textbooks and the catechism, proposing instead the ancient *narratio* of St. Augustine. While serving as bishop of Hippo (AD 430), St. Augustine was

---

20. Jungmann, *Good News*, 7
21. Michael Warren, "General Conclusions of the Eichstätt Week, 1960," in *Sourcebook for Modern Catechetics*, ed. Warren (Winona, MN: St. Mary's Press, 1983), 30.
22. Jungmann, *Good News*, 3.
23. Jungmann, *Good News*, 4.

asked by one of his catechists to give advice on the best method for catechizing beginners in the faith. St. Augustine's written response, aptly entitled "On Instructing Beginners in the Faith" (*De catechizandis rudibus*), proposed the telling of salvation history (the *narratio*) as an appropriate and meaningful start.

The *narratio* recounts the critical events of salvation history beginning with the creation of the world and the fall of Adam and Eve and continues through the Old Testament covenants leading up to the New and Everlasting Covenant established by Jesus Christ. The *narratio* offers an overarching framework for those receiving instruction in the faith and serves as a "golden thread" that allows all other doctrines to be woven into the one story of salvation. In recommending the *narratio*, St. Augustine proposes a particular catechetical content that is offered in a particular method for instructing beginners in the faith as well. Eager catechists often get carried away and try to teach everything. St. Augustine cautions that "we should not allow the introduction of these other dimensions of meaning to make us lose track of the exposition and cause our heart and our tongue to rush off into the intricacies of an over complicated discussion."[24] In other words, teach only what people need to know, when they need to know it.

Jungmann saw perennial value in St. Augustine's seminal text on catechesis. He writes,

> [I]t is indispensable for catechesis at the primary age level to present Christian doctrine in such a way that notions are joined as far as possible to concrete images, preferably and most effectively in the form of a narrative. Catechesis can meet this need by recounting to the children in simple terms the history of redemption and basing further instructions upon this.[25]

While he never sought to create new doctrine with the concept of *kerygmatic* catechesis, Jungmann most certainly worked to create a new mode—*a renewed language*—for the transmission of the Church's doctrine. The language of *kerygmatic* catechesis was biblical and liturgical. In the Scriptures and the prayers of the liturgy, Jungmann saw an essential form of the Gospel itself: the very words and actions of Christ. In proposing a *biblical-liturgical* catechesis, Jungmann offered a content that was in the form of its initial proclamation without sacrificing the doctrine contained in the

---

24. Augustine of Hippo, *Instructing Beginners in Faith (De catechizandis rudibus)*, ed. Boniface Ramsey, trans. Raymond Canning (New York: New City Press, 2006), 25.

25. Jungmann, *Handing on the Faith*, 79; emphasis mine.

catechism. In this regard, Jungmann foreshadows the 2020 *Directory*, which calls for a variety of catechetical language (DC, 204ff.).

Biblical-Liturgical Catechesis

A unique aspect of Jungmann's *biblical-liturgical* catechesis was his method of allowing the child to access the Scriptures directly as opposed to reading paraphrases in a textbook. Jungmann recognized that when they were guided adroitly by a catechist, the children were capable of engaging with the biblical texts firsthand. He introduced to children's catechesis the medieval practice of *lectio divina*, which is a contemplative reading of the Scriptures.

Lectio divina is a marvelous technique for engaging the child on a number of levels. The child touches, reads (*lectio*), and hears the Sacred Word. His intellect is engaged because he must think and make connections (*meditatio*) about the text. As he ponders the meaning of the text and strives to be in dialogue with God (*oratio*), his heart is engaged. On a few occasions, I have observed a child in the CGS atrium seeming to rest in quiet prayer during a time of *lectio*. Was this a kind of *contemplatio* in which the soul simply enjoys God's presence? I certainly never doubted the possibility, knowing that "it is to such as these that the kingdom of heaven belongs" (Matthew 19:14).

Rich as it is, the biblical expression of the *kerygma* is incomplete without its liturgical expression. In fact, the liturgy is the preeminent expression of the *kerygma*, for it allows us to participate in the actual events that the *kerygma* proclaims. In the liturgy, the suffering, death, resurrection, and ascension of Jesus is not merely proclaimed, it is re-presented (CCC, 1104). Thus, the liturgy is the "communication, realization, and participation in this message of salvation."[26]

Even though the liturgy's primary purpose is not to catechize, but to bring people into union with God, Jungmann recognized in the liturgy "an imperishable treasure full of pedagogical principles."[27] "In the liturgy," he writes, "we do not philosophize about God, but we adore him. In the liturgy we do not attempt to analyze faith, hope and charity, we practice them."[28] Dogma that is lived and prayed "will prove to be the best school: and so far as prayer is concerned, the prayer of the Church—the liturgy—takes first

---

26. Jungmann, *Good News*, 26.
27. Jungmann, *Handing on the Faith*, 98.
28. Jungmann, *Handing on the Faith*, 99.

place."[29] For this reason, Jungmann saw the liturgy as a primary place and a primary source for catechizing children.[30]

In *Handing on the Faith*, Jungmann offers a few of the educational consequences of the liturgy. Doctrines that are studied in a notional manner are apt to fade from the memory but doctrines that are prayed and celebrated in a regular manner, Sunday and holy days, become assimilated into our very being.[31] When Christians fully participate in the liturgy, they "will come to see that worship—divine service—must be nothing but the distillation of a way of life in which men serve God, that divine service, in the sense of worship, and the service of God must merge into one another.[32] Such is the meaning of the Church's axiom *lex orandi, lex credendi, lex vivendi*: the law of worship is the law of faith is the law of life. Catechesis seeks to form all aspects of the disciple: his belief, prayer, and life. "If in catechesis we should succeed in introducing children to the content of the liturgy, we would open up a well which could supply the adult Christian with 'waters of eternal life' his whole life through." [33]

Of course, Jungmann recognized that formal catechetical instruction on the liturgical signs and symbols is needed for a person to fully engage in the liturgy. Liturgical catechesis aims at "clarifying the meaningful relationships of the events of salvation and of the Church's institutions with the hope that, as instruction progresses, this objective order may find a subjective reflection in the mind of the student."[34] This is especially necessary in a secular age that lacks a sacramental imagination. The "altar with the tabernacle before which the vigil light flickers displays most forcibly the living heart of Christian dogma."[35] Yet is this dogma always recognized? Returning to image of education, we could say that liturgical catechesis teaches children the "ABCs" of worship so that they can read its signs and symbols.

In Jungmann's view, good liturgical catechesis provides a child with a faith that is "built to last a lifetime."[36] Unfortunately, his view—and his legacy—was eclipsed because of its focus on children's catechesis as opposed to adult catechesis. In the years after the Council, a few prominent

---

29. Jungmann, *Good News*, 114.

30. Jungmann, *Handing on the Faith*, 98.

31. Jungmann, *Handing on the Faith*, 99.

32. Josef Jungmann, "The Liturgy, a School of Faith," in *Pastoral Liturgy* (New York: Herder & Herder, 1962), 334.

33. Jungmann, *Handing on the Faith*, 99.

34. Jungmann, *Good News*, 103.

35. Jungmann, *Handing*, 100.

36. Jungmann, *Handing*, 99.

catechetical theorists in the United States challenged the traditional structure of the Catholic school and its place in the overall mission of a parish. One of the more vocal objectors was Mary Perking Ryan, who envisioned "parish schools of education" as adult centers of religious formation within the context of the whole community.[37] Ryan's views were supported by several prominent catechetical theorists in the United States—Gerald Sloyan, Gabriel Moran, and Maria Harris, to name a few. The 2020 *Directory*'s emphasis that adult catechesis be considered "the chief form of catechesis" (DC, 77) might seem to support their view. I do not agree and caution my reader to weigh carefully the innumerable factors that have contributed to the crisis in catechesis. To skip over the tender years of a child's faith formation is to deprive that child of innumerable graces and the necessary foundation upon which to build his life of faith. The child is not the problem—rather, as the CGS approach demonstrates, it is our ignorance of the child's religious potential.

Conclusion

The second phase of the modern catechetical movement, which was championed by Josef Jungmann, sought to recapture the vibrancy of the early Church's catechetical mission by proposing a more essential proclamation of the Gospel. Jungmann's *kerygmatic* catechesis aligned itself with the theological *ressourcement* of the 1950s relying on Sacred Scripture and the Church's liturgy for its primary source of catechetical content. It is unfortunate that Jungmann's call for a more biblical-liturgical catechesis was rejected by a generation of catechetical theorists who sought to make the content of catechesis so subjectively relevant that it lost all objective standing. In the next chapter we will examine the anthropocentric turn that catechesis took in the 1960s that continues to impact catechesis negatively.

---

37. Mary Perkins Ryan, *Are Parochial Schools the Answer?: Catholic Education in Light of the Council* (Chicago: Holt, Rinehart and Winston 1964), 108.

Chapter 4

In Search of Relevancy

Phase III (1970–2000): Concern for the Person

The Second Vatican Council (1962–1965) is at times referred to as "the people's council."[1] Unlike previous Church Councils, the thrust of Vatican II was pastoral, not doctrinal, and this was intentional. In his opening address to the Council Fathers, Pope St. John XXIII expressed that the Council would not concern itself so much with defining dogmas as with "discovering new and effective ways of presenting and defending the sacred deposit of Christian doctrine."[2]

The Holy Father was anything but cavalier toward the teachings of the faith. He expressed deep concern that the Council should "transmit whole and entire and without distortion the Catholic doctrine which, despite difficulties and controversies, has become the common heritage of humanity" (GM, 14). Yet the greater concern to the Holy Father and many cardinals at the time was the average person and the need for the Church to be in dialogue with the individual—embracing as its own concern, his or her "joys and hopes, . . . griefs and anxieties" (GS, 1).[3] Highlighting its anthropological core, one bishop remarked during the Council that, "[i]n this central question of man which still remains of the greatest importance, all the human problems of our time converge."[4]

As noted in chapter 2, catechesis in the nineteenth and early twentieth centuries was negatively influenced by the propositional model of revelation

---

1. Basil Pennington, OCSO, *Vatican II: We've Only Just Begun* (New York: The Crossroad Publishing Co., 1994), 15.
2. St. Pope John XXIII, *Gaudet mater ecclesia*, Opening Speech to the Second Vatican Council (October 11, 1962), 11.
3. See C. Moeller, "History of the Constitution," in *Commentary on the Documents of Vatican II*, vol. 5, ed. H. Vorgrimler (New York: Herder and Herder, 1969), 8–9.
4. See Josef Cardinal Ratzinger, "The Dignity of the Human Person," in *Commentary on the Documents of Vatican II*, vol. 5, 118.

that "tended to reduce [divine Revelation] to a series of propositions about Christ, without acknowledging that Christ himself was Revelation."[5] While maintaining the importance of objective truth, the propositional model failed to "address adequately the manner in which objective revelation is subjectively received."[6] The purpose of divine Revelation is not merely to save *humanity* but to save *this person*. "The believer longs for an experience of God that cannot be answered on the level of the intellect alone; it must also involve the longings of human affectivity."[7]

An Anthropocentric Shift

The efforts to reform or renew catechetical praxis have had at their core a concern for the person receiving catechesis. It certainly became the critical concern for the series of six International Catechetical Study Weeks held in Assisi (1956), Nijmegen (1959), Eichstätt (1960), Bangkok (1962), Katigondo (1964), Manila (1967), and Medellín (1968). The International Study Weeks on Catechetics served as a think tank for theorists seeking catechetical renewal. These Study Weeks reflect the theological developments regarding the nature of Revelation, and the political and societal unrest throughout the world. It is easy to recognize in their proceedings the shifting nature in catechesis from a doctrine-centered emphasis to a person-centered emphasis. According to Louis Erdozian, an early commentator on this historical period, failure to use a person's life experiences as a point of reference in catechesis was criticized as "abstract" and "disincarnate."[8] Monsignor Michael Wrenn, another commentator of this era, observes: "It is possible to trace . . . the gradual loss of interest in the content of the faith—the Christian message itself . . . through these proceedings."[9]

Most catechetical theorists recognize the conference at Medellín as the final turning point to an anthropocentric focus in catechesis. According to Hofinger, the turn to the person had already begun to happen at Nijmegen and Eichstätt. In fact, Hofinger attributes the anthropological considerations of the Decree on the Church's Missionary Activity (*Ad gentes*) to these gatherings.[10] Participants at the 1968 Conference recognized that

---

5. Gerald O'Shea, "Historical Discontinuity," 334.
6. O'Shea, "Historical Discontinuity," 334.
7. O'Shea, "Historical Discontinuity," 378.
8. L. Erdozian, "The Evolution of Catechesis," in *Lumen Vitae* (Brussels: International Centre for Studies in Religious Education, 575–599. See English translation, *Lumen Vitae* 25, no. 1 (1970): 7–31.
9. Msgr. Michael Wrenn, *Catechisms and Controversies* (San Francisco: Ignatius Press, 1991), 92.
10. Hofinger and Buckley, *The Good News*, 30–33nn1–5.

catechesis had matured in its progression by rediscovering its doctrinal, biblical, and liturgical sources.[11] The complete renewal would come by means of "a new reference to the person."[12] The shift truly was Copernican. Prior to Medellín, the emphasis in catechesis was on learning the teachings of Christ (or the teachings of the Church), what is known as a *Christocentric* catechesis. After Medellín the emphasis became the person's lived experience, often referred to as an anthropocentric catechesis.

The term *anthropocentric catechesis* is open to broad interpretation. At one extreme, it refers to a viewpoint that represents a complete disregard for the Church's teachings, especially when those teachings "no longer reflect the lived experience of the persons being catechized."[13] Reflecting on this kind of catechesis, Pope Emeritus Benedict XVI draws attention to the inherent problem with this kind of catechetical approach when he writes, "a catechesis that is turned inward and not upward, the person is left to his own subjectivity."[14] Underlying this anthropocentric approach is a true "crisis of faith, or, more precise . . . a crisis of the faith shared with the Church of all ages."[15]

In contrast to this inward, downward spiral, there is on the other hand the praxis of examining a person's lived experience and from this going to God. The Church recognizes that this existential or ascending method is valid so long as there is a true movement from the person to God, and that "human problems and conditions" are enlightened with the word of God (GDC, 151). The purpose of this kind of existential approach is to recognize, as Pope John XXIII desired, that the Church's doctrine needs to relate directly to the person's life and not be taught in theoretical abstraction or isolation.

Two of the most influential leaders in the catechetical movement who championed an *anthropocentric catechesis* were Gabriel Moran and Thomas Groome. According to their view, the focus of catechesis should be less on the objective teachings of the Church and more on the person receiving catechesis: his experience of God—his story of life and faith.

---

11. Hofinger and Buckley, *The Good News*, 27.
12. Medellín Documents, *Liberation: Towards a Theology for the Church in the World*, according to the Second General Conference of Latin American Bishops, Medellín, 1968 (Rome: Catholic Book Agency, 1972).
13. Thomas Groome, "Toward a Theory/Method of Liberating Catechesis," (ED diss., Columbia University Teachers College, New York, 1976), 3–4.
14. Ratzinger, "Handing on the Faith," 16.
15. Ratzinger, "Handing on the Faith," 17.

Catechetical Response in Phase III

The Second Vatican Council was a watershed for the Church. It was equally so for catechesis. [16] We can observe a clear paradigm shift during the 1970s and 1980s among theologians who challenged the Church's authority to define and teach doctrine.[17] Cardinal Ratzinger attributes this shift, in part, to the influence of *liberation theology*, a neo-Marxist view of the Gospel that valued praxis over truth to the detriment of truth itself. [18] During Phase III, catechetical content and methodology placed less emphasis on the communication of doctrine and more attention to matters of social action. The focus of catechesis changed from "proclaiming the good news of salvation in Jesus Christ and everything that follows from that to espousing a purely human kind of effort featuring a struggling humanity trying to save itself by political means from oppression and injustice."[19] The shift in emphasis redefined the nature and purpose of catechesis altogether.[20]

Catechesis of Revelation

Gabriel Moran (1935–) was an early theorist on the matter of revelation and catechesis. From his early studies in the School of Catechetics at the Catholic University of America, under the tutelage of Gerald Sloyan (an equally prodigious catechetical theorist), Moran dedicated his life to improving religious education. His approach "took religious instruction out of the revelation-as-concept model."[21] To some degree, this was a positive development, for reasons already noted. The propositional model of revelation tended to reduce catechesis to mere religious knowledge, fostering a catechetical methodology that over-emphasized instruction in and memorization of a catechism. Yet on another level, Moran's approach has been problematic. Though he promoted his teachings under the auspices of renewal by frequently citing *Dei Verbum*, Gabriel Moran actively sought a catechetical revolution by way of a particular reconfigured Christology and theology of ongoing revelation.

---

16. Joseph Cardinal Ratzinger, "Handing on the Faith and Sources of Faith," in *Handing on the Faith in an Age of Disbelief*, trans. Michael Miller (San Francisco: Ignatius. 2006), 16.

17. Sr. Johanna Paruch has given painstaking study to this negative influence in catechesis.

18. Caroline Farey, "A Metaphysical Investigation of the Anthropological Implications of the Phrase '*Ipse enim, Filius Dei, incaranatione sua cum omni homine quodammodo se univit*' ['For he, the Son of God, has united himself in a certain way with every man by his incarnation'] (*Gaudium et spes*, 22)" (PHD diss., Pontifical University of the Lateran, Rome, 2008), 28–34.

19. Msgr. Michael Wrenn, *Catechisms and Controversies* (San Francisco: Ignatius Press, 1991), 90.

20. René Marlé, "The Concentration on Hermeneutics in Catechesis: The Interpretation of Experience," in *Lumen Vitae* 25, no. 4 (1970): 545–550.

21. Anne Marie Mongoven, *The Prophetic Spirit of Catechesis: How We Share the Fire in Our Hearts* (New York: Paulist Press, 2000), 61.

In Moran's catechetical model, Jesus is *not* the fullness of God's revelation and the Church does *not* have a specific deposit of faith or specific content per se because divine revelation is ongoing. He writes: "I hope . . . to show that revelation may be viewed as a process which only begins in its fullness with apostolic times, a process now extending to all history and never to cease."[22] Moran's application of this teaching in catechesis was to make the *individual* person a direct recipient of God's ongoing revelation *independent* of the Church.

It should be apparent why Moran's view of revelation and catechesis is problematic and even heretical. Integral to the mission of Jesus Christ to save us was his mission to reveal the truth of who God is and the truth of who we are. It is not by chance that Jesus commanded his apostles (the Church) to teach all nations and "to obey everything that [he] commanded" (Matthew 28:20). To say yes to Jesus is to say Amen to the teachings that he entrusted to the Church. If his teachings are not faithfully proclaimed to a person, then that person's yes is incomplete. In the words of Pope St. John Paul II, "Unfaithfulness on some point to the integrity of the message means a dangerous weakening of catechesis and putting at risk the results that Christ and the ecclesial community have a right to expect from it" (CT, 30).

Moran's influence on catechetics remains unparalleled. In her analysis of post-Vatican II catechesis, Sr. Johanna Paruch, FSMG, identifies Gabriel Moran and his new model of catechesis as one of the primary catalysts of the deconstruction of catechetical content. His academic criticisms on Jungmann's *kerygmatic* and *liturgical* catechesis caused them to fall out of favor almost immediately. Moran actively sought to revolutionize the Church's understanding of divine revelation and the nature of catechesis by making the person the center of catechesis.

God revealed *and* God revealing

The Church provides clarification to Moran's misunderstandings regarding the nature of divine revelation, while offering something of a reconciliation between Moran's desire that God continue to speak personally to the individual and the truth that divine revelation is objective and definitive. Drawing from the theological insights of St. John Henry Newman, the *Catechism* teaches that, "even if Revelation is already complete, it has not been made completely explicit, it remains for Christian faith gradually to grasp its full significance over the course of the centuries" (CCC, 66).

---

22. Gabriel Moran, *Theology of Revelation* (New York, 1966), 28.

The Church's dogmatic constitution on the nature of divine revelation, *Dei Verbum*, speaks of revelation in terms of God's self-manifestation. God revealed himself through Jesus Christ, so that "we might have access to the Father through the Holy Spirit and come to share in His divine nature" (DV, 2). Through this revelation, "the invisible God, out of the abundance of His love, speaks to men as friends and lives among them so that He may invite and take them into fellowship with Himself" (DV, 2). Writing then as Joseph Cardinal Ratzinger, Pope Emeritus Benedict XVI comments:

> The word ["Revelation"] refers to the act in which God shows Himself, not to the objectified result of this act. And because this is so, the receiving subject is always also a part of the concept of "Revelation." Where there is no one to perceive "Revelation," no revelation has occurred, because the veil remains. By definition, revelation requires someone who apprehends it.[23]

It is true that God still speaks to his people yet the Word he speaks, "Jesus Christ is the same yesterday and today and forever" (Hebrews 13:8).

Shared Christian Praxis

As with the catechetical theorists before him, Thomas Groome (1945–), prolific writer and professor of catechetics at Boston College, criticized catechesis for its reliance on the scholastic approach because it was "too theoretical, too abstract and too ahistorical."[24] For Groome, the shift in catechesis from knowledge to the person—or as he saw it, from doctrine to real life—reflects "the immanent anthropocentric situation in which the Word (of God) is to be announced."[25]

In the 1970s, Groome created a new approach to catechesis that emphasized human experience, called *Shared Christian Praxis* (SCP). When first introduced, Shared Christian Praxis was revolutionary in its inductive approach to catechesis. Countering all other methods that began with God, Scripture, or the catechism, Groome's method begins with the person. He explains,

> The purpose of [step 1] is to bring to group awareness the participants' present action in regard to a particular focus of the Christian faith (e.g., "What does the Eucharist mean to you?"). This is the

---

23. Joseph Cardinal Ratzinger, *Milestones: Memoirs 1927–1977* (San Francisco: Ignatius, 1998), 108–109.
24. Thomas Groome, "Christian Education: A Task of Present Dialectical Hermeneutics," in *Living Light* 4, no. 3 (1977): 420.
25. See Groome, "Toward a Theory/Method of Liberating Catechesis," 24–25.

opening of attention to our present action. It is beginning with the present life situation and experience of the participants.[26]

In step 2, "The task . . . is to return to the biographical and social genesis of the participants' present action ('Why do you believe that? Think that? Do that?') and to become aware of the future consequences of those actions."[27] Step 3 introduces the "Christian Community Story and Vision." Though Groome readily admits that there exists past tradition and teaching of the Church (what he calls "the Story"), he insists that,

> God shows up in a different light when his people find themselves in different historical situations. [Thus], the continued activity of God in our present, requires a critical appropriation of our past tradition and creative adding to the Story.[28]

Groome's ideas reveal a kind of *historicism*, which claimed that there could be no objective, universal truth for all ages; truth is in flux and must be nuanced according to the lived experience of each age.

Those who ascribe to the theory of *historicism* argue that whatever was true for one age need not be true for the current or future age. In the case of the Church's moral teachings, *historicism* translates into something detrimental to the deposit of faith: maybe the person should change his life in response to Church teaching; but then again, maybe the Church's teachings no longer inform the person's lived experience and so the Church is in need of creative change. According to Groome, the matter is left to be "worked out."[29]

With regard to catechetical content, Groome is insistent, "[n]othing is complete and final."[30] He continues, "as Vatican II pointed out we are only on our way toward the fullness of truth. Along the way we must realize that there is non-truth among us. This calls for a creative suspicion in the midst of our commitment to 'the way.'"[31] Groome's ideas here are not completely original. Jesuit theologian Juan Luis Segundo (1925–1996) used ideological suspicion as an exegetical technique, which enabled him to reinterpret the teachings of Christ as calling for mere political liberation. Groome credits

---

26. Groome, "Christian Education," 421.
27. Groome, "Christian Education," 422.
28. Groome, "Christian Education," 422.
29. Groome, "Christian Education," 420.
30. Groome, "Christian Education," 420–421.
31. Groome, "Christian Education," 420–421.

the views of this liberation theologian as a significant influence on his revolutionary model of catechesis.

If the Church does not have the fullness of truth, and truth is to be worked out, then catechesis can only take a *Hegelian* approach to dialogue or what Groome calls a "dialectical approach." He explains,

> The meaning I intend for *dialectical* here is the basic Hegelian one of affirming, denying and moving beyond. A dialectical relationship must be maintained between the present and past Story because the Story must be critically appropriated and is yet to be accomplished.[32]

In Groome's method of dialectics, the Church's Story (its teachings) can only affirm or deny a person's story (his personal belief or moral choice) if that person *accepts* the Church's authority. Each person in the catechetical session stands in equal authority with the Church in evaluating the validity or applicability of any doctrine.[33] The Church cannot promulgate or hand on her teaching, but must always and only be in dialogue with each person's life.

It should be clear that Groome's approach to catechesis is in direct contrast to God's pedagogy. Our Lord was a master at dialogue and he certainly left others free to accept or reject his teachings. Nevertheless, it could never be said that Jesus lacked a clear intention of trying to bring others to a deeper understanding of what it means to live in the Kingdom of God. The 2020 *Directory* reminds catechists that we are to develop a "pastoral dialogue without relativism, which does not negotiate one's Christian identity" while it "seeks to reach the heart of the other . . . and there sow the Gospel" (DC, 54).

Reconciling Knowledge and Experience

Moran and Groome represent a phase of intense experimentation in which the focus falls too heavily on the living subject in his intersection with the Church. As history demonstrates, the crisis in catechesis is not solved by simply addressing religious illiteracy. Nor is it solved by focusing exclusively on a person's subjective experience of God. The goal of catechesis is to provide a way for God's objective revelation to be received by the personal subject. We need to discover a catechetical approach that links "the objective truths of Christian revelation in Christ with the requirements of human

---

32. Groome, "Christian Education," 417.
33. Groome, "Christian Education," 420–421.

subjectivity, while avoiding the pitfall of 'ongoing revelation.'"[34] The Church points to God's *original pedagogy of faith* as the way:

> The irreducible originality of Christian identity has for corollary and condition no less original a pedagogy of the faith. Among the many prestigious sciences of man that are nowadays making immense advances, pedagogy is certainly one of the most important (CT, 58).

A proper understanding of God's pedagogy needs to find that balance between objective teaching and personal reception of that truth.[35] I am convinced that such balance is to be found in the CGS approach.

Conclusion

The 2020 *Directory* identifies *human experience* as an integral component of catechesis recognizing that "God acts in every person's life *and* in history" (DC, 197; emphasis mine). The concern for the person receiving catechesis that was seen in Phase III was a valid concern. People in the 1970s and 1980s were struggling to make sense of events in the world, in the Church, and in their lives. The disconnect between life and faith was tangible. People had questions—deep, genuine, existential questions; but many who served in the name of the Church had lost confidence that God had the answers. They certainly lost confidence that the Church had the answers and this caused the separation between doctrine and life to widen.

It has always been the case that when "catechesis neglects to correlate human experiences with the revealed message, it falls into the danger of artificial juxtapositions or misunderstandings of the truth" (DC, 199). It has also always been the case that when catechists fail to proclaim the Gospel with *paresia* (*boldness*) their witness is unconvincing. In every age, people need the Gospel proclaimed to them with the same vigor and boldness of the apostles. The anthropocentric experiment failed not because catechetical theorists turned to the human person; it failed because they did not turn together with the person to God. God always has the answer—he always *is* the answer.

---

34. O'Shea, "Historical Discontinuity," 363.
35. Pierre de Cointet et.al., *Craft of Catechesis and the Catechism of the Catholic Church* (San Francisco: Ignatius, 2008), 41–59.

PART II

The Catechesis of
the Good Shepherd

Chapter 5

We Need to Do It the Way God Does

Phase IV (2000–Present): Rediscovering God's Pedagogy

Following years of experimentation, some of which was helpful and some of which was not, the Church has consistently asked that catechesis be understood and conducted in accordance with God's pedagogy—*his way*—of forming his people in faith. Drawing upon the insights of Vatican II regarding the nature of divine revelation (DV, 2), the 1971 *General Catechetical Directory* (GCD) specifies:

> In the history of revelation God used pedagogy in such a way that he announced his plan of salvation in the old Covenant prophetically and by means of figures, and thus prepared the coming of his Son, the author of the New Covenant and the perfecter of the faith. (GCD, 33)

Since the time of Adam and Eve, God has demonstrated a unique way of revealing himself and inviting humankind to enter into covenant with him. Jesus perfected for us this *Way* (see John 14:6). Just as there is a way of *being* Christian (see Acts 2:42), there is a way of *forming* others to be Christian. God has shown us this way in his *divine pedagogy* (DC, 166). Even in the face of dynamic historical and cultural changes among God's people, the catechetical process must always remain inspired by *God's way*.

In his post-synodal apostolic exhortation *Catechesi tradendae (On Catechesis in our Time)*, Pope St. John Paul II insists that "the irreducible originality of Christian identity" should have for its corollary God's "original pedagogy of the faith" (CT, 58). The 2020 *Directory* proposes an authentic *ressourcement* that returns the Church's catechetical work to its "original existence" (DC, preface). The 1997 *General Directory for Catechesis* offered numerous principles and characteristics of God's pedagogy to help catechists align their various catechetical activities with "The Pedagogy of Faith" (GDC, 137–162).

If we hope to renew catechesis and resolve the catechetical crisis that continues to put in opposition religious knowledge and religious experience, continues to separate doctrine from life, continues to fragment the head from the heart (cf. DC, 4), then we must be even *more* intentional that our catechesis be conducted according to God's pedagogy—it must have a distinctly educative nature. The closer and more fully catechists align their work with God's pedagogy, the richer and more effective their catechesis will be in nurturing and encouraging a "true experience of the Faith and thus a filial encounter with God" (GDC, 143).

Characteristics of God's Pedagogy

Characteristics of the divine pedagogy include its adaptive and personal nature. "The invisible God, from the fullness of his love, addresses men as his friends, and moves among them, in order to invite and receive them into his own company" (DV, 2). God speaks to the Hebrew people in the events of their lives and transforms these events "into lessons of wisdom, adapting himself to the times and situations" in which they live (cf. DC, 158).

Another characteristic is the gradual and progressive nature of God's pedagogy (DC, 158). God takes his time and he waits for his people to respond. Consider the number of years between the time of creation and the call of Abraham, and again between Abraham and Jesus. Consider how our Lord gradually revealed his divinity to the apostles. Consider his unique catechetical session with Nicodemus and the Samaritan woman: how he slowly brought them to the truth of who he was.

In Jesus there are still other discernible characteristics. He "welcomed the poor, the simple, the sinners" (DC, 159). He proclaimed the "kingdom of God as good news" (DC, 159). He manifested a "style of love which frees from evil and which promotes life" (DC, 159). Jesus was an "expert in interpersonal communication" (GDC, 140). His "[w]ord and silence, parable and image become authentic pedagogical methods for revealing the mystery of his love" (DC, 159). His manner of leading others to full discipleship is marked by a "pressing invitation" (GDC, 140) which, though always allowing for the free response of the other (DC, 161), nevertheless left no doubt that the aim of his preaching was always to open the person's mind and the heart to the fullness of the Kingdom (see DC, 160).

The Church, too, has its own pedagogical action inspired by the features of God's pedagogy (DC, 164). Its characteristics include the witness of saints and catechists, various forms of religious life, and communities of faith (see DC, 164). Included in this pedagogy is the Church's "precious patrimony of catechetical teaching of faith culture, and of catechetical institutions and services" (DC, 164). Thus the Church remains a vital, indispensable, and primary locus of catechesis forming new disciples in the *sequela Christi—the way of following Christ* (see GDC, 141; see also DC, 164).

Inspired by the pedagogy of God, as displayed in Christ and in the Church, catechesis thus becomes a "pedagogical action at the service of the dialogue of salvation between God and humanity" (DC, 165). A catechetical process inspired by God's pedagogy

- makes present the initiative of God's gratuitous love;
- brings into focus the universal destination of salvation;
- evokes the conversion necessary for the obedience of faith;
- adopts the principle of the progressive nature of Revelation and the transcendence of the word of God, as also its inculturation in human cultures;
- recognizes the centrality of Jesus Christ, Word of God made man, which establishes catechesis as *pedagogy of incarnation*;
- values the community experience of the faith as proper to the people of God;
- puts together a pedagogy of signs, where actions and words are in mutual relationship;
- recalls that God's inexhaustible love is the ultimate reason for all things (see DC, 165).

Finally, though the Church encourages "plurality of methods" (DC, 195), God's pedagogy should have direct bearing on catechetical methodology. The 2020 *Directory* offers guidelines for catechists, reminding them that their choices of method should

- take into consideration *human experience* (DC, 197);
- value the role of *memory* (DC, 201);
- utilize a variety of *language* (DC, 204ff.);
- draw strength and influence from the Christian community—*the group* (DC, 218ff.);

- include an appropriate *space* where the sacred mysteries can be proclaimed, pondered, and celebrated (see DC, 221ff.).

The list of characteristics of God's pedagogy, which the Church offers, is intended to provide catechists with a general vision of what catechesis should entail. They serve as principles, by which we can make faithful choices regarding catechetical content and method. At the same time, these principles allow us to be innovative. The Church has not instituted one way of conducting catechesis recognizing that every catechetical circumstance is unique. The unifying principle for faithful diversity is God's pedagogy.

The Primacy of God's Action

While the Church offers several principles regarding God's pedagogy, we should recognize that the true reference point is not these principles in themselves, but in the activity of God. Only God can open the mind to receive the light of faith and move the will to respond generously. By drawing attention to the pedagogy of God, the Church points out that the path to catechetical renewal is to allow *God* to be the primary agent of formation and transformation (DC, 174). The Church has always cautioned against confusing God's pedagogical action with human pedagogy, but we must also not create an artificial contrast (DC, 181). God invites us to be collaborators with him in this sacred work of catechesis (DC, 174). Primarily, our work is to provide him with the greatest opportunity to act.

Of all the catechetical approaches I've seen, none provide God with as much *opportunity* to work as the CGS approach affords. The material content of the CGS is God's Word and the Church's liturgy. The proclamation of this content is limited to only what is essential, providing time and silence for the child to converse with God. Even the posture taken by the catechist while giving a presentation—often sitting next to the child, instead of across from the child or standing above the child—communicates that it is *God* who is teaching and that both catechist and child are invited to listen to his voice.

Catechetical Response in Phase IV

The notion of God's pedagogy as a source of renewal in catechesis has elicited the attention of some, but not all, catechetical theorists. Leading catechetical theorist Thomas Groome took issue with the 1997 *Directory*'s focus on

God's pedagogy, criticizing the Christian *paideia* of early catechetical schools as the beginning of the end of the Apostolic way of catechesis.[1]

In 2010, a small group of catechetical theorists from around the world gathered in Rome to discuss the concept of God's pedagogy as delineated in the 1997 *Directory*, and how it could be a source of catechetical renewal. The collected wisdom from this gathering has been published in the book *The Pedagogy of God: Its Centrality in Catechesis and Catechist Formation.*[2] I was present at that gathering and am pleased to recognize in the 2020 *Directory* many of the themes discussed there.

While there have been a number of good catechetical initiatives in the recent phase of catechesis, I draw attention here to those that are directly related to the concept of the divine pedagogy as it is particularly addressed in the 2020 *Directory*.

An Educational Catechesis

Dr. Petroc Willey, director of the Catechetical Institute at Franciscan University, has dedicated his professional career to renewing catechesis specifically under the Church's renewed emphasis on the educational nature of catechesis. He argues convincingly the Church's reasons for asking catechists to reconceive catechesis as a "school of faith" (GDC, 30).[3] Drawing from the unparalleled research of twentieth-century classicist Werner Jaeger (1888–1961),[4] Willey explores God's pedagogy within the context of the early Church's assimilation of the ancient Greek *paideia*.

The Greek word *paideia* refers to the program of education used in the ancient Greco-Roman world. While most people recognize the term as having to do with education, the Greek notion of *paideia* is, in fact, difficult to define in contemporary Western concepts. Words such as "civilization, culture, tradition, literature, or education" fail to grasp the full meaning.[5] More than the mere transfer of information, the Greek *paideia* was a complete *formation* of the human person—"the process of educating man into

---

1. Thomas Groome, "Total Catechesis/Religious Education: A Vision for Now and Always," in T. Groome and H. D. Dorrell, *Hopes and Horizons* (Mahwah, NJ: Paulist Press, 2003), 26.

2. Caroline Farey, Waltraud Linnig, Sr. M. Johanna Paruch, eds., *The Pedagogy of God: Its Centrality in Catechesis and Catechist Formation* (Steubenville, OH: Emmaus Road Pub, 2011).

3. Petroc Willey, "Philosophical Foundations for Catechesis in the Light of the Pedagogy of God," (PHD diss., Pontifical University of the Lateran, Rome, 2010). A consolidation of Willey's arguments may be found in chapters 1–4 in *The Pedagogy of God*.

4. See Werner Jaeger, *Paideia: The Ideals of Greek Culture*, trans. Gilbert Highet (New York: Oxford University Press, 1945).

5. Jaeger, *Paidea*, vol. 1, vi.

his true form, the real and genuine human nature" in the Greek heritage.[6] Hence, the Greek *paideia* included both the *aim* and the *process* of formation; both the development of the whole of a culture and the enculturation of a person into the developing heritage of Greek society, which was transmitted from generation to generation.[7]

Not everyone would agree that the Greek influence on Christianity was positive. Notably, Thomas Groome blamed the Greek influence on the ancient catechetical schools for causing catechesis to become hyper-rational.[8] Certainly, an exclusively rational approach to catechesis, one that fails to excite the will, is detrimental. On the other hand, an approach that neglects the cognitive dimension of the faith is equally problematic (DC, 80).

In asking catechists to conceive catechesis as a school of faith, the Church is asking for a Christian *paideia* that offers a formation of the whole person: heart, mind, body, and spirit; a formation that brings together in a symphonic way all dimensions of Christian discipleship: belief, worship, life, and prayer. Willey observes, "Such an integrated account of human development necessarily takes one beyond many of the dichotomies which bedevil contemporary catechetical thinking" (such as the polarizations that can arise between followers of a 'praxis' approach and those arguing for a more cognitive approach)."[9] With the promulgation of the 2020 *Directory*, we can hope that the polemics in catechesis that have arisen from misconceptions and over-corrections can come to an end.

Willey's research on the *paideia* of the ancient catechetical school offers an excellent reference for us as we explore the pedagogy of the CGS approach. For one, as with ancient Greco-Roman *paideia*, the praxis of CGS is an all-encompassing approach to the formation of the child: his heart, mind, and body. The materials used in the atrium are designed to appeal to the child's senses. The doctrines proclaimed are carefully chosen for their greatest intelligibility. The themes for each level of CGS correspond with the child's heart and hunger for God. In subsequent chapters, we will look at the many other ways in which the CGS approach is intentionally designed to catechize the *whole* child so as to foster a *whole* response of faith.

---

6. Jaeger, *Paideia*, vol. 1, introduction, xxiii.

7. Willey, "Pedagogy of God," 17.

8. Thomas Groome, *Christian Religious Education: Sharing Our Story and Vision* (San Francisco: Jossey-Bass, 1980), 158.

9. Willey, "Pedagogy of God," 21.

A Narrative Catechesis

The 2020 *Directory* gives considerable attention to the art of storytelling and its effectiveness as a method for catechesis (DC, 171, 173, 270, 363). Through the stories of the saints, ordinary Christians, the catechist, and even those being catechized, Church doctrine can be conveyed in a manner that is engaging because it is accessible. Storytelling "fosters the experiential dynamism of the faith because it involves all dimensions of a person: affective, cognitive, volitional" (DC, 208). Youth, in particular, are drawn to this approach (DC, 363). Of course, the one story that has universal appeal is God's story of salvation—the *narratio*.

In chapter 3, I mentioned that Josef Jungmann made appeal to St. Augustine's *narratio* as a means of giving catechesis an authentic *ressourcement*. Dr. Sean Innerst of the Augustine Institute has been promoting Augustine's *narratio* as a valid catechetical approach for a number of years.[10] Innerst explores the *narratio*, or the narration of salvation history, through the lens of God's pedagogy, observing that the *narratio* shares "the same principles."[11] Innerst insists that the *narratio* is not merely information *about* salvation history nor is it a clever method of catechizing: it is a "transformational practice that works to incorporate the person into the shared faith of the Church."[12] Notwithstanding, the *narratio* does serve both *content* and *method*. Innerst explains why this is so:

> [I]f God has been revealed in a narrative mode in salvation history, then perhaps a narrative account of that revelation in catechesis will most closely comport with that divine mode, not merely with reference to the ordering of the *content* of revelation but with the very *method* of its disclosure.[13]

"The personal quality of faith (the *fides qua*) is ordered to and consistent with the personal quality of revelation (the *fides quae*) which is the whole history of God's personal self-disclosure."[14] In other words, faith is the appropriate *personal response* to a *personal revelation* on the part of God.

Dr. Gerard O'Shea, professor of religious education at the University of Notre Dame (Australia), likewise gives voice to the power of the *narratio*,

---

10. Sean Innerst, "The Ancient *Narratio* as an Ecclesial Participation in the Divine Pedagogy," (STD diss., University of South Africa, 2010).

11. Innerst, "The Ancient *Narratio*," 10.

12. Innerst, "The Ancient *Narratio*," 16–17.

13. Innerst, "The Ancient *Narratio*," 16–17.

14. Innerst, "The Ancient *Narratio*," 44–45.

recognizing its ability to bridge the objective (content) and subjective (person) dimensions of catechesis. He writes:

> The merits of such an approach are immediately evident. It places emphasis on the individual's relationship with God and picks up Biblical themes, which tend to be understated in the propositional model. . . . In so doing, it opens up the Scriptures for personal reflection, and the possibility of personal encounter with the real source of Revelation, the Word of God himself—Jesus Christ.[15]

The 2020 *Directory* supports Innerst's and O'Shea's understanding of the significant contribution that the *narratio* offers catechesis, stating that the narrative quality of the biblical account provides a way to insert the person being catechized into salvation history so that he may realize "that this history is also a part of his or her own life" (DC, 145).

Though Innerst fails to make reference to Cavalletti or to the CGS approach in his writings, I think it important to point out that, from the beginning of their work in 1954, Cavalletti and Gobbi gave primacy of place to the narration of salvation history (the *narratio*). Cavalletti observes, "The history of salvation is the history of all peoples and of each person." [16] As the *narratio* is recounted and its significance pondered, the person comes to appreciate that the story of salvation is in fact their own story. When we reflect on the events of salvation history, God's unfathomable face gradually takes shape. We come to recognize his pattern of loving and providing for his people and this in turn helps us to recognize how he loves and provides for us. In this way, the Bible serves as a sacramental portal, through which we can encounter the God of Abraham, Isaac, and Jacob, as well as the God of Peter, James, John, Mary, Martha, and Lazarus.

A Liturgical Catechesis

Liturgical catechesis aims to initiate people into the mystery of Christ "by proceeding from the visible to the invisible, from the sign to the signified, from the sacrament to the mysteries" (CCC, 1075). It has always been a necessary component of catechesis as Pope St. John Paul II observes in *Catechesi tradendae*:

---

15. O'Shea, "Historical Discontinuity," 329.

16. Sofia Cavalletti, *The History of the Kingdom of God: From Creation to Parousia; Part 1*, trans. Rebekah Rojcewicz (Chicago: Catechesis of the Good Shepherd Publications, 2012), 1.

Catechesis is intrinsically linked with the whole of liturgical and sacramental activity. . . . Sacramental life is impoverished and very soon turns into hollow ritualism if it is not based on serious knowledge of the meaning of the sacraments, and catechesis becomes intellectualized if it fails to come alive in the sacramental practice. (CT, 23)

The liturgy is one of the "essential and indispensable sources of the Church's catechesis because from it, catechesis draws its content, vocabulary, actions, and words of faith" (DC, 95). It is also our privileged place of encountering God (DC, 96). The liturgy is the communication, realization, and participation in the mystery of salvation where religious knowledge and religious experience most perfectly converge.

A number of catechetical theorists, indeed too many to list, have promoted liturgical catechesis as a principal approach to catechesis. Another contemporary scholar, Dr. James Pauley, professor of catechetics at Franciscan University and editor of the *Catechetical Review*, would agree.[17] In his doctoral research, Pauley revisits the genius of Josef Jungmann and Cipriano Vagaggini, osb, two catalysts in the liturgical *ressourcement* of the 1940s.[18] While venerating their legacy, Pauley recognizes that a new manner of conducting liturgical catechesis is necessary if we hope to engage a contemporary audience.[19] Pauley's new approach calls for a person-to-person liturgical catechesis, or what he calls a catechesis of apprenticeship.[20]

Liturgical catechesis, given in the context of apprenticeship, moves catechetical practice from a one-size-fits-all model to a person-to-person experience of accompaniment that imitates the unique way in which Jesus formed his apostles and the early Church formed new disciples. Given the limited resources both in personnel and finances, is such an approach practical or even possible? Pauley thinks so and he is not an idealist. Prior to becoming an academic, Pauley served catechists on the parish and diocesan levels. He understands the challenges that parish leaders face. However, the failure to form others in a person-to-person apprenticeship model is to

---

17. Published by the Catechetical Institute at the Franciscan University, *Catechetical Review* has replaced Drinkwater's *The Sower* as a periodical aimed at forming catechists in the craft of catechesis.

18. James Pauley, "On the Necessity of Rediscovering the Theological Orientation of Liturgical Catechesis: An Analysis and Application of the Relevant Writings of Josef A. Jungmann, sj, and Cipriano Vagaggini, osb," (std diss., University of St. Mary of the Lake, Mundelein Seminary, 2014); James Pauley, *Liturgical Catechesis in the 21st Century: A School of Discipleship* (Chicago: Liturgy Training Publications, 2017).

19. Pauley, *Liturgical Catechesis*, 30.

20. Pauley, *Liturgical Catechesis*, 80–81. Pauley recognizes the Catechesis of the Good Shepherd approach as a model of apprenticeship catechesis.

continue along the trajectory of an ever-increasing number of empty church-es.[21] The stakes are simply too high to not do so.

An Evangelizing Catechesis

The term *evangelization* is best understood as "making present and announc-ing Jesus Christ" (DC, 29). In his encyclical *Evangelii nuntiandi* (1975), Pope St. Paul VI makes the bold affirmation that the Church "exists in order to evangelize" (EN, 14). Already, in the 1971 *Directory*, the Church put forward the need to renew the work of evangelization so that the faith could be trans-mitted to a new generation (see GCD, 2), and it challenged catechists to form others in a dynamic faith capable of changing their lives (see GCD, 6). Thus, the Church insists that "any form of catechesis must also perform the role of evangelization" (GCD, 18).

The emphasis on evangelization has at times eclipsed the work of cat-echesis, leaving some well-intentioned authors to claim that people have been catechized but not evangelized. Even the full text of the 2020 *Directory for Catechesis*, paragraph 29, is open to misunderstanding and runs the risk of perpetuating the bifurcation between religious knowledge and religious experience. There can be no authentic announcement of Jesus except through doctrine. The proclamation "Jesus Christ loves you; he gave his life to save you; and now he is living at your side every day to enlighten, strengthen and free you" (EG, 164) is not only doctrinal: it is *dogmatic*.

Sherry Weddell, speaker and author of *Forming Intentional Disciples*, offers a better explanation: "The majority of Catholics in the United States are *sacramentalized* but not *evangelized*."[22] In other words, they might be Catholic, but they are not *disciples*. Weddell sparked a rigorous discussion in the catechetical world by identifying the underlying cause for an increas-ing exodus from the Church. Too many Catholics, though they have received all of the sacraments, do not possess an explicit, personal attachment to Jesus Christ.[23] These same Catholics not only lack a personal relationship with Jesus, they "don't even know that this personal, interior journey exists."[24] Sometimes Weddell criticizes catechesis as the problem, stressing the need to form intentional disciples. Because the Church sees evangelization and catechesis as one work with differing moments, I would simply suggest that

---

21. Pauley, *Liturgical Catechesis*, 7.
22. Sherry Weddell, *Forming Intentional Disciples: The Path to Knowing and Following Jesus* (Huntington, IN: Our Sunday Visitor, 2012), 46.
23. Weddell, *Forming Intentional Disciples*, 46.
24. Weddell, *Forming Intentional Disciples*, 57.

what we really need is for catechists to be more *intentional* in forming disciples of Christ through a distinctive *evangelizing catechetical education*.

In most of the post–Vatican II documents related to evangelization or catechesis, the two terms are often joined with the conjunction *and* to delineate their respective characteristics. Pope Francis, in his apostolic exhortation *The Joy of the Gospel*, unites the terms in a more symbiotic manner:

> On the lips of the catechist the first proclamation must ring out over and over: "Jesus Christ loves you; he gave his life to save you; and now he is living at your side every day to enlighten, strengthen and free you." This first proclamation is called "first" not because it exists at the beginning and can then be forgotten or replaced by other more important things. It is first in a qualitative sense because it is the principal proclamation, the one which we must hear again and again in different ways, the one which we must announce one way or another throughout the process of catechesis, at every level and moment. (EG, 164)

An evangelizing catechesis recognizes that *every* catechetical session must proclaim the *kerygma* and invite the person to an intentional, personal response to Jesus, who is that Good News.

The Good Shepherd Catechesis

The Catechesis of the Good Shepherd approach began in 1954 in the home of Sofia Cavalletti. Cavalletti was approached by Adele Costa Gnocchi, who asked if she would help prepare the grandson of a friend for First Holy Communion. Cavalletti was an unlikely choice for this task. She was an academic—a university professor—accustomed to teaching adults. Her own protest, that "she had no experience working with children," was to no avail.[25] Her friend Adele persisted, and in the end, Cavalletti acquiesced. It was to be a most providential decision.

Enrico was a typical child who was not excited over the loss of his Saturday afternoon for the sake of religious education class.[26] On the day of their first appointment, he and his friends Paolo and Massimo appeared at Cavalletti's apartment, and he boldly "announced that he did not plan on

---

25. Scottie May, "Sofia Cavalletti," electronic personal correspondence with Cavalletti (Oct. 21, 2006), http://www.talbot.edu/ce20/educators/catholic/sophia_cavaletti/.
26. Cavalletti, "Searching among Memories . . . ," in *The Catechesis of the Good Shepherd Journal* 25 (2010): 6.

returning because that day of the week was his only free day."[27] Undeterred, Cavalletti began the session by recounting the story of salvation beginning with the story of Genesis. Cavalletti recounts the wonder of that first catechetical session and the discovery of a new approach to catechesis:

> As for my involvement with children, I would never have thought that Catechesis would have become the work of my life, until I saw a child's eyes filled with tears. It happened after having had a meeting with three or four children, a meeting that I thought would be followed with a few other meetings and then stop forever. Paolo, after having spent two hours with me, reading the first account of creation in Genesis, did not want to leave. I was very impressed and I asked myself, "What have we done? Why did Paolo not want to leave?" His mother had told me [earlier] that he had not been very willing to come.[28]

When Cavalletti began working with children, the use of the *narratio* in catechesis was enjoying a renewal due to the work of Josef Jungmann. While Jungmann appears in Cavalletti's writings, it does not seem that he had any direct influence on her choice to begin with a study of the book of Genesis. A more plausible reason for Cavalletti's choice was her own studies in Hebrew and Comparative Semitic Languages. Given that Cavalletti was a scholar of St. Augustine, it is equally plausible that her choice to start with the *narratio* was influenced by his treatise *De Catechizandis Rudibus* (On Instructing Beginners in the Faith). The point is that Enrico, Paolo, and theirfriends responded favorably to Cavalletti's choice of religious content.

As the catechetical sessions continued, Adele introduced Cavalletti to Gianna Gobbi, a master educator who studied under and worked with Dr. Maria Montessori. Gobbi provided for Cavalletti anthropological principles that addressed the unique nature of the child.[29] Together they experimented with a Montessorian and what I call "rabbinic" or "Hebraic" method for presenting the faith in a manner that was dialogical, reflective, and incarnational.[30]

---

27. Cavalletti, "Searching among Memories," 6.

28. Scottie May, "Sofia Cavalletti."

29. The reasons for this claim will be further argued in chapter 6. Cavalletti did go on to receive training in Montessori education, but I find in the CGS approach a very strong influence from her Hebrew studies and her personal tutelage under Eugenio Zolli.

30. The term *rabbinic* is my own way of describing what I see as their unique method of engaging the child in a dialogical reflection on the Scripture texts and other catechetical proclamations that I believe Cavalletti learned from her Hebrew studies.

Throughout their fifty years of catechizing children and studying the Church's catechetical documents, Cavalletti and Gobbi came to realize that the Church's mission of catechesis requires all-encompassing *pedagogy* that includes not only sound catechetical content, but a method worthy of that content. Most critically, they came to recognize that the content-method relationship in catechesis is incomplete without a deep understanding of the child who receives catechetical formation. They came to see that the child needs more than information about God; she needs a formation in how to be with God—how to speak to him and listen to his voice. The child needs more than sensory materials that correspond with catechism statements; the child needs a catechetical language that is intelligible and stimulates wonder. The child needs faithful doctrine that satisfies his religious hungers and methodology that corresponds with his existential needs. In truth, these two women came to see that the child requires—*deserves*—an approach to his faith formation wherein the theological, methodological, and anthropological components are interrelated: *this* content, proclaimed in *this* manner, because of *this* child. The approach that the child needs is the Catechesis of the Good Shepherd.

Conclusion

The various attempts to renew catechesis in this current age highlight one or another of the principles of God's pedagogy. Catechesis must indeed be educative, personal, liturgical, and evangelizing. Yet it must be all of these *simultaneously.* As we will see, each of these aspects of God's pedagogy, and more, are found in the unique approach of the Catechesis of the Good Shepherd. It is my hope that the previous chapters on the history of modern catechesis have provided you with the necessary background for evaluating the positive contribution that the CGS model offers catechetical practice in our time. In the subsequent chapters of this book, I offer a thorough examination of the nature of the CGS approach that responds to the theological, methodological, and anthropological concerns that catechetical theorists throughtout the twentieth century sought to address.

Chapter 6

Converging Gifts:
Sofia Cavalletti and
Gianna Gobbi

Introduction

In an investigation of the pedagogical components of the Catechesis of the Good Shepherd approach, it seems essential to know something about the women who began this work, Sofia Cavalletti and Gianna Gobbi. Though they never sought to draw attention to themselves, Patricia Coulter, an early disciple of Cavalletti and Gobbi, as well as coauthor and translator of a number of Cavalletti's books, confirms that the principles of the CGS approach draw from the strength of each woman's personal and professional formation.[1] Sofia's was a "strong theological foundation, with its reverence of the Bible and the liturgy as direct sources of God's self-communication to us."[2] Gianna's was a solid pedagogical foundation, "with its respect for the person and the potential of the child."[3]

In chapter 5, I recounted Cavalletti's catechetical session with Enrico, Paolo, and friends. In this chapter, I would like to bring to light some of the reasons for the unconventional choices that Cavalletti and Gobbi made in developing the CGS approach, prompted by their observations: *What was different about that first day with Enrico and Paolo? What had they done? Why did the boys want to return?* In probing their choice of catechetical content and method, we find in Cavalletti's biographical information the significant influence of many theologians. The shelves of her personal library

---

1. Patricia Coulter, "Appendix B: A Brief History of the Catechesis of the Good Shepherd," in Cavalletti et al., *The Good Shepherd and the Child: A Joyful Journey,* 101–104.
2. Coulter, *The Good Shepherd and the Child: A Joyful Journey,* 102.
3. Coulter, *The Good Shepherd and the Child: A Joyful Journey,* 102.

were lined with the works of Augustine, Aquinas, Chenu, Vagaggini, Rahner, Ricoeur, Daniélou, Bouyer, and de Chardin. I would also argue that the first and fundamental influence was her biblical professor, Eugenio Zolli, chief Rabbi in Rome during World War II, who later converted to Catholicism. Likewise, biographical reflections on Gianna Gobbi reveal her to be an outstanding educator, formed extensively by the work of Dr. Maria Montessori.

As they journeyed together through the course of their fifty-year adventure in catechesis, Cavalletti and Gobbi were tethered to two grounding principles, which enabled them to remain faithful to the Church even while experimenting with catechetical content and methodology. Coulter identifies these two principles most eloquently:

> The first rests on the belief that God, who is Love, seeks to love us and for our love, and that the human heart hungers to receive and return this love. The second pillar rests on the belief that since God's love is unconditional, including the condition of chronological age, even the very young child is invited into this covenant relationship.[4]

These particular positions, from which the theologian and the educator approached children's catechesis, converged in such a manner as to create a unique catechetical approach that bears the critically important catechetical hallmark of *fidelity to God and fidelity to man* (see DC, 179).

The Theologian: Sofia Cavalletti (1917–2011)

Sofia Cavalletti was born August 21, 1917, in the heart of Rome, Italy. She lived, worked, and died within walking distance of the Vatican. Though she never spoke of her ancestral pedigree and conducted herself with all humility and simplicity, those who knew her personally remarked that she was "a woman of great refinement and education."[5] Only once did Cavalletti allude to her social standing when she reminisced, "I did not go normally to school until I was ten years old because little girls of my social level usually had teachers who taught them at home."[6]

---

4. Coulter, *The Good Shepherd and the Child: A Joyful Journey*, 102.
5. Augusta Poluzzi shared this with me in a personal conversation on October 4–6, 2014, at the international *Consiglio* gathering in Phoenix, Arizona.
6. May, "Cavalletti." Talbot School of Theology, https://www.biola.edu/talbot/ce20/database/sofia-cavalletti.

Marchesa

As was a woman of high social status, Cavalletti bore the title of *Marchesa* (Baroness).[7] Other clues to her social and intellectual standing include her access to a private tutor during World War II and her subsequent matriculation to Rome's prestigious Sapienza University, where she received a doctorate, holding the distinction of being the first woman to do so.[8] Her home on the Via degli Orsini, where she established the Catechetical Center of the Good Shepherd Catechesis, was the same building that served as Pope Pius XII's ancestral home.

In an interview with Scottie May, Cavalletti shared that she received her religious education primarily from her parents, something for which she was particularly grateful since it "contrasted greatly from that of the parish churches and convents [which] offered—just catechism!" Her comment elicits wonder about the nature of the approach used by her parents and whether its method of catechesis influenced the CGS approach. Likewise, her secular education was rather remarkable for today's standards. She learned to read at home and was sent to grammar school (*ginnasio*), where she received a classical education studying, among other things, Latin and Greek. These she "learned with great joy and pride." During her extended years at the *ginnasio*, she received a secondary school education that was in her opinion "very unsatisfactory."[9] At the end of World War II, she began private studies and eventually entered the university. The fact that Cavalletti could afford private studies in the aftermath of the war is a further indication of her high social standing.

Biblical Scholar

Cavalletti was a true intellectual. As mentioned, she studied Hebrew and comparative semitic language, receiving a doctorate in the field. She could converse in five modern languages and was proficient in Latin, Greek, and Hebrew. A voracious reader who loved to study, she went daily to the library to study and read Hebrew. Reminiscing upon how the CGS experiment had changed her, she quipped, "The children saved me from becoming a mouse in the library."[10] Cavalletti was a prolific writer, as her own bibliography

---

7. E. M. Standing, *Child and the Church*, 124.
8. May, "Cavalletti."
9. May, "Cavalletti."
10. Sofia Cavalletti, "The Adventure of the Catechesis," trans. Rebekah Rojcewicz, in *Catechesis of the Good Shepherd: Essential Realities*, ed. Tina Lillig (Chicago: Catechesis of the Good Shepherd Publications, 2004), 7.

testifies. A recent biographer, Scottie May, records 165 entries, many of which are biblical commentaries.[11]

Around the age of twenty, Cavalletti began reading the Old Testament.[12] She remarked that this was highly unusual since "in the Catholic world of [this] time the Bible had become somewhat relegated to the church sacristy."[13] While at university, a friend encouraged Cavalletti to take a class in Hebrew offered by Dr. Eugenio Zolli, who not only ignited in her a passion for the Old Testament, but also reoriented her whole approach to the Bible. She recalled,

> with Zolli, the Bible began to open totally new horizons for me. I came to discover a profundity and multiplicity of meanings in the Bible that I had never imagined. I came to realize the enormous value of the Old Testament, not only in relation to the New Testament, but in itself. . . . I came to discover what Augustine calls the "golden thread"; that is, the constant presence of God, of God's plan, in which all the events are linked together, one to the other, in their movement forward to the fullness that all are looking forward.[14]

Cavalletti presents many of the insights that she gleaned from Augustine and her biblical studies in *History's Golden Thread: The History of Salvation*.[15]

In time, Cavalletti became Zolli's colleague, working together on Jewish and Christian relations and earning notice in the Church. She was among the first lay persons to receive an appointment to an ecumenical committee, serving on, among others, the Vatican Commission on Jewish-Christian relations and the Italian Ecumenical Commission.[16] They remained close friends until his death in 1956.

Under the mentorship of Zolli, teaching and studying Scripture was to become a lifelong passion for Cavalletti. Coulter recounts that

> Hebrew scholarship became shared work, continuing up to the time of Zolli's death. It has occupied an important position in Sofia's life ever since, with contributions to various editions of the Bible,

---

11. May, "Cavalletti."
12. Cavalletti, *Way of Holy Joy*, 61.
13. Cavalletti, *Way of Holy Joy*, 62.
14. Cavalletti, *Way of Holy Joy*, 62–63.
15. Cavalletti, *History's Golden Thread: The History of Salvation*, trans. Rebekah Rojcewicz (Chicago: Catechesis of the Good Shepherd Publications, 1999).
16. Coulter, *Joyful Journey*, 101.

translating and annotating original texts, and extensive writings on post-biblical Hebraic tradition and ecumenical matters.[17]

Like Zolli, Cavalletti was to become an established biblical scholar, publishing official commentaries on the Books of Esther and Ruth. Recognizing the genius of Cavalletti's scholarship, noted American biblical scholar Dr. Scott Hahn invited her to make a submission to his inaugural issue of *Letter & Spirit*.[18]

Rabbi Eugenio Zolli (1881–1956)

Eugenio Zolli was born Israel Anton Zoller. During World War II, he was the chief rabbi of Rome and an eyewitness to the cruelties of Rome's Nazi occupation. Zolli recounts these events and his own journey to the Catholic Church in his 1954 autobiography *Before the Dawn*.[19] After the war, Zolli entered the Catholic Church, taking the name Eugenio in gratitude to Pope Pius XII (Eugenio Pacelli), who did so much to save the Jewish people of Rome from the atrocities of Hitler's SS.

Zolli's conversion to the Catholic Church was a long journey of prayer and study. In 1945, his questions regarding the truth of Christianity were settled by a vision of Christ. As he was celebrating the liturgy of Yom Kippur, he saw Jesus and heard him say, "You are here for the last time."[20] Zolli was asked in an interview why he had given up the Synagogue for the Church. He replied, "But I have not given it up. Christianity is the integration (completion or crown) of the Synagogue."[21]

One account from Zolli's youth stands out. When he was a boy, his teacher (a rabbi) humiliated him for reasons Zolli never knew or understood. The event left an indelible mark on his character. Zolli reflects,

> In the afternoon of that memorable day, I returned to school. It was toward the end of the week, and I kept repeating to myself, "Justice: follow justice and fear thy God." In the evening home, my eyes kept gazing at the stars while I repeated to myself: "But does the *teacher* follow *justice* and fear God?" A serious question was shaping itself in my mind: to become a rabbi one has to study and to know many

17. Coulter, *Joyful Journey*, 101.
18. Cavalletti, "Memorial and Typology in Jewish and Christian Liturgy," in *Letter & Spirit, Vol.1: Reading Salvation Word, Worship, and the Mysteries* (Steubenville: St. Paul Center, 2005), 69–86.
19. Eugenio Zolli, *Before the Dawn: Autobiographical Reflections* (1954; reprinted, San Francisco: Ignatius Press, 2010).
20. Zolli, *Before the Dawn*, 8.
21. Zolli, *Before the Dawn*, 17.

things. That is true. But . . . [i]s not the Torah rather something that must be *lived*?[22]

It is likely that Zolli shared this memory with Cavalletti, for she too believed that there was more to catechesis than simply knowing many things *about* God. Faith in God was a way of life—a way of being in relationship with God.

Of the many things that Cavalletti learned from Zolli, she was especially appreciative of learning his Rabbinic way of approaching the Sacred Scriptures—the way of *midrash*. She writes, "The *midrashic* method takes seriously the fact that the Bible is ONE book in which there is always the ONE God."[23]

The Hebrew term *midrash* is derived from the root *drsh* which has several meanings: *to ask, to study, to investigate, or search out*.[24] Though the term has come to be used to describe a way of doing biblical exegesis, rabbis and biblical scholars insist that it entails more than mere exegetical method and technique.[25] As an exegetical method, *midrash* "attempts to penetrate into the spirit of the Scriptures, to examine the text from all sides, and thereby to derive interpretations which are not immediately obvious."[26]

Cavalletti's pleasure with the *midrashic* approach to Scripture is apparent in the CGS method of reading the Scriptures with the children. Cavalletti and Gobbi emphasize repeatedly that, in the CGS approach, the catechist and the child sit together to ponder the Scriptures. While each lesson has a direct aim (a doctrinal proclamation), the child's insights are equally welcomed during the catechetical session. One of my religious Sisters who uses the CGS approach shares the following story,

> A few days after I had given the presentation of the True Vine to the children, one of them stood next to me during dismissal waiting to speak with me. She said to me, "[Sister] have you been thinking about the vine?" I replied, "Yes. Have you been thinking about it too?" She said, "Yes," and continued to explain that just as the real vine takes a long time to grow fruit, it can take us a long time to do our kind deeds.

---

22. Zolli, *Before the Dawn*, 35
23. Cavalletti, *Way of Holy Joy*, 63. Italics and use of capitalization are original. It was a technique she would use in her writings to emphasize a point. I have chosen to retain it for this reason.
24. Joseph Jacobs and S. Horovitz, "Midrash (מדרש, from the root דרש, 'to study,' 'to investigate')," *The Jewish Encyclopedia* (1906), http://www.jewishencyclopedia.com/articles/10805-midrash.
25. Jacobs, "Midrash."
26. Jacobs, "Midrash."

She continued to elaborate on how some actions take a long time to perform.[27] Another Sister shares,

> Once I was pondering the Prophecy of the Names with a group of three-to-six-year-olds. One little boy on being asked, "What did you hear?" responded, "FOR US! God did this FOR US!" All of a sudden, he began to tear up . . . a five-year-old . . . overcome with joy. I suppose that the statement, "for us" is inherent in the phrase that Jesus is a gift, but this child's emphasis on "for us" exceeded my expectation of the aims of the lesson.[28]

Cavalletti's formation in the rabbinic method of reading the Scriptures gave her an experience of what first-century catechesis would have been like. As Jews, all the apostles would have teased out the meaning of the Scriptures with Jesus, their rabbi. Jesus asked his disciples probing questions and we can easily imagine that this became their own model for introducing others to the Lord.

Biblical Criticism

Cavalletti equally credits Zolli for helping her navigate through the Church's fruitful, though tumultuous, use of biblical criticism. Biblical interpretation, especially in the wake of the Enlightenment, was at the center of the twentieth-century theological project, engaging both Protestant and Catholic biblical scholars.[29] The emergence of the historical-critical method of biblical exegesis raised serious questions against the Catholic Church, especially since much of its theology was built upon particular interpretations of the Scriptures.[30]

Biblical criticism in its fullest understanding "is the examination of the literary origins and historical values of the books composing the Bible, with the state in which these exist at the present day."[31] It is a method for evaluating the objective historical value of Scripture "in light of modern philological, historical, and archeological science, and subjects to severe tests the previously accepted and traditional views on the human authorship, the

---

27. Personal account of Sr. Imelda Garrison, OP.

28. Personal account of Sr. Anna Christi Solis, OP.

29. See Ford, ed., *The Modern Theologians: An Introduction to Christian Theology Since 1918* (Hoboken, NJ: Wiley-Blackwell, 2005).

30. For a superior scholarly treatment of biblical criticism, see Scott Hahn and Ben Wiker, *Politicizing the Bible: The Roots of Historical Criticism and the Secularization of Scripture 1300–1700* (New York: Herder & Herder Books, 2013).

31. George Reid, "Biblical Criticism (Higher)," *The Catholic Encyclopedia* (1908), http://www.newadvent.org/cathen/04491c.htm.

time and manner of composition of the sacred writings, and discriminates as to their objective historical value." [32]

While Cavalletti notes that there is much good in the various methods of interpreting the Scriptures, in the end, these methods lack the substantial spirit in which the Scriptures were written and by which they should be read. She clearly breaks from the overly technical approach to reading the Scriptures in favor of the method of reading the Scripture with the heart.[33] Notwithstanding, though Zolli opened Cavalletti's heart to the Scriptures, he no less opened her mind. Indeed, her own commentaries on Ruth and Esther demonstrate rich study and analysis of the Scriptural texts.[34]

Scripture and Catechesis

It is clear that Cavalletti's biblical studies influenced the catechetical praxis of CGS. Cavalletti is helpful in identifying the influence herself:

> Consigning the historical-critical method to second place I discovered many methods of reading the Bible that were in tune with the new currents of scholarship (structuralism, narrative, etc.) and in which it was not easy to get one's bearings. I note especially the scholars of the Biblical Institute which I read with interest and benefit. . . . Of course, these books from the best scholars in the biblical field are important and very useful. Nevertheless, they are insufficient to help give that lift to one's wings, which is capable of placing the person who is reading in a stance of listening to a Word, a Word which has not limits and yet is addressed personally to each individual.[35]

The comment above serves to illustrate Cavalletti's concern that a highly critical approach to Scripture study can easily become a method that seeks to dominate, objectify, and dissect the biblical text, rather than foster an encounter with the Mystery it contains. It is a position she would carry into her work with children's catechesis.

Cavalletti rejected the practice of reducing catechesis to the memorization (even in a clever manner) of definitions contained in a catechism. As her understanding of the child grew, Cavalletti came to believe that this method seemed to close the door on any further reflection or meditation. In Montessorian terms, such a method conveys to the child that "all the work

---

32. Reid, "Biblical Criticism (Higher)."
33. Cavalletti, *Way of Holy Joy*, 64.
34. May, "Cavalletti."
35. Cavalletti, *Way of Holy Joy*, 64.

has been done" and there is nothing left for her to do but be a passive spectator, stifling the child's existential need to be fully engaged in her own learning. Here again, a critical parallel emerges between Cavalletti's biblical studies and the CGS approach. The Scriptures contain a Voice to be heard and a Person to be met. Just as the methods of textual analysis can lead to an objectification of the Word of God, so too the formulaic approach to catechesis can lead to an objectification of God, fostering an attitude that "we have God all figured out," closing the door on any fresh wonder of his Mystery.

Cavalletti credits Dominican moral theologian Dalmazio Mongillo for helping her to recognize that an overly technical and intellectual approach to catechesis is problematic. Father Mongillo was a professor of moral theology at the University of St. Thomas Aquinas (the Angelicum) in Rome. Cavalletti recalls a conversation they had about the nature of catechesis, when Father mentioned in dismay, "God [has become] an abstraction to be thought about rather than a Person to be encountered and enjoyed."[36] Many years after Father Mongillo's voiced concern, the greatest theologian of our time, Pope Benedict XVI, would write in his inaugural encyclical, "Being a Christian is not the result of an ethical choice or a lofty idea, but the encounter with an event, a person . . . " (*Deus caritas est*, introduction).

Liturgy and Catechesis

Cavalletti's study of the Jewish Passover liturgy, the *haggadah* or *seder*, was also extremely formative for her. Her understanding of the liturgy as *memorial* enabled her to penetrate the reality of the Paschal Mystery made present at every liturgical celebration. She writes, "[T]hrough the liturgy the great events of the history of salvation are made present *here* and *now, for me*."[37] The Eucharistic liturgy is the central theme—indeed the apex—of the CGS approach. In some fashion, all the doctrinal proclamations and works in the CGS approach prepare for a full participation in the Eucharist or guide the children in how to live from these sacred mysteries.

Another strong influence on Cavalletti's liturgical formation was Father Cipriano Vagaggini, osb. Vagaggini was personally appointed by Pope St. John XXIII to serve as an expert at the Second Vatican Council and was one of the chief architects of the *Dogmatic Constitution on Sacred Liturgy*,

---

36. Cavalletti, "Christianity? To Enjoy a Person," in *Journals of the Catechesis of the Good Shepherd, 2003–2008*, ed. Mary Fox, trans. Patricia Coulter (Chicago: Catechesis of the Good Shepherd Publications, 2009), 113–115.

37. Cavalletti, *Way of Holy Joy*, 69.

Sacrosanctum concilium. His work *Theological Dimension of the Liturgy*, first published 1957, remains an important text in liturgical studies today. Cavalletti relied on Vagaggini's advice, particularly in the early stages of the Catechesis, when she was preparing her lectures for the adult formation classes.[38] She notes that Vagaggini helped her to recognize that the liturgy did not "speak a language of abstract theology." Rather, the liturgy is a language of "signs—the universal, concrete language that is grasped not only with the mind, but with the eyes, by looking, touching."[39]

Helping children read the language of the liturgy is a fundamental task in the CGS approach. It begins with the three-year-old, who learns the articles of the altar and liturgical colors, and continues with the twelve-year-old, who orchestrates and leads a prayer service modeled on the Easter Vigil's Liturgy of the Word.

The Educator: Gianna Gobbi (1919–2002)

Gianna Gobbi was born on December 15, 1919. She lived her entire life just outside of Rome, in the Italian countryside. Fifty-one of those years were spent working side-by-side with Sofia Cavalletti, crafting the Catechesis of the Good Shepherd approach. Though Gobbi does not write about their providential meeting, she must have recognized something unique in Cavalletti's approach to catechesis, since at the time of their meeting, Gobbi had already experienced success with Montessori's approach to catechesis. The fact that Gobbi remained Cavalletti's faithful collaborator for fifty years confirms that she believed that the CGS approach had something deeper to offer catechesis. Something that completed Montessori's approach. Perhaps it was Cavalletti's biblical and specifically "rabbinic" contribution.

"Country Mouse"

In contrast to the *Marchesa*, Gianna Gobbi was born and raised on a farm and possessed a "'peasant' soul."[40] The accounts of Gobbi's life do not suggest opulent wealth, though she was the daughter of a lawyer. Her house was "modest—even rustic—yet her fields were vast."[41] She delighted more in the countryside than the city; overjoyed by "every rose that bloomed, the mushrooms we would look for in the morning under the poplar trees, and above all, by the summer

---

38. Cavalletti, *Way of Holy Joy*, 70.
39. Cavalletti, *Way of Holy Joy*, 70.
40. Cavalletti, "Gianna," in *Catechesis of the Good Shepherd: Essential Realities*, ed. Tina Lillig (Chicago: Catechesis of the Good Shepherd Publications, 2004), 48.
41. Cavalletti, "Gianna," 48.

harvest."[42] Cavalletti would refer to Gobbi as "the country mouse," an allusion to Aesop's fable "The City Mouse and the Country Mouse." Those familiar with the story immediately recognize a term of endearment and compliment given to Gianna's industriousness and practical wisdom.

Cavalletti always believed that Gobbi's remarkable insights into the nature of the child and catechesis, as well as her own personal gifts, flowed from her life on the farm. She reflects that in the person of Gianna Gobbi,

> the "peasant" patience . . . linked in an absolutely natural way with her Montessorian attitude . . . that [wished] the educator to know and respect the time of each child's maturation.[43]

As a woman of the soil, Gobbi understood the rhythm of preparing, planting, waiting, and harvesting. Formed by the seasons of farming, she "had learned very well how to wait." [44] Cavalletti reminisces,

> The second rhythms of the countryside entered into Gianna and forged in her a discipline she brought to her work as an educator. The countryside rhythms impose a discipline because they cannot be rushed but require you to wait patiently; they do not allow you to pretend, for example that a geranium flowers out of season.[45]

Just as she had watched the slow changes in nature, Gianna knew how to watch, "without attempting to hasten, the slow normalization of the child and his or her manifestation as a child of God." Hers was "the expression of a deep respect—a religious respect—in front of the manifestations of the miracle of life, in all its forms."[46]

As with Cavalletti, the gifts that Gianna Gobbi brought to the work of the CGS were both personal and professional. Gobbi's personal qualities had direct bearing on the development of the CGS approach that embodies so perfectly the gradual and progressive nature of God's pedagogy. Like the farmer, the catechist must recognize and appreciate the work that is his; but he also—and perhaps more importantly—must recognize that the work is *beyond his control.* The farmer understands that the seed bears within its nature the power to bring forth fruit; he does not create this. The soil too possesses its own natural nutrients. The farmer can supplement the soil's richness, but he cannot entirely change its constitution. For a rich harvest,

---

42. Cavalletti, "Gianna," 48.
43. Cavalletti, "Gianna," 48.
44. Cavalletti, "Gianna," 48.
45. Cavalletti, "Gianna," 48.
46. Cavalletti, "Gianna," 49.

the farmer certainly has his work of preparing the soil and caring for the sapling plants, but in no way can he hurry, much less control, the seed's natural process of growth. Our Lord drew the parallels between farming and catechesis in his Parable of the Sower (Matthew 13:1–9) and from this parable the Church draws critical lessons pertaining to its work of catechesis.[47]

A Montessorian Master

Like Cavalletti, Gianna Gobbi also had a mentor who affected the direction of her life, Italy's most famous educator of children, Dr. Maria Montessori. While still in her teens, Gobbi received training in the Montessori pedagogy and began her apprenticeship in Montessori's approach to education. At the age of twenty, Gobbi attended the Montessori course held by Adele Costa Gnocchi and Maria Antonietta Paolini. This was one of the few parallel AMI courses held in the 1930s in Europe while Maria Montessori was in India. According to Coulter, Gobbi received her Montessori training "clandestinely under the fascist government."[48]

Gobbi's studies led her to choose early childhood education, working with children as young as two years of age.[49] Only after she had begun her work as a Montessori teacher did Gobbi have the privilege of meeting Dr. Montessori. At the completion of her formation, Gobbi worked for fifteen years in various *Casa dei Bambini* (Children's House) schools with Adele Costa Gnocchi. In 1951, after many years of experience with children and one year before Montessori's death, Gobbi was invited to assist in a Montessori teacher training course. Her involvement in the training continued beyond the formation of teachers. By 1960, this included the "Assistants to Infancy," a specialized work of forming adults to care for children from birth to three years of age. Eventually, her work in this field would extend beyond Italy, leading her to direct adult formation courses in Mexico and in the United States.[50]

It is easy to recognize the professional gifts that Gobbi brought to the work of CGS. As a Montessori master, she was instrumental in creating materials that would help the child enter into the mystery of God's revelation, which Sofia understood so well. The gift of understanding the pedagogy of the child would be Gobbi's special strength and contribution in the partnership. As one ex-atrium "bambini" reminisced at Gobbi's funeral:

---

47. See also GDC, 15–33.
48. Cavalletti, "Gianna," 42.
49. Cavalletti, *Joyful Journey*, 102.
50. Cavalletti, *Joyful Journey*, 102.

"In my memory, it was Gianna's work to take the children by the hand and lead them to the Word of God, while Sofia brought the Word of God to the children."[51] This is not to say that Cavalletti was not involved in the formation of materials for the atrium. On a visit to Cavalletti's apartment, Augusta Poluzzi showed me the workroom full of wood and woodworking tools that Cavalletti used to create the CGS materials. As I marveled over the display, Poluzzi humorously pointed out, "Gianna had the ideas, but Sofia had the tools."

Although Cavalletti and Gobbi differed in their backgrounds and styles, they were the dearest of friends. In a tribute following Gobbi's death, Cavalletti reminisced:

> Everything was so intertwined between us. . . . In every material that I look at, I see Gianna's pencils and pens, and also my saws. There is no material that was only her work or only mine. This intertwining, so evident and visible in the atrium, corresponds to an intertwining of feelings, of agreements, of passions, that our relation created between us. I will never be grateful enough to Gianna for this friendship, and to Adele Costa Gnocchi, who made us meet.[52]

Always, Cavalletti was struck by Gobbi's wisdom and her insight into the nature of children, marveling at the juxtaposition between the peasant and the researcher. "It is not possible to separate the peasant Gianna from the researcher and Montessori educator," Cavalletti recalls. "In [Gianna], the soul of the educator and the soul of the 'peasant' were combined in perfect unity, and both constituted her person."[53] With deep admiration and appreciation for Gobbi's wisdom regarding the child, Cavalletti would often speak of her as the greater gift of the CGS partnership.

Maria Montessori (1870–1952)

Already in chapter 1, we briefly considered Maria Montessori's contribution to the modern catechetical project, but her influence on Gianna Gobbi, and thus the CGS approach, was so significant, Montessori deserves a fuller consideration. Without exaggeration, Montessori ranks among the great

---

51. Cavalletti, "Gianna," 49.
52. Cavalletti, "Gianna," 49–50.
53. Cavalletti, "Gianna," 48.

thinkers of her time and ours.[54] She lived during a time when women were not regularly admitted to the university, yet she undauntedly pressed for admittance into Rome's school of medicine and was awarded a degree in 1896. According to biographer Rita Kramer, Montessori claimed that "Pope Leo XIII got [her] in."[55] She was a student of philosophy and pedagogic anthropology and then became a professor of pedagogic anthropology at the University of Rome, a position she held until Mussolini and the Fascists drove her out of the city. It is easy to conclude that her method of forming children in truth and freedom was seen as a threat to their political agendas.[56]

The late nineteenth century was a time of exciting and rapid advancements in the modern sciences. Anthropologists, psychologists, sociologists, and educational theorists all asked questions regarding the nature of the human person—specifically the nature of the child. Scientists of great fame—Itard, Seguin, Froebel, Rousseau, and Pestolozzi—approached their investigations with the rigor of the scientific method, through repeated observations, procuring great insight into who and what is the child. Unfortunately, their insights were incomplete and distorted. Lacking faith in God, they were unable to recognize the human person's true nature as *imago Dei*. This biased them against recognizing the most essential truth about the human person—namely his origin, his purpose, and his destiny in God. While recognizing the important discoveries of her contemporaries, Montessori was forthright in critiquing their limitations.

In a lecture given in California in 1915, Montessori remarked that Rousseau's work "remained in the field of theory" and was never put to "practical application." Pestalozzi produced "results very far from those which [his] theory promised." His method "failed as a result of too much mechanism and pedantry" and in the end could not "free the child from scholastic slavery." Froebel's method remained "too systematic, too mechanical and parroted." Froebel's idea of kindergarten actually did violence to "the faculty of the child's will, compressing and distorting it with rigid discipline."[57]

---

54. A few outstanding resources on her life and her work include E. Mortimer Standing, *Maria Montessori: Her Life and Work* (1957; reprinted, New York: Plume, 1998); Rita Kramer, *Maria Montessori: A Biography* (New York: Putnam, 1976); Angeline Stoll Lillard, *Montessori: The Science Behind the Genius* (Oxford: Oxford University Press, 2005); Robert Buckenmeyer, *The Philosophy of Maria Montessori: What It Means to Be Human* (USA: Xlibris, 2009).

55. Kramer, *Montessori*, 35.

56. Buckenmeyer, *Philosophy of Maria Montessori*, 73.

57. Montessori, *1915 California Lectures*, 361.

Montessori believed there was a better way to help a child develop and she made it her life's work to discover that way.

Montessori's Discovery of the Child

Following the work of Seguin, Montessori's original experiment was with children who were classified as intellectually disabled. Her measurable success in being able to teach such children to outperform their non-disabled peers caused Montessori (and others) to wonder what the results might be if the non-disabled child was given a similar opportunity to learn and develop.[58] Fifty years of observation and experimentation around this question produced a *method of life* that resonates with the deepest reality of who and what the child is. Gianna Gobbi reflects,

> Montessori's discovery . . . of the characteristics of the child was completely new and previously unsuspected. This discovery of the child's true nature forms the basis of her work in education. What is often referred to as "the Montessori Method" is a view of education as "an aid to Life itself."[59]

At the time of Montessori's work, children's education focused on "forcing them into the adult world."[60] In response to this, Montessori devoted her life to discovering the "secret in the child which was being overlooked."[61] Based on the meaning of "discover"—*de* (away) and *coverir* (to cover)— Montessori considered the discovery of the child as an unveiling or uncovering of the child's true, God-given nature. [62] From her years of observing children, Montessori concluded that the child possessed unique psychological, physical, emotional, and spiritual exigencies that must be met if education had any hope of being effective.[63] She taught emphatically that the "process of education would continue to *damage the child* until adults accepted that children were persons in their own right."[64]

From the beginning, Montessori was adamant that she sought not just a better way of teaching children, but a better way of aiding their natural

---

58. Montessori, *The Montessori Method*, originally published as *Scientific Pedagogy as Applied to Child Education in "The Children's Houses" with Additions and Revisions by the Author*, trans. Anne George (New York: Frederick Stokes Company, 1913), 41–42.

59. Gianna Gobbi, *Listening to God with Children: The Montessori Method Applied to the Catechesis of Children*, ed. and trans. Rebekah Rojcewicz (Loveland, OH: Treehaus Publications, 1998), 69.

60. Montessori, *Secret of Childhood*, 110.

61. Montessori, *Secret of Childhood*, xi.

62. Montessori's second book published in 1948 is entitled *The Discovery of the Child*.

63. Montessori, *Absorbent Mind*, 3–17.

64. Montessori, *Secret of Childhood*, 110; emphasis added.

development. Her approach—the Montessori Method—seeks to assist children, from birth to maturity, along the path of reaching their full human potential. Montessori's method did not correspond to what is generally understood by school; her method was an education to *life*, and for this reason, she named her early educational institution the "Children's House" (*Casa dei Bambini*).

In truth, Montessori never intended for her educational approach to be called a "method." "There was no method to be seen," she insisted. "What was seen was the child. A child's soul freed from impediments was seen acting according to its own nature."[65] Montessori was never really pleased that her work with children was reduced to a method of education, and she repeatedly offered corrective clarification, especially to her followers in America. She emphasized that her work was a help to life and not merely a technique for schools. Montessori's approach was a radical appreciation for the child's whole development as a human person and not merely his acquisition of reading, writing, and arithmetic.

Montessori's Method

Observing how children absorb their culture, Montessori proposed a similar method of assimilation in education, rather than direct instruction. In the Montessori Method, the teacher assumes the role of guide, who helps the child to discover truth for herself through the proper use of didactic materials. The educational environment for the child is fitted according to her size and filled with activities that she can carry out without the help of adults.[66] This approach to education speaks to the delicate interplay between discipline and liberty and is deeply rooted in the Catholic notion of freedom in the formation of the human person. This notion of freedom is especially critical in the moral formation of the child.[67]

Against popular perception, the Montessori Method of instruction is not an aimless free-for-all, but a technique of instruction within the context of a *prepared environment* that enables the child to assign meaning to the objects used for instruction. Montessori writes: "The principal agent is the object itself and not the instruction given by the teacher. It is the child who uses the object; it is the child who is active, and not the teacher."[68]

---

65. Montessori, *Secret of Childhood*, 136.

66. See Montessori, *Secret of Childhood*, 110–113.

67. See Montessori, "The Teaching Methods Employed in Children's Houses," ch. 3 in *Discovery of the Child*, 41–63.

68. Montessori, *Discovery of the Child*, 149.

On this point Montessori relies on the realist epistemology of St. Thomas Aquinas and that of Aristotle before him. Epistemological realism recognizes the existence of objective truth in reality and, most importantly, the intellect's power to know that truth. In chapter 11, we consider more fully the contributions of Aristotle and Aquinas regarding the nature of knowledge as it relates to the work of education.

Montessori's Discovery of the *Religious* Child

Montessori's concern for pedagogy did not stop at the secular education of children, but extended to her treatment of catechesis as well. While it is not apparent in Montessori's writing that she had a direct intention of uniting herself to the catechetical movement of the twentieth century, she nevertheless joined its criticism of the prevailing manner of children's catechesis. Montessori insisted that education in the faith requires a unique pedagogy more fitting to its subject matter and more faithful to the child's way of learning and relating to God. In her lectures, Montessori often challenged the manner in which religion class was treated the same way as "history, geography and any other subject." Children need to have their "religious sentiment developed" and this requires an altogether other way of educating them in the faith.[69] According to Montessori, the problem was "not so much a question of *what* to teach as of *how* and *when*."[70] In due time, Cavalletti and Gobbi would offer the corrective nuance that it most certainly is a question of *what* to teach as well.

In her work *The Child in the Church*, first published in 1929, Montessori criticizes the manualist method that relied on the memorization of the catechism. She writes,

> [T]he preparation of the child for his full participation in the life of the Church is a much wider thing than the learning by heart of certain intellectual truths. *It is life in itself.* . . . All these things are to be *done* rather than things to be *read*.[71]

Given her understanding of the role of memory in the educative act, it does not seem likely that Montessori rejected altogether the task of memorizing doctrine. In fact, she recommends that the children *do* learn things by heart. "Yes, of course," she writes, "I would have certain things learned

---

69. Montessori, *The 1946 London Lectures*, 199. See *Child in the Church*, 15–17; *The 1913 Rome Lectures*, 259–275.

70. Montessori, *Child in the Church*, 54.

71. Montessori, *Child in the Church*, 33.

by heart; but I would have the memorizing come *at the end, as a summing up after the experience.*"[72] Hence, a more faithful interpretation of her criticism would be that she was against the manner in which memorization took primacy, disconnected from an authentic learning experience.

Throughout his formative years, a child experiences reality and is given terms by which to hold that experience in his memory. The richer the experience and the more intelligible the term, the greater the retention. Montessori points to the "pedagogical method of the Church" found in the liturgy as an example.[73] The Church's liturgy engages the whole child—body, mind, and heart—in the active learning of his faith. Montessori's insight is a tremendous contribution to catechetical education and one upon which the CGS approach stands.

Another of Montessori's significant insights regarding the child was the recognition of the child's religious potential, which creates in him the aptitude for hearing God's voice, receiving his instruction, and entering into a deep relationship with him.[74] She was greatly disturbed by the failure to recognize and respect the child as one who "has a principle within him," orienting him to truth and, more essentially, to God.[75] Yet for this potential to reach its fullest expression, the catechetical setting in which the child is placed is vitally important, to foster silence and contemplation.

To foster the child's silence and contemplation, Montessori retrieved from the early Church the concept of the *atrium*. An atrium is an entryway into something greater. In the first century, the atrium was the place of instruction for the catechumens before they could enter the Church. Montessori's retrieval of both this space and its purpose indicates her attempt to revolutionize the manner of catechesis through a return to the Church's heritage of catechesis. With a new emphasis, the 2020 *Directory* recognizes the importance of the "space" where catechesis is conducted (DC, 221). In chapter 13, I examine the significance of the atrium as the sacred environment, where the child learns how to listen to God's voice and to speak to him.

Though she was very much aware that her catechetical experiment with children was reaping abundant fruit, Montessori believed that her work would be picked up one day and brought to its fullness by others. I see her prophecy fulfilled in the CGS approach. Many of the principles she observed

---

72. Montessori, *Child in the Church*, 33; original emphasis.
73. Montessori, *Child in the Church*, 22.
74. Montessori, *Child in the Church*, 22.
75. See Montessori, *Child in the Church*, 55.

and defended regarding the nature of the child and the nature of catechesis figure significantly in the Catechesis of the Good Shepherd.[76]

The CGS Adventure

Reflecting on the personal and professional formation of Cavalletti and Gobbi helps us to see how God prepared these two unassuming women for a critical mission in the Church: to propose a new model of children's catechesis that is faithful to God and faithful to the child. Cavalletti confessed readily that she and Gobbi "had no preconceived idea of what should happen when working with those first few children."[77] They had embarked on what they affectionately called "an adventure" in catechesis.[78] Their only confirmation that their new approach might be working was the joy and peace observed in the children.[79] Watching the face of the child became a marker for Cavalletti and Gobbi, who understood that the children's joy, peace, and serenity were the fruit of the Holy Spirit. Having authentically encountered Jesus the Good Shepherd, the children would rest in deep satisfaction.

While they certainly drew from the wisdom of their distinct, yet complementary, backgrounds, Cavalletti and Gobbi maintained that the project they came to pursue was always beyond their intentional manufacturing. Cavalletti recounts:

> We realized that we had been working without any secret, not mine, not ours. We had worked, following the child and adjusting our work according to the child's responses. It was only much later that we consciously realized what we had done. Initially, we just did what we did; that's all. We did what it seemed to us the child was asking us to do. And the child led us to what is essential![80]

Though both women brought their own theological and pedagogical expertise to the catechetical experiment, they remained open to the child's reception of particular themes and materials. In the end, it was the children who showed Cavalletti and Gobbi "that God not only communicates with the young child, but that in the child God finds a partner especially

---

76. Chapters 9 and 10 of this book explore more deeply the insights of Dr. Maria Montessori and their application in the CGS approach.

77. May, "Cavalletti."

78. Sofia Cavalletti, "An Adventure: The Catechesis of the Good Shepherd," trans. Patricia Coulter, in *The Way of Holy Joy* (Chicago: Catechesis of the Good Shepherd Publications, 2012), 29.

79. Cavalletti, "The Child and Peace," in *Way of Holy Joy*, 21–28.

80. Cavalletti, "Searching among Memories," 4.

responsive to the overture of love." [81] Cavalletti and Gobbi discovered that young children are not only able to enter into this profound partnership with God, but that they have a unique capacity to experience and enjoy his holy presence.[82]

Conclusion

This chapter has identified the converging gifts that Cavalletti and Gobbi brought to the development of the CGS approach. Sofia Cavalletti and Gianna Gobbi were experts in their respective fields of biblical theology and children's education. Cavalletti brought to the work a deep appreciation for the pedagogy of revelation, while Gobbi brought a deep understanding for the pedagogy of the child. These two components of catechesis interweave in the CGS approach as harmoniously as the two women who discovered it.

Neither woman set out to discover—much less invent—a new catechetical approach *per se*, yet they did. Had they attempted to create a new approach independent of each other, their efforts would have failed. The expertise of both women was necessary to complete and complement the other. The Scripture scholar needed a deeper understanding of the child; the educator needed a deeper understanding of God's pedagogy of salvation.

The Church has called for a renewal in catechesis that is faithful to God *and* faithful to man, and this requires a proper understanding of both (DC, 179). It is clear that Cavalletti and Gobbi achieved this fidelity by operating from very clear and discernible principles regarding the nature of the child and the nature of God's revelation, which enabled them to maintain the integrity of the content-method-child relationship so necessary in faithful catechesis.

---

81. Coulter, *Joyful Journey*, 102.

82. Cavalletti, "And a Little Child Shall Lead Them . . . ," in *Journals of the Catechesis of the Good Shepherd 1984–1997*, ed. Victoria Tufano (Chicago: Catechesis of the Good Shepherd Publications, 1998), 167.

Chapter 7

The Mystery of God: The Content of CGS

Introduction

In this chapter we begin our consideration of the religious content in the CGS approach. In an educational setting, the term *content* refers to that body of information also known as *content knowledge*. Content is "what" a teacher is expected to teach and "what" a student is expected to learn, and this varies greatly according to the educating institution's philosophy of education. We have already established that catechesis is an education in the faith (DC, 31), yet we also know intuitively, and the *Directory* has confirmed, that catechetical education differs from an education in grammar, math, science, or history precisely in this matter of *content* (see DC, 13–14, 58, 197). Hence, there is a primary question for all of us involved in catechesis regarding the nature of *religious education content*: *What* are catechists expected to teach and *what* are students of catechesis expected to learn?

The Church maintains that "Catechesis will always draw its content from the *living* source of the word of God transmitted in Tradition and Scriptures [that] make up a single sacred deposit of the word of God" (GDC, 94; see CT, 27; emphasis added). In other words, the very *what, why* and *how* of catechesis—its constitutive character—is drawn from the very *what, why* and *how* of divine revelation (GCD, 143). For this reason, one's concept of divine revelation has a direct bearing on one's concept of catechesis (GDC, 30). Gabriel Moran correctly identified that "[d]isagreements about catechetical theory are based on different assumptions about the nature of revelation."[1]

---

1. Gabriel Moran, *Catechesis of Revelation* (New York: Herder & Herder, 1968), 15–16.

If, for example, we think that divine revelation is propositional *truths about God*, then our catechesis will take on a more notional approach that focuses on teaching *religious knowledge*. If, on the other hand, we think that divine revelation is an *encounter with God*, then our catechetical approach will take on a more affective and existential approach that strives to foster a *religious experience*. Of course, by now, you should be wary of false dichotomies; catechesis requires *both* religious knowledge *and* religious experience as Cavalletti and Gobbi understood. How the CGS approach manages to provide both is the thesis of this book.

This chapter briefly explores the theological debates regarding the nature of divine revelation to which Cavalletti would have been exposed during the early development of the CGS approach and introduces her understanding of the Church's declaration on divine revelation *Dei Verbum* especially as it relates to the specific content of catechesis. First, a little background.

The Nature of Divine Revelation

In the years between Vatican I and Vatican II, especially in the years leading up to the Second Vatican Council, theologians fiercely debated the nature of divine revelation.[2] The discussion centered around this basic question: Is divine revelation an event—*an encounter*—or is it propositional truths that follow from the event? The polemic is not new.[3] Dominican master of theology Romanus Cessario traces the debate to similar arguments debated in the thirteenth century regarding the nature of faith: Is faith an adherence to the event, or is faith adherence to the statement about the event?[4] The answer to this directly impacts not only catechetical content but catechetical methodology as well. Is catechesis the handing on of a *what* or a *who*?

Though theologians struggled with the technical issues at hand, it would be historically inaccurate to suggest that the *neo-scholastics* rejected outright the notion of a personal dimension to revelation; they certainly did not reject that God was *personal*. Still, in the face of repeated attacks to the

---

2. Tracey Rowland, *Ratzinger's Faith* (Oxford University Press, 2008), 38–63. See also John Montag, sj, "The False Legacy of Suarez," in *Radical Orthodoxy*, ed. John Milbank, Catherine Pickstock, and Graham Ward (New York: Routledge, 1999); Aidan Nichols, *Engaging Theologians* (Milwaukee: Marquette University Press, 2013), in particular chapter 5, "De Lubac and Reginald Garrigou-Lagrange."

3. Yves Congar, op, offers a masterful treatment of the issues and debates in *Tradition and traditions: A Historical and a Theological Essay* (London: Burns & Oates, 1966). Rene Latourelle, sj, likewise provides an excellent history of the theological discussions and developments in *Theology of Revelation* (New York: Alba House, 1966). See in particular part 3, chapter 4, "The Theology of Revelation in the XX Century."

4. Romanus Cessario, *Christian Faith and the Theological Life* (Washington: CUA Press, 1996), 63–68.

validity of Church doctrine, especially during the Modernist crisis, in the years following Vatican I, it is not surprising to find an overemphasis and at times exclusive emphasis on the propositional character of God's revelation. Noted Scripture scholar Gerald O'Collins observes,

> Vatican I did speak expressly of God "revealing himself" but the trend to depersonalize was unmistakably there, so that revelation was presented as the disclosure of new truths about God, the communication of a body of doctrine, a privileged enriching of our knowledge about God. The upshot was that revelation came to be closely associated with notions of creed, correct doctrine or a collection of doctrines. The assent of faith was understood as assent to doctrine. It was believing "the things" to be true which God has revealed.[5]

Thus, it comes as no surprise that catechesis inherited a restricted view of catechetical content that became synonymous with propositional statements of faith. As theologians of the *nouvelle théologie* challenged the propositional view of divine revelation, in time catechetical theorists would challenge the propositional view of catechetical content.[6]

While not dismissing the propositional character of revelation, the Fathers of the Second Vatican Council recovered for the Church (and for catechesis) a fundamental understanding that Jesus Christ is the *living deposit*, sent by the Father, revealed by the Spirit, and who remains present in the Church. *Dei Verbum*, paragraph 2, reads:

> It pleased God, in his goodness and wisdom, to reveal himself and to make known the mystery of his will (see Eph 1:9). His will was that men should have access to the Father, through Christ, the Word made flesh, in the Holy Spirit, and thus become sharers in the divine nature (see Eph 2:18; 2 Pet 1:4).

Reflecting on this passage from *Dei Verbum*, Jesuit theologian Avery Dulles comments, "Revelation is presented, not simply as a communication of knowledge, but as the dynamic process by which the divine persons invite men to enter into a relation of fellowship."[7] Revelation is not merely truth bearing statements, but *Truth Himself* (DV, 6). With careful distinction,

---

5. Gerald O'Collins, *Foundation of Theology* (Chicago: Loyola Press, 1971), 24.

6. Karim Schelkens, *Catholic Theology of Revelation on the Eve of Vatican II: A Redaction History of the Schema "De fontibus revelationis"* (1960–1962) (Boston: Brill, 2010). Tracey Rowland, *Ratzinger's Faith* (Oxford University Press, 2008). Victor White, *Scholasticism* (London: Catholic Truth Society, 1959). See also Flynn and Murray, Kerr, Nichols, Montag, and Mettepenningen cited above.

7. Avery Dulles, *Revelation and the Quest for Unity* (Washington: Corpus Books, 1968), 86.

Cessario engages the false dichotomy that Dulles seems to introduce. He writes, "There can be no opposition between *First Truth-Speaking* and 'truth-bearing-statements.'"[8] Truths about God serve as necessary portals to his reality. Because our intellect can only think in terms that are intelligible, we need intelligible terms in order to think about God and thus to be in conversation with him.[9]

The matter of *intelligibility* remains a question regarding children's catechesis as well as of adults. The language of a catechism is often not easily intelligible. On the other hand, the rejection of the symbiotic relationship between God who is First Truth-Speaking and those statements that are truth bearing has produced disastrous results in the faith formation of at least four generations of Catholics who have little if any knowledge of the teaching of Jesus or his Church. It is unfortunate that, in the wake after the Council, many prominent catechetical theorists, such as Gabriel Moran and Thomas Groome, misinterpreted the theological insights of *Dei Verbum* and promoted a "content-less catechesis" (see GDC, 30).

Cavalletti's Theology of Revelation

In my estimation, Cavalletti did not have an original theology of revelation, as did Gabriel Moran, for example. Her view of divine revelation is similar to what Dulles calls the "Revelation as History Model," which gives "priority of event over interpretation."[10] First there is an encounter with God; and after this comes the understanding of that encounter. In other aspects she aligns herself with the symbolic approach of Paul Tillich and Paul Ricoeur,[11] relying especially on Ricoeur's understanding of "signs."[12] Of the five models proposed by Dulles, it seems to me that Cavalletti aligns most with the "cross-fertilization" approach, gathering from each model elements that she considers valid and synthesizing them into a cohesive whole.[13] One thing

---

8. Cessario, *Christian Faith*, 62.

9. Cessario, *Christian Faith*. Chapter 2 is particularly relevant for understanding this relationship.

10. Avery Dulles, *Models of Revelation* (1983; reprinted, Maryknoll, NY: Orbis Books, 2005), 54.

11. Paul Tillich (1886–1965) was a Lutheran theologian who was influenced by Heidegger's existentialism. Tillich's theological tome *Systematic Theology* (published in three volumes, 1951, 1957, 1963) emphasizes the symbolic nature of the Christian religion which he understood as God's way of revealing infinite Truth through finite means. His Christology was unorthodox in so far as he taught that Jesus was not substantial God but only a symbolic revelation. Paul Ricoeur (1913–2005) was a French philosopher who was influenced by Husserl's existential phenomenology. As a philosopher, Ricoeur explored the nature of many things but a primary interest was the human person, specifically the person's reflexive consciousness and the language to describe one's experience.

12. Cavalletti, *Religious Potential 1*, 131.

13. See Dulles, "The Models Compared," in *Models*, 128.

seems clear: Cavalletti opposed any reduction of divine revelation to theological propositions. She writes,

> In the past thousand years, much of theological thinking tended toward the abstract and intellectual. As a result, catechesis often abandoned the eloquent language of images in favor of theological definitions or explanations.[14]

For Cavalletti, the content of catechesis is not "abstract information" but "the Mystery of the infinite God, revealed as an inexhaustible source of richness for us."[15] For Cavalletti, the inexhaustible mystery of God is not "definable" and when we try to do so in catechesis, we risk causing "dangerous confusion . . . in the mind of the person to whom we wish to communicate the mystery."[16]

Cavalletti's view may sound critical of the Church's doctrinal heritage. If that were true, she would find herself in direct opposition to the Church and to Pope St. John Paul II, whom she held in high regard and affection.[17] We must, therefore, interpret Cavalletti's comments about theological definitions as a pedagogical concern. To the unprepared heart and mind, doctrinal definitions can obscure the doctrinal mystery leading to misunderstanding rather than clarity.[18]

For Cavalletti, divine revelation is primarily "the encounter with a living Person"[19]—the "encounter of the infinite mystery of God."[20] Drawing from her Hebrew studies, Cavalletti came to appreciate the intimate knowledge that the Israelites had of God. "Israel does not know God merely because it has heard about him," she explains, "Israel knows God because it encountered him in its own life."[21] Of course this view that revelation is the encounter with God is not without its potential risk, especially when it is applied to catechetical practice. Moran's application caused him to dismiss the Church's doctrine altogether. Cavalletti, however, maintained that the

14. Cavalletti, *Joyful Journey*, 31.

15. Cavalletti, *Joyful Journey*, 32.

16. Cavalletti, *Religious Potential 1*, 126.

17. Pope St. John Paul II writes: "Catechesis is an education in the faith of children, young people, and adults which includes especially the teaching of Christian doctrine imparted, generally speaking, in an organic and systematic way, with a view to initiating the hearers into the fullness of Christian life" (*Catechesis tradendae*, 1, 2).

18. Pope Francis addresses the same concern in *Evangelii gaudium*.

19. Cavalletti, *History's Golden Thread*, 1.

20. Cavalletti, *Joyful Journey*, 32.

21. Cavalletti, *History's Golden Thread*, 12.

primary place of encounter with God was in his word and, in a special way, in the Church's liturgy.[22]

Word *and* Event: Knowledge *and* Experience

Because sacred events, past and present, are the meeting place between God and mankind, they serve as the meeting place of religious knowledge *and* religious experience. On this point, Cardinal Ratzinger is most helpful in reconciling potential polemics:

> [I]nstead of a legalistic view that sees Revelation largely as issuing of divine decrees, we have a sacramental view, that sees law and grace, word and deed, message and sign, the person and his utterance within one comprehensive mystery [sic] from this there follows the understanding of revelation as dialogue. . . . Revelation in totality equals "Word & Event"—touches man in his totality, not only challenging his reason, but, as dialogue, addressing him as partner.[23]

Ratzinger's insight is significant in that he became a chief architect of *Dei Verbum*, as well as an authoritative voice for its interpretation. He maintained his theological position while serving as the secretary for the Congregation of the Doctrine of the Faith and then as the Holy Father.

Where can we experience the events of God's revelation today? In the events of salvation history proclaimed and made present in the celebration of every divine liturgy. Cavalletti explains:

> Liturgy . . . frees the historical occurrence from its limits in time and space and constantly re-presents it throughout all time. . . . In this way, persons of every age, as each one enters into history, can become active participants [in the saving events] and enjoy the richness of divine life that springs forth from it.[24]

The events of salvation history recorded in the Scriptures are celebrated in the Church's liturgy (CCC, 1145ff.). Through the signs and symbols of the liturgical rites, the events of salvation become intelligible for the child. The mind grasps their meaning on the level of truth, the heart on the level of experience. The words of Scripture and the liturgical signs and gestures serve as portals to God's reality and, as such, allow the child to experience

---

22. See Cavalletti, *Religious Potential 1*, 135–136.

23. Joseph Ratzinger, "Revelation as Dialogue," in *Commentary on the Documents of Vatican II*, ed. H. Vorgrimler (New York: Herder and Herder, 1969), 171–172.

24. Cavalletti, *History of the Kingdom of God 2*, 6–8.

God. Cavalletti's emphasis on the experience of God is an intentional attempt to broaden the concept of catechetical content and to see it as the *inexhaustible mystery* of God.[25]

"Inexhaustible Mystery"

The Word that unfolds itself to the catechist and the child is "unfathomable."[26] In saying this, Cavalletti makes the point that, while there is much that we can know about God (the Church's rich doctrinal heritage indicates no dearth of insight), there is always more to discover. Not only that; in light of the unsurpassable mystery of the divine, any knowledge of God must always be regarded as incomplete. God is an inexhaustible mystery. Hence, the material content of catechesis (its sources, curricular themes, and proclamations) likewise must bear an inexhaustible quality.[27]

Scripture and the liturgy are inexhaustible and for this reason they are the most fitting and intelligible portals to God, who is himself an inexhaustible mystery. We could also say that the lives of the saints (those canonized and those "next door") serve as portals to God's inexhaustible mystery as well. Their splendid array of ethnicity, personality, talents, and even struggles bear witness to the manifold ways in which God is encountered and known (see DC, 100).

The Church has "always venerated the divine Scriptures just as she venerates the body of the Lord . . . [f]or in the sacred books, the Father who is in heaven meets His children with great love and speaks with them" (DV, 21). There is a particular grace that accompanies the reading of and meditation upon the Sacred Scriptures, one that is tangible to the soul who encounters the very presence of God in the Scripture. And how can this be? The Scripture is a true portal to God because it is his inspired word. The Holy Spirit did not simply inspire the Sacred Scriptures, "He inhabits it. His breath permanently animates it."[28] The oft quoted saying of St. Jerome, "Ignorance of Scripture is ignorance of Christ" refers not merely to notional knowledge about Jesus; from our prayerful reading of Scripture we *encounter* the Lord.

As with Sacred Scripture, God is truly present and active in the Sacred Liturgy (*Sacrosanctum concilium*, 7). The word *liturgy* (*leitourgia*) literally means "work *for* the people." In the Christian tradition the term *liturgy* refers

25. See Cavalletti, *Religious Potential 1*, 126.

26. Cavalletti, *Religious Potential 1*, 126.

27. Cavalletti, *Joyful Journey*, 32.

28. Francis Martin, "Sacred Scripture: The Disclosure of the Word" (Naples, FL: Sapientia Press, 2006), xii. Martin references Marcellino D'Ambrosio's unpublished dissertation on Henri de Lubac.

to "the participation of the People of God in 'the work of God'" (CCC, 1069), highlighting the fact that God has done a great work for us in redeeming us from sin. It is through the liturgy, especially in the Eucharist, that the "work of our redemption is accomplished" (SC, 2). Drawing forth from the heritage of their Catholic liturgy, Cavalletti and Gobbi knew that if they put the child in touch with the inexhaustible treasures of the liturgy, they would put the child in touch with the inexhaustible treasure of God.

Inexhaustible *and Objective*

Though Cavalletti was opposed to using a catechism with children, she was not opposed to objective religious knowledge. Indeed, no properly trained CGS catechist would ever say that doctrine is not essential to the CGS pedagogy without betraying Cavalletti's own view of the work. "Wishing to stay on a vague level, without any specific content," she once reproached, "is the same as wanting the child to talk but without using any particular language. If we want to speak of the religious reality, we need to use language."[29] "In regard to content," she continues, "we have a wealth of sources at our disposal: the Bible, the liturgy, and the magisterium of the Church. *If we hold faithfully to these, we will have a secure foundation.*"[30]

The curriculum[31] in the CGS approach is doctrinally rich, containing an abundance of the itemized doctrines in the *Catechism of the Catholic Church*. The national CGS office for the United States of America provides an analysis chart demonstrating CGS's conformity with the documents of the Church, including the *Catechism of the Catholic Church.* [32] In addition, CGS catechist and formator Dr. Gerard O'Shea has carefully aligned the CGS curriculum with the *Catechism of the Catholic Church*, highlighting the extent of objective doctrine proclaimed throughout the three levels.[33]

---

29. Cavalletti, *Joyful Journey*, 12.

30. Cavalletti, *Joyful Journey*, 31; emphasis added.

31. By "curriculum" I simply mean the sequence of doctrinal presentations that span the three levels. Though the term is not used by CGS, I am using it because within the CGS approach there exists a very clear—though not rigid—course of study. The genius of Cavalletti and Gobbi is that they discovered the best course for presenting doctrine to the child at a time when the child is most eager to listen to and receive a particular doctrine.

32. The United States Association of The Catechesis of the Good Shepherd, "Catechetical Themes in Levels I, II, III CGS and Relevant Church Documents" https://www.cgsusa.org/resources/.

33. O'Shea, "Appendix A: Organization of Content in Liturgical Spiral Curriculum, Kindergarten-Gr. 7 (US Schools)," *Educating in Christ*, 215–241. O'Shea's book, *Educating in Christ: A Practical Handbook for Developing the Catholic Faith from Childhood to Adolescence*, is an invaluable resource for all catechists and a masterful application of the pedagogy of CGS. O'Shea's work makes several additions to the CGS curriculum which have proven to be beneficial to children in the catholic school setting.

Each presentation (what non-CGS catechists might call a "lesson") in the CGS cycle of presentations has both direct and indirect aims. The direct aims include the doctrinal point(s) proclaimed by the catechist as well as other unquantifiable aims of catechesis, such as greater participation in the liturgy (see DC, 95). The indirect aims are those additional doctrinal points that the Holy Spirit may lead the child to grasp.

Though Cavalletti would say that catechesis should not be *intellectualized*, she placed great value on truth, study, and the Church's doctrinal legacy. Her own CGS formation courses were appropriately doctrinally intense, drawing from a variety of theological sources within the Church's tradition, especially from the Church Fathers, the *Catechism of the Catholic Church*, and documents of Vatican II.

There is a valid concern that not every CGS formation course offers the same doctrinal legacy that Cavalletti handed on to her catechists. While most of my training courses were exemplary, I have participated in others that rarely mentioned a Church document or the *Catechism of the Catholic Church*. This to me seems to compromise Cavalletti's intention that the CGS catechist herself be well formed in matters of the faith and not merely in a catechetical technique. Nevertheless, though anomalies exist in current formation practices, such do not represent the true nature of the CGS approach or invalidate Cavalletti's personal concern for *orthodoxy*, which was consistent while she lived. In a 1998 message to CGS catechists throughout the world, she emphatically reminded her catechists to be faithful in their proclamation of the Church's doctrine. She writes:

> Every catechist should be able to apply to himself the mysterious words of Jesus: "My teaching is not mine, but his who sent me" (John 7:16). St. Paul did this when he was dealing with a question of prime importance, "I received from the Lord what I also delivered to you" (1 Cor 11:23)—what detachment from self must a catechist have to be able to say, "My teaching is not mine!" (CT, 6). The text cited establishes a principle of the utmost importance in catechesis: the need for the catechist to be rigorously objective in the transmission of the message.[34]

Recognizing the symbiotic relationship between the *fides quae creditur* and the *fides qua creditur* (the faith believed and the faith by which we believe), Cavalletti insisted that doctrinal "vagueness violates the Incarnation—there

---

34. Cavalletti, "The Objectivity of Catechesis," in *Journals of the Catechesis of the Good Shepherd 2003–2008*, ed. Mary Fox, trans. Maureen Armas-Wess (Chicago: Catechesis of the Good Shepherd Publications, 2009), 100.

must be a message," she insists. "[I]t must be announced."[35] Indeed, to do otherwise violates the incarnational dimension of God's pedagogy.

Objective *and Essential*

Though Cavalletti cherished the Church's doctrinal legacy, she did not agree that its traditional form of presentation, namely a catechism, was suitable for the *child*. In her view, children need simple language—*essential* language. If the child is to advance in knowledge of God and understanding of the magisterial teachings of the Church, she must first be taught the "ABCs of Christianity."[36] Cavalletti explains,

> [T]he ABCs are an ensemble of signs relating to fundamental sounds, an indispensable instrument to place us in communication with reality. Obviously, they do not give me reality in its entirety, but signs are a means of being able, potentially, to reach everything. They serve to open infinite horizons for us, always taking as our departure point that ensemble of signs.[37]

To impose upon children words that are beyond meaningful understanding is equivalent to giving a child a book to read before teaching him the alphabet, an exercise that Cavalletti considered futile.

Cavalletti and Gobbi discovered that certain themes and proclamations in the Scripture and liturgy serve as an *essential alphabet* for the child's faith, opening her to the infinite horizons of faith. Scripture and liturgy are more intelligible to the child because they are more essential. Let us not forget that Cavalletti's choice for biblical-liturgical language was likewise motivated by the inexhaustible nature of God. "[B]iblical-liturgical language knows that its contents are greater than the container, because in bringing us close to the Mystery it cannot speak other than by means of allusions."[38]

Regarding language, Cavalletti's position seems to contradict the 2020 *Directory*, which states that catechesis is the bearer of a specific "*biblical . . . symbolic-liturgical . . . doctrinal . . .* and *formative language*" (DC, 204–205; italics original). Indeed, the question has been asked by non-CGS catechists, "Why are some doctrinal words such as *grace* or *Trinity* not

---

35. Cavalletti, *Religious Potential 1*, xxxv.
36. Cavalletti, "ABCs of Christianity," in *Journals of the Catechesis of the Good Shepherd 2014–2018*, ed. and trans. Patricia Coulter (Chicago: Catechesis of the Good Shepherd Publications, 2018), 100–103.
37. Cavalletti, "ABCs of Christianity," 100.
38. Cavalletti, *Way of Holy Joy*, 45.

found in the CGS curriculum?" First of all, some CGS catechists do actually use the terms *grace* and *Trinity* when reflecting on their theological reality. Some children seem to embrace these terms, other do not. Notwithstanding, the doctrine of grace is certainly proclaimed in many of the CGS presentations, but Cavalletti observed that the child's meditation on the reality of grace was aided better with the image of *sap flowing through the True Vine* and terms that convey the same theological meaning as grace such as "*God's life,*" "*God's love,*" or "*God in us.*" It is a matter of pedagogy. Catechetical terms must be intelligible if the child is to cogitate and meditate on their reality.

Arguing from the standpoint of the faith of the early Christians, Cavalletti would remind her catechists that "there was a Church . . . that preceded the great councils."[39] In other words, prior to the more explicated doctrines promulgated by the Councils, there existed an essential, objective doctrine that drew directly from the life and teachings—particularly the parables—of Jesus. As the first-century martyrs attest, the *kerygma* sufficed as doctrine (*orthodoxy*) that was more than sufficient to evoke in the hearts and minds of the early Christians a response to God that was not only faithful (*orthopraxis*), *it was heroic to the point of death.*

"We should not think," Pope Francis exhorts, "that the Gospel message must always be communicated by fixed formulations learned by heart or by specific words which express an absolutely invariable content" (EG, 129; DC, 59). The same essential doctrine that inspired martyrs and saints in the early Church is the same essential doctrine proclaimed to the child in the CGS approach. This essential doctrine not only fits the child, but it also actually prepares him for more advanced knowledge about God, as well as a deeper knowledge *of* him.

Essential *and Existential*

Cavalletti had a deep appreciation for the Hebrew tradition of knowing God—what she called a "Semite knowledge" of God. [40] "Israel's knowledge of God [was] not merely speculative," she writes. It was "experiential or, more precisely, existential."[41] Traditionally, this knowledge has been referred to as *heart* knowledge. Cavalletti refers to it as "affective integration"—an "awareness grasped by the heart and mind *together.*"[42]

---

39. Cavalletti, *Way of Holy Joy,* 67.
40. Cavalletti, *Religious Potential 2,* 52.
41. Cavalletti, *History of the Kingdom 1,* 10. See also Cavalletti, *Religious Potential 1,* 6.
42. Cavalletti, *Joyful Journey,* 66; emphasis added.

"Friendship with God follows the same rule as friendship with people," Cavalletti observes. "One cannot know another person if one has only heard about him or her, but has not actually met him or her."[43] This seems self-evident. Whatever can be said about a person—his description, his interests, his preferences, his actions—certainly leads to some knowledge of who that person is and may even be helpful in recognizing that person in a crowd. Nevertheless, to truly *know* another person, there must be an encounter, even multiple encounters. The same is true with God. "As an active God and a person," Cavalletti insists, "God is not known through speculation; (but) rather, . . . by entering into communion with him, assenting to dialogue with him."[44] We must be careful to not take Cavalletti's words out of context, for properly speaking, she herself was a speculative theologian. From the Latin *spectare*, to speculate is "to look." Authentic speculation is an *intelligent contemplation* of truth.

It seems clear to me that the entire CGS project is the fruit of Cavalletti and Gobbi's intelligent contemplation of God and his children. These women looked and looked and *looked again*. From their observations of the child's responses to God, Cavalletti and Gobbi found confirmation that they were indeed on the right path of helping the child to see—*to contemplate*—God's loving, merciful, and beautiful Face. Furthermore, we know that Cavalletti was not entirely biased against "speculative theologians" for she herself makes appeal to one of the Church's greatest speculative theologians, St. Thomas Aquinas.[45] We have testimony from the canonization process of St. Thomas Aquinas that when he was perplexed by a theological difficulty, he found his answer while on his knees in prayer.[46] Hence, Cavalletti's criticism can only refer to a too often caricatured *method* of theology attributed to scholasticism.

Despite Cavalletti's repeated criticism of the scholastics, I maintain that she is not anti-intellectual. Her concern is pedagogical. To her, catechesis had become *hyper*-intellectual, reduced to a mere mastery of information about God, with little opportunity to speak to him or delight in him. On this point, Cavalletti is a prophet of the 2020 *Directory*, which likewise proposes a more well-rounded catechetical pedagogy (DC, 165).

---

43. Cavalletti, *History of the Kingdom 1*, 11.

44. Cavalletti, *History of the Kingdom 1*, 11.

45. See Cavalletti, "The Water and the Wine of the Eucharist," in *Journals of the Catechesis of the Good Shepherd 1984–1997*, ed. Victoria Tufano (Chicago: Catechesis of the Good Shepherd Publications, 1998), 34–35.

46. As cited in Mary Carruthers, *The Book of Memory: A Study of Memory in Medieval Culture* (New York: Cambridge University Press, 1990), 6.

Knowing God . . .

What is the role of the intellect in catechesis? How *does* one come to *know* the inexhaustible mystery that is God? What does it actually mean to *know* God? These are critical questions that require our serious consideration if we are to avoid one or the other extremes that continue to negatively impact catechesis. For Jesus Christ clearly taught that eternal life is this: "to know" both him and the Father (see John 17:3). In chapter 11, we will examine the technical aspects of what it means to know. For now, let us consider a more biblical understanding of knowledge.

There is a kind of knowledge gained only through personal intimacy, as when Adam "*knew* his wife Eve and she conceived and bore Cain" (Genesis 4:1).[47] Such knowledge is what some Scripture scholars call "biblical knowledge."[48] Biblical scholar Dr. Mary Healy explains that the Hebrew verb *yāda'* (*to know*) suggests much more than theoretical apprehension of an objective reality.[49] Though this knowledge does not exclude what is theoretical, it entails much more.[50]

The desire to foster *a biblical knowledge* of God forms an important principle for the CGS approach as it strives to fulfill the aim of catechesis, which is to "put others not only in touch but in communion, in intimacy with Jesus Christ" (CT, 5). The specific choice of doctrinal content in the CGS approach and the method, by which that content is proclaimed, work together to satisfy both head *and* heart.

. . . through the Events of Salvation

Dei Verbum states that "[t]he works performed by God in the history of salvation show forth and bear out the doctrine and realities signified by the words; the words, for their part, proclaim the works, and bring to light the mystery they contain" (DV, 2). Commenting on this passage, Cavalletti writes,

> [T]he priority given to God's works by the Dogmatic Constitution on Divine Revelation *Dei Verbum* is noteworthy . . . and witnesses

---

47. Emphasis added.

48. See Mary Healy and Robin Parry, eds., *The Bible and Epistemology: Biblical Soundings on the Knowledge of God* (Milton Keynes, UK: Paternoster, 2007). See also Ian Scott, *Paul's Way of Knowing: Story, Experience, and the Spirit* (Grand Rapids, MI: Baker, 2009).

49. Mary Healy, "Knowledge of the Mystery: A Study of Pauline Epistemology," in *The Bible and Epistemology: Biblical Soundings on the Knowledge of God* (Milton Keynes, UK: Paternoster, 2007), 141.

50. While not dismissing Healy's insights, Gregory Vall counters the modern rejection of the propositional or theoretical dimension of knowledge of God. See Gregory Vall, "An Epistemology of Faith: The Knowledge of God in Israel's Prophetic Literature," in *The Bible and Epistemology: Biblical Soundings on the Knowledge of God* (Milton Keynes, UK: Paternoster, 2007), 30–31.

to a God who is active in the history of humankind, which cannot encounter God except by participating in divine activity.[51]

According to the *Catechism of the Catholic Church*, the events of salvation history—in particular those of Jesus—are not "swallowed up in the past" but become moments of experience for each generation (see CCC, 1085). Christ is present in each of his sacraments, effecting the same transformation in grace today that he offered while on this earth. The source and summit of the sacraments is the Holy Sacrifice of the Mass, wherein the Paschal Mystery of Christ is re-presented (see CCC, 1085). Echoing the Church's teaching, Cavalletti writes,

> In [all the events of sacred history], humankind encounters God and comes to an ever deeper knowledge of him. This knowledge that God bestows on humankind is never abstract, but is tied to and rooted in human life. In the Bible God does not explain who he is in conceptual terms; rather, God enters into communion with human beings, allowing them to experience divine love, justice and tender mercy.[52]

The child is called to communion with God through our Lord's same saving events. For these events to become meaningful, the child must experience them:

> If our reading of the Bible is truly to be an encounter with the living God, we must be aware of the *reality* of the biblical events in our lives. We must realize that those ancient events preserved for us in the Bible are *present* in our lives today in some way.[53]

In the Church's liturgy, these same events of salvation history are experienced, "those acts through which the Church makes present Christ's redemptive work in all times and places."[54]

If the purpose of catechesis is to insert others into the mystery of Christ—*and it is* (CT, 5)—then the fullest place of encountering and being inserted into his mystery is in the divine liturgy. Citing Vatican II's Dogmatic Constitution on the Sacred Liturgy *Sacrosanctum concilium*, the *Catechism* states:

> The liturgy is the summit toward which the activity of the Church is directed; it is also the font from which all her power flows. It is

---

51. Cavalletti, *History of the Kingdom 1*, 11.
52. Cavalletti, *History of the Kingdom 1*, 11.
53. Cavalletti, *History of the Kingdom 1*, 12.
54. Cavalletti, *History of the Kingdom 1*, 14.

therefore the privileged place for catechizing the People of God. "Catechesis is intrinsically linked with the whole of liturgical and sacramental activity, for it is in the sacraments, especially in the Eucharist, that Christ Jesus works in fullness for the transformation of men." (CCC, 1074)

The Eucharist is the central theme of the CGS curriculum because "the Mass is the place and time in which we encounter our Good Shepherd in a most particular way."[55] At Mass, the Good Shepherd "calls His sheep to come around His altar to feed them with Himself in a special way."[56] For this reason, all three levels of CGS present the events of salvation history as *leading to* and *for the sake of* fostering a rich *participation in* the liturgy.

Conclusion

At the beginning of this chapter we asked the question: "What is the nature of catechetical content?" Throughout the chapter we have considered the Church's answer to this question as well as Cavalletti's understanding of the answer: the *content* of catechesis is nothing less than *God himself*! In studying the unique pedagogy of the CGS, we discover an original understanding of catechetical content. By original, I mean at the *origin* of catechesis itself. *Catechesis tradendae* asserts, "At the heart of catechesis we find in essence the Person of Christ" (CT, 5). The inexhaustible nature of divine revelation serves as one of the foundational principles for the CGS approach, guiding its choice of material content (the doctrinal proclamations). It is for the sake of preserving the quality of God's unfathomable mystery that CGS relies on the words of the Scriptures and liturgy for its primary text.[57] Cavalletti never wanted the child to have the impression that "everything has already been researched and resolved and that nothing remains for the individual to do."[58] The words of the Scriptures and the liturgy possess an inexhaustible nature providing for the child a rich source for continuous contemplation.

This chapter explored the mystery of God and pointed to biblical-liturgical language as the best means for communicating his mystery. In chapter 8 we will discuss the particular manner in which the CGS approach reveals the mystery of God to the child.

---

55. Cavalletti, *Religious Potential 1*, 49.
56. Cavalletti, *Religious Potential 1*, 49.
57. See Cavalletti, *Way of Holy Joy*, 45.
58. Cavalletti, *Religious Potential 1*, 126.

Chapter 8

Revealing the Mystery of God

Introduction

As mentioned in chapter 4, one of the theological and catechetical conundrums regarding revelation that theologians tried to reconcile in the years before and after Vatican II was how Jesus could be the definitive and sum total of God's revelation in history, and yet still reveal himself to each person. This is a critical point to be settled if we are to reconcile religious knowledge and religious experience. While some theologians, such as Gabriel Moran, have proposed a theory of ongoing revelation (that is, there is new revelation still coming), Cavalletti rejects this proposal and reconciles the tension by first affirming that in the Word become flesh, the mystery of God has been revealed and realized among us. Jesus is the culminating point of God's economy of salvation.[1] Yet God "continues to make Himself known through the sacraments, in which there is always present a material and perceivable element[2]" Because he is God, our Lord's words and actions do not remain in the past; they are an ever-present reality in the liturgy (CCC, 1083).

This chapter will explore specifically how Cavalletti navigates the discussion of God revealed and God revealing by examining her understanding of typology and memorial. "The mystery *speaks* and *acts*," she writes. One reaches it by listening and participating in the sacramental celebration. When the mystery speaks and we listen to it, the method of listening is *typology*. When the mystery is celebrated and we participate in it, the way of

---

1. Sofia Cavalletti and Patricia Coulter, *Drinking from the Sources: How Scripture and Liturgy Shape Our Christian Life* (Chicago: Catechesis of the Good Shepherd Publications, 2015), 62. See also *Dei Verbum*, 4.

2. Cavalletti, *History of the Kingdom 1* (first edition), 6.

participating is *memorial*.[3] The convergence of typology and memorial offers a way for God's revelation to be simultaneously historical *and* experiential. Let us explore more deeply the meaning of these terms and how each provides a way to reconcile the catechetical conundrum.

Typology and Memorial

"Typology and memorial," Cavalletti writes, "are bound together at the level of the Reality that draws us near: the infinite mystery of God."[4] *Typology* refers to a way of reading the Scriptures that enables one to see the unity between the events of the Old Testament and those of the New. The explanation of typology is best summarized by St. Augustine: "The New Testament lies hidden in the Old and the Old Testament is unveiled in the New."[5] *Memorial* carries a deeper reality than a simple mindfulness. From the Jewish understanding of *zakar* and *zikkaron* we inherit a concept of memorial that means to make present again or to *re-present*. God says to Noah, "I will remember (*zakar*) my covenant . . . between me and you" (Genesis 9:15). "*Memorial* renders the event it celebrates objectively present, thereby making it possible for us to participate in [those events] today."[6] "We must say," Cavalletti writes, "that typology and memorial are *the methods* connatural to the mystery of God revealing himself in history."[7]

Typology and memorial exhibit a kind of freedom from time. "The distance between events seems to disappear, and the events merge into one unified expression of God's salvation and love, in which the past and future are fused."[8] Memorial expresses in the present those saving events of the past and prepares us for their eschatological completion, anticipating it and preparing for it in prayer and hope.[9] Together, typology and memorial converge in the liturgy, where the events of the Bible continue to touch our lives, and the history of God's people becomes our history in a most particular way.

Drawing from the Church's own catechetical tradition, Cavalletti understood that the Bible and the liturgy are not two separate entities but

---

3. Cavalletti, *History of the Kingdom 1*, 23; emphasis added.
4. Sofia Cavalletti, "Memorial and Typology," in *Letter & Spirit I* (Steubenville: St. Paul Press, 2005), 85.
5. St. Augustine, *Questions on the Heptateuch*, 2.73; and *Catechism of the Catholic Church*, 129.
6. Cavalletti, *History of the Kingdom 2*, 7.
7. Cavalletti, "Memorial and Typology," 85; original emphasis.
8. Cavalletti, *History's Golden Thread*, 22.
9. Cavalletti, *History of the Kingdom 1*, 23–24.

are two distinct moments of one, lived reality.[10] "The events of the Bible are made present once again in the liturgy and for this reason the Bible is a book that contains both the prehistory and the history of each of us."[11] As the Israelites crossed through the Red Sea into the Promised Land, so too the baptized person passes through the blessed waters that provide passage to his heavenly homeland. As God fed the Israelites manna in the desert, so does he continue to feed his faithful people with the Bread of Life.[12]

Everything in the CGS approach is oriented to the liturgy—to helping the child perceive the biblical events of salvation history in the liturgy and to see those same saving events relating to his own life. In this way, CGS prepares the child for full and active participation in the liturgy that celebrates his personal *narratio* of salvation and that of all mankind. Initiation into the Church's liturgical celebration is thus an initiation into the very mystery of God.[13]

Covenant

Cavalletti's theological understanding of divine revelation as the encounter with God is best expressed thematically as *covenant*.[14] "God's covenant relationship with each of us is the central theme of the Bible. . . . [It] is the core of the Christian message."[15] Covenant denotes a particular relationship between persons—a relationship that is personal while carrying a specific, objective response or obligations. The covenant that God made with the people of Israel affected the whole life of the whole people.[16] Cavalletti offers an important consideration and clarification of this term *covenant*:

> The terms *pact* and *covenant* point to a relationship that is not biological nor a given fact as is the relationship between parents and their offspring. Such a relationship does not require an agreement but is already established naturally. *Pact* and *covenant* indicate an

---

10. See Cavalletti, *History of the Kingdom 1*, 117. Writing in the fourth century, St. Ambrose illuminates the relationship between Scripture and the liturgy in his seminal works, *De Mysteriis* and *De Sacramentis*. More recently Pope Emeritus Benedict XVI refers to the integral relationship between typology and memorial as *mystagogical catechesis*. See *Sacramentum caritatis*, 64.

11. Cavalletti, *History's Golden Thread*, 16.

12. See Cavalletti, *History of the Kingdom 2*, 5–11.

13. Cavalletti, *History of the Kingdom 1*, 22.

14. See Cavalletti, "Religious Formation and Later Childhood," in *Journals of the Catechesis of the Good Shepherd 1984–1997*, ed. Victoria Tufano, trans. Patricia Coulter (Chicago: Catechesis of the Good Shepherd Publications, 1998), 5.

15. Cavalletti, *Joyful Journey*, 1.

16. See Cavalletti, *History of the Kingdom 1*, 82.

act of the will, a free choice resulting in a bond that did not previously exist.[17]

The notion of "[c]ovenant means relationship between the One who calls and the one who answers."[18] "God seeks [mankind]" who responds to "the divine voice" calling all persons to new life.[19] Simply put, covenant entails both gift and response. It indicates a free choice on God's part, as well as a free choice on the part of human beings, who accept the gift of God.

An intriguing way that the CGS approach educates the child in the covenantal relationship with God is through its unique choice of themes and the manner of their presentation. Some of the themes that run through the CGS curriculum include the Plan of God, the Good Shepherd, the Vine and Branches, the Maxims, and the Mass.[20] In a seminal text, *Ways to Nurture the Relationship with God*, Cavalletti and Coulter examine more specifically how these themes nurture the child's covenantal relationship with God.[21]

Gift and Response

At the heart of the covenant is the "double movement of gift and response."[22] We hear the echo of this in God's words spoken through the prophet Jeremiah: "[Y]ou shall be my people, and I will be your God" (30:22). Every gift includes a giver. "Gift is not a unilateral action," Cavalletti observes, "but, by its very gratuitousness, it elicits a response."[23] When a gift is received, there is a natural response of gratitude and a desire to return the gift as well. The response to a gift becomes a "bilateral act that aspires above all to establish a relationship."[24]

Thus, the concept of covenant embraces the threefold reality of gift, giver, and receiver. One of my religious Sisters tells the story of a child in her

---

17. Cavalletti, *History of the Kingdom 1*, 82.
18. Cavalletti, "The Source of the Moral Life," in *Journals of the Catechesis of the Good Shepherd 1998–2002*, trans. Alan Perry and Rebekah Rojcewicz (Chicago: Catechesis of the Good Shepherd Publications, 2003), 38.
19. Cavalletti, "Source of the Moral Life," 38.
20. Other themes include the Kingdom Parables: the parables of the Mustard Seed, Pearl of Great Price, Leaven and Bread, and the Ten Bridesmaids. For an excellent analysis of how these various themes and others in the CGS curriculum convey the covenantal relationship see Cavalletti, "The Source of the Moral Life."
21. See Sofia Cavalletti and Patricia Coulter, *Ways to Nurture the Relationship with God* (Chicago: Catechesis of the Good Shepherd Publications, 2010).
22. Cavalletti, "Source of the Moral Life," 38.
23. Cavalletti, "Religious Formation," 5. See also Cavalletti, *Religious Potential of the Child 6 to 12 Years Old: A Description of an Experience*, trans. Rebekah Rojcewicz and Alan R. Perry (Chicago: Catechesis of the Good Shepherd Publications, 2002), 29–32. See also Aquinas STh I-II, q. 110, a. 1.
24. Cavalletti, "Religious Formation," 5. See also Cavalletti, *Religious Potential 2*, 29–32.

atrium, who upon receiving a presentation on the history of the Kingdom of God and the Blue Unity Strip, erupted with a spontaneous joyful, "For me! For me! He's given this all for me!"[25]

In catechesis we know that the Gift is both the *Person* of God and his *Plan* for our salvation (see CCC, 51). These are not two opposing realities; rather, each serves the other. The personal dimension of God giving himself to mankind includes an objective path by which we fully receive him, dwell in him, and in the end, become one with him. Jesus, as God's perfect gift of himself to us, not only shows us the way: he *is* the Way (see John 14:6). In recognizing this, the child comes to discover the Giver of these gifts. Recognizing that he is loved by a personal God, the child seeks to respond by loving him in return. The child seeks to be with God and to follow his way.

One of the most significant strengths of the CGS approach is that from the child's first days in the atrium, she is invited to reflect not only on the gifts received through creation and redemption, but also on her response to those gifts—her own reception and use of these gifts. The child comes to recognize that, every day, each person makes choices for how she is to live the *objective* events of salvation history, thus writing her own *subjective* page in salvation history. In CGS this is referred to as *the blank page*.[26] Of the many works that the children complete during their time in the atrium, this work that invites the children to write their own page in salvation history is perhaps the most concrete expression of how the CGS approach unites doctrine and life.

Kerygma and *Parenesis*

Cavalletti sees the double movement of *gift and response* in the relationship between the *kerygma* and *parenesis*—between hearing and receiving the Gospel and the living of that Gospel. Referencing the meaning of the word *catechesis*, which is "to echo" or "to resound," Cavalletti explains:

> The "sound" to which we seek to give voice in the CGS has two fundamental notes: *kerygma*, which is the proclamation of the Christian message, the transmission of what God makes known to us of himself; and *parenesis*, or moral exhortation, which indicates the appropriate response to what God has made known to us.[27]

---

25. For a sample presentation on the Blue Unity Strip, see appendix A.
26. For a sample of a child's blank page, see appendix B.
27. Cavalletti, "The Source of the Moral Life," 36.

The 2020 *Directory* addresses this delicate relationship between *kerygma* and *parenesis*, reminding catechesis that proclamation of God's saving love precedes any moral or religious obligation (DC, 59). Any tension between the two falls away when the material content (the specific doctrinal proclamations) is expressed in covenantal terms or in the language of *gift and response.* God offers himself to us in a covenant of love and invites our free response in love.

In Cavalletti's estimation, the purpose of catechesis is to serve the covenant relationship between God and the person.[28] In the "covenant relationship with God, children find what is most precious in themselves: the capacity to love."[29] Thus catechesis or "religious education should focus on helping the child to enjoy the relationship with God with deep awareness and great wonder."[30] With great insight Cavalletti writes:

> Relationship with God is founded on a deep, existential level that stems from the certitude of a presence, a presence of love that attracts with the great force of "seduction," but not more than the child [is] inclined toward and [has decided] to follow; therefore, a presence that does not impose but appears to await a response.[31]

For this reason, the CGS catechetical education is marked by a certain quality of freedom and patience. The goal of the CGS approach, if it can be expressed as a goal, is to aid the child in her discovery of God's love and to show her how to live with gratitude for the saving actions of Christ, which the child experiences in and through the liturgy.[32] Does the CGS approach fulfill this educational goal? Once, Cavalletti asked a group of older children, "What is the connection between the Bible and the Eucharist?" "The God who gives," a child responded.[33]

The Plan of God

A second aspect of divine revelation, and thus a prominent theme in the CGS curriculum, is God's plan of salvation (DV, 11). Inspired by St. Paul's letter to the Ephesians, Cavalletti observes, "A plan has always existed in the mind of God, the aim of which is to bring humankind to the full enjoyment of

---

28. Cavalletti, *Joyful Journey*, 13.
29. Cavalletti, *Joyful Journey*, 12.
30. Cavalletti, *Joyful Journey*, 95.
31. Cavalletti, *Religious Potential 1*, 6.
32. Cavalletti, *Joyful Journey*, 13.
33. Cavalletti, *Religious Potential 2*, 122.

God."[34] This plan, also known as sacred history, or God's "plan of loving goodness" (CCC, 51), is the account of God's interaction with mankind to bring man to his greatest glory.[35] Throughout all three levels of CGS, the child reflects upon the theologically rich and profoundly mysterious theme of the *Plan of God*.

The Plan of God is composed of two principal phases—as recounted in the Old Testament and the New Testament—and is marked by three principal moments in biblical history: creation, redemption, and *parousia*.[36] The term *parousia* is a transliteration of the Greek word παρουσία. In classical Greek, the word had the meaning of "presence" or "arrival." In the Old Testament, *parousia* refers to the day of the Lord (YHWH), and it is a technical term for God's saving acts in history. In the New Testament, *parousia* is an eschatological concept expressing faith in a final act of God that is to occur when human history has reached its divinely determined goal. This act of God will usher in a life in which all humanity is completely under the rule of God.[37] In CGS terms, *parousia* is when "God may be all in all" (1 Corinthians 15:28).

Together, these three moments—creation, redemption, and *parousia*—serve as a "golden thread" for all of the presentations in the CGS curriculum.[38] Cavalletti observed that the children's responses to these three presentations of biblical history were always encouraging, but the children's response to the presentation on the *parousia* has traditionally been the most evocative. She reflects,

> In relation to these presentations [Creation, Redemption and Parousia], we have been given to see how deeply satisfied the children are in discovering themselves to be essential "collaborators"—even if very small—in a history that is moving toward a goal [the Parousia], which will come through God's gift and also through the commitment of each one of us engaged in it.[39]

The emphasis given in the CGS approach to the third moment of salvation history—the *parousia*—is significant in light of the catechetical

---

34. Cavalletti, *History of the Kingdom 1*, 1.

35. Cavalletti, *History of the Kingdom 1*, 1.

36. Cavalletti, *History of the Kingdom 1*, 2.

37. "*New Catholic Encyclopedia*, c.v. "parousia," http://www.encyclopedia.com/article-1G2 -3407708486/parousia.html.

38. "Golden thread" is a reference to St. Augustine who saw the story of salvation as a golden thread woven through the Scriptures giving unity to all doctrine.

39. Cavalletti, 'The Catechesis as Adventure," 39.

bifurcation between doctrine and life, which the Church so eagerly wishes to reconcile. In Cavalletti's estimation, to merely reflect on the Plan of God as past events of salvation history is no different than reflecting on propositional statements of faith. Somehow, these moments in Salvation History must become relevant to the child, relating to his or her life. She explains,

> In Christ, history reaches a moment of unique importance signifying a new and particular instance of divine intervention. [B]ut sacred history is not yet completed. The history of salvation continues in every person who enters into the plan of God and participates in it with his or her life.[40]

As the child comes to recognize that the third moment of salvation history is still unfolding, she wonders what her mission is and how she will help to bring about God's kingdom. One of the concepts in the atrium that encourages the child's meditation on how she will be God's coworker is the "blank page." She is in dialogue with God about her mission and seeks God's help to fulfill it. The greatest collaboration is the child's participation in the liturgy, another golden thread that runs through the CGS curriculum, tying all of the doctrines together. The liturgy is God's cosmic plan "embracing all things that are in heaven and on earth."[41] It is primarily through the liturgy that the child becomes deeply and personally engaged in participating in the building of God's kingdom as his collaborator.

The Dialogue of Salvation

In both the 1997 and the 2020 catechetical directories, the Church points to the dialogical nature of God's revelation (GDC, 143; DC, 53). According to its etymology, *dialogue* means "to speak" (*legein*) "across" (*dia*) and from this we understand dialogue as "to converse together." Drawing upon the covenantal nature of revelation, Cavalletti asserts that "covenant means dialogue."[42] God himself testifies through the words of the prophet Jeremiah that Israel's covenant with God was not one sided: "[Y]ou shall be my people, and I will be your God" (Jeremiah 30:22).

To be in covenant with God is to be in dialogue with him. How could it be otherwise? God himself is speech.[43] Yet God has not only *spoken* to mankind, he also *speaks* in the depths of each person's heart and soul.

---

40. Cavalletti, *History's Golden Thread*, 16.
41. Cavalletti, *History of the Kingdom 2*, 1.
42. Cavalletti, "The Source of the Moral Life," 38.
43. Joseph Cardinal Ratzinger, *Feast of Faith* (San Francisco: Ignatius Press, 1986), 25.

As catechists we have a twofold task in fostering the dialogue of salvation. First, as catechists, we must faithfully proclaim God's Word. Second, we must teach the child how to listen and receive God's Word.

In 1977, Cavalletti contributed a chapter on the nature of Jewish pedagogy for an Italian anthology on education.[44] Though it does not address catechesis directly, I find her insights immensely applicable to our discussion on the pedagogy of the CGS.[45] Cavalletti observed a fundamental difference between Jewish and Greek pedagogy, a difference that is ontological—at the root of being. The identity of the Jewish people was that of being a *chosen* people. They already belonged to God. While the Greeks sought Truth, the Jews were pursued by him. They simply needed to listen (*obaudire*) to his voice. Israel's *Shema* proclaims this: "Hear O Israel: The Lord is our God, the Lord alone" (Deuteronomy 6:4).

Cavalletti's insights provoke a critical question: In what manner would our catechetical practice be impacted if we were to envision catechesis as an *education in listening*? To use educational terms, what would be the unique scope and sequence of our catechetical content? What would be the unique model of presenting that content? What would be the anticipated outcomes from each presentation? Cavalletti and Gobbi had tremendous trust in God's love for the child and the child's capacity to hear his voice. Guided by this trust, they looked for themes in the Scriptures and the liturgy (sources of content) that best fostered the dialogue between God and the child. They then sought a model of presentation that helped the child to hear God's voice. Finally, they measured the success of their approach by observing in the child joy, peace, and contentment, which are the fruit of having heard God's voice and delighting in his presence.

The Call to Intimacy

As the CGS experiment continued, Cavalletti became more and more convinced of the personal nature of divine revelation and thus catechetical content. She cites the influence of the Dominican Father Dalmazio Mongillo as sparking a "Copernican moment" for her.[46] Father Mongillo, OP (1928–2005) was a professor of moral theology at the University of St. Thomas Aquinas (the Angelicum) in Rome from 1963 to 2001, during the years that Cavalletti

---

44. Cavalletti, "L'Educazione Ebraica" (Hebrew Pedagogy), in *Nuove Questioni di storia della pedagogia* (New Issues in the History of Pedagogy), vol. 1 (Brescia: Editrice La Scuola, 1977), 11–62. A publication of my translation is pending.

45. We will examine the text more fully in chapter 11.

46. Cavalletti, *Way of Holy Joy*, 72.

and Gobbi were developing the CGS approach. Cavalletti took several courses from him and consulted him on many aspects of CGS, especially in the area of the child's moral formation. She credits Father Mongillo for showing her the best approach to moral formation.

Mongillo once lamented to Cavalletti, "We have made Christianity into a lot of rules. Christianity is to enjoy a *Person*." [47] He writes,

> [C]atechesis with children is the "joyful contemplation" of the action of the Holy Spirit in the hearts of the children whom the Spirit loves; as such, it is the respectful attentiveness to the ways that nourish their growth, so that the dialogue between the Spirit and the bride [the child] not be disturbed. [48]

Though Mongillo's view had particular resonance with the *ressourcement* theologians of the 1930s and '40s , his insight was still not widely held in the 1950s, making him a rather prophetic voice for Cavalletti. Reflecting on his statement several years later, Cavalletti wrote:

> The orientation of the moral formation in the Catechesis of the Good Shepherd came from a felicitous meeting between the positive vision of the moral life from Father Dalmazio and the capacity of the children to fall in love. [49]

Here, in this discussion of catechetical content, it helps to recognize the intimate nature of the *fides quae creditur*—the Gift of God himself—and the *fides qua creditur*—the child's response to that Gift. As Innerst points out:

> [T]he personal *quality* of the *fides qua* [the faith that believes] is ordered to, or consistent with the personal *quality* of the *fides quae* [the faith that is believed], that is the whole history of God's personal self-disclosure. [50]

There can be no real opposition between the content of catechesis and its recipient. Rather, there is a harmony; and this harmony finds consonance in the child's desire to *know* and to *love* God and God's desire to reveal himself to the child.

---

47. Cavalletti, "Christianity? To Enjoy a Person," 113.

48. Dalmazio Mongillo, OP, "Preface to the Italian Edition of Religious Potential of the Child," in *Journals of the Catechesis of the Good Shepherd 1984–1997*, ed. Victoria Tufano (Chicago: Catechesis of the Good Shepherd Publications, 1998), 19.

49. Cavalletti, *Way of Holy Joy*, 72.

50. Innerst, "Narratio," 45.

Conclusion

The question "What is the *content* of the CGS approach?" has thus far been answered: "the whole *inexhaustible mystery of God.*" God, who is infinite mystery, is known and experienced through inexhaustible sources, primarily the Scriptures and liturgy. Within the category of Scripture and liturgy, there is the more precise nature of CGS content that focuses on specific themes that convey the covenantal relationship and that foster the dialogue between the mystery of God and the mystery of the child. The themes are intentionally limited in number so as to allow substantial time for the child to ponder and delight in their doctrinal mystery—the inexhaustible Love of God.

Over the course of their fifty-year experiment, Cavalletti and Gobbi recognized that certain biblical themes nourish the child's mind and heart while providing an objective proclamation of doctrine that reveals the truth of who God is and what he wants of us. The unique themes that make up the CGS curriculum invite the child to reflect on God's many gifts (creation, redemption, grace, love) while they inspire within the child a natural response of gratitude and a desire to be faithful to God's gifts. In writing his own blank page, the child grows in his awareness of how he participates in the Plan of God and comes to recognize that in the liturgy, he becomes a coworker in God's greatest work of salvation.

Chapter 9

The Mystery of the Child

Introduction

The importance of catechetical content cannot be overemphasized. When content is lacking or distorted, its recipient does not have the Gospel preached to him, and for this reason he cannot make a "sacrificial offering of his life" (CT, 30). At the same time, the content of catechesis must be conveyed in a manner befitting both the message and its receiver. The 1997 *General Directory* (GDC) draws particular attention to the "person who is catechized" (GDC, 145), emphasizing in particular that the person receiving catechesis "must be an active subject, conscious and co-responsible, and not merely a silent and passive recipient" (GDC, 167). The 2020 *Directory* exhorts us to "keep in mind that the educational goal of catechesis determines the methodological choice" (DC, 194). The 2020 *Directory*, likewise, draws our attention to the "authentic demands of human experience" (DC, 194). While the Church cautions against reducing God's "original pedagogy of faith" to a mere technique of educational psychology (see CT, 58; GDC, 30), the Church's equal insistence on fidelity to man necessitates a closer consideration of the recipient of catechesis. Who is he? How does he learn? What are his existential needs? It is easy to see that content and method cannot be considered except in relation to the child.

Catechesis does not occur in a theoretical vacuum. We teach actual people with real intellectual capacities and real existential needs. Just as catechesis must reverence the mystery of God, so too it must reverence the mystery of the child. At a decisive point in the beginning of their catechetical experiment, Cavalletti and Gobbi asked themselves the question: "How do we speak about God to *children*?"[1] At first glance, this may appear to be a question regarding methodology—and it is. It is also a question regarding

---

1. Cavalletti, *Joyful Journey*, 31; emphasis added.

content as described in chapter 4. Yet the question at hand is equally and deeply anthropological. *Who is this child? What is his mystery?* The following two chapters provide an answer to these questions.

An Anthropological Focus

In chapter 4, I offered an overview of the anthropocentric shift in catechesis that took place over a series of International Catechetical Study Weeks. Cavalletti recognized that the 1968 Study Week at Medellín was a "reaction to the intellectualistic and abstract catechetical formation of the pre-Vatican II stage."[2] Though Cavalletti and Gobbi agreed that catechesis needed more attention to life experiences, their CGS approach differs from other major interpretations of Medellín.

"The interpretation of Medellín," writes Cavalletti, "has been restricted to mean 'the reference to man should be looked for in the experience of everyday life.'"[3] Cavalletti challenged this interpretation proposing instead that the point of departure in catechesis is the person's nature. She writes,

> [W]e have even greater doubts regarding anthropological catechesis, understood in the sense of catechesis linked to—and therefore in some manner dependent on—everyday experiences. We ask ourselves in fact, if it is not the fundamental structure of the child that should be taken as the basis and reference point for that necessary "attention to man."[4]

The child's nature is rooted more deeply in his psychological configuration than what he may or may not have experienced in life. "How else can we explain," she writes, "that even children who have been abandoned and without parental affection respond with joy to the Good Shepherd?"[5]

An anthropocentric catechesis tends to focus on a person's experiences of life, and this can become shallow even with the best intentions. On the other hand, a catechesis in tune with the foundational structure of the human person and his vital exigencies—or life forces—is authentically *anthropological*.[6] An authentically anthropological catechesis rightly considers the physical, emotional, spiritual, moral, and existential needs that animate the child.

---

2. Cavalletti, *Religious Potential 1*, 141; see footnote 1.
3. Cavalletti, *Religious Potential 1*, 136.
4. Cavalletti, *Religious Potential 1*, 136.
5. Cavalletti, *Religious Potential 1*, 135.
6. Cavalletti, "Characteristics of the Good Shepherd," in *Journals 1984–1997*, ed. Victoria Tufano, trans. Patricia Coulter (Chicago: Catechesis of the Good Shepherd Publications, 1998), 27.

Though the CGS approach is preeminently concerned with the child, it is not anthropocentric—it is anthropological. The difference is worthy of our recognition and understanding.

Properly speaking, authentic catechesis must be *Christocentric* because Christ is the aim of catechesis (CT, 5) and his teachings are the heart of the catechetical proclamation (CT, 6). While addressing the need to be attentive to the person receiving catechesis, the 1997 *General Directory* presents catechetical renewal specifically in terms of a return to Christocentric catechesis (GDC, 98–100, 114, 235). I would simply argue that an *authentic* anthropological catechesis *is* Christocentric because man is made in the image and likeness of God.

Content-Method—*Child*

The GDC emphasizes that the content of catechesis cannot be subjected indiscriminately to any method (see GDC, 149). The method must serve the content. Thus, the is certainly true. Yet it is equally true that the content must serve *the child*. Thus, the content-method relationship finds its fullest expression when considered in relation to in the nature of the child following the Thomistic principle "whatever is received, is received according to the mode of the receiver."[7] In other words, the child has a particular way of receiving the Gospel that is in accordance with her very nature, and we must be willing to recognize and appreciate that way.

We read in the GDC that in the catechetical process, "the recipient must be an active subject, conscious and co-responsible, and not merely a silent and passive recipient" (GDC, 167). Hence, the solution to the problem in catechesis that history has identified as the separation of religious knowledge and religious experience is not to be found only or mainly in the proper understanding of catechetical content or proper catechetical method: it must include a proper understanding of the child who is served by both. "The child demands full respect and help in its spiritual and human growth" (GDC, 77).

In a seminal text entitled *Listening to God with Children*, Gianna Gobbi addresses the need to reconcile catechetical practice with the child's nature. She writes,

> A greater understanding of the needs of the child in the psychic sphere can aid us in understanding and respecting the needs of the child in the religious sphere. To know, at least to some degree, the

---

7. *"Quidquid recipitur ad modum recipientis recipitur."* See STh, I, q. 75, a. 5; III, q. 5.

true nature of the child means to help the child in ways that will allow him or her to develop as an integrated or "whole" person, one who is in right relationship with self, with God, and with others.[8]

God has created the child with a unique nature, possessing unique needs, desires, and stages of development. The child will only reach his full potential (physical, psychological, moral, and spiritual) when his true nature is responded to and nurtured.[9]

The *true* child, or what Montessori called the *new* child, is the child that emerges when his nature is understood and allowed to be nurtured. Indeed, the real problem of childhood is that the child's nature is rarely *nurtured*, but instead is acted upon, sometimes violently, in a manner that hinders the child's psychic development. This is done most often by those adults to whom God has entrusted the child's care.[10] As educators of the faith, catechists most especially should find the prayer of Maria Montessori readily in our hearts and on our lips: "Help us, O God, to enter into the secret of childhood, so that we may know, love and serve the child in accordance with the laws of thy justice and following thy holy will."[11]

The *New* Child

Through her observations and educational experiments with children, Maria Montessori discovered that the true nature of the child includes "inborn qualities [such as] a powerful, self-creative instinct; love of order; precocious intelligence and attachment to reality; spontaneous self-discipline and complete harmony with others in the environment."[12] "A child is mysterious and powerful and contains within himself the secret of human nature." Montessori continues, "Whoever wishes to confer some benefit on society must preserve [the child] from deviations and observe his natural ways of acting."[13]

The idea that children bear a secret is simply the recognition that "adults have failed to notice their true identity."[14] While it should seem obvious that the child should have a nature quite different from the adult,

---

8. Gianna Gobbi, *Listening to God with Children: The Montessori Method Applied to the Catechesis of Children*, trans. Rebekah Rojcewicz (Loveland, OH: Treehaus Communications, 1998), 78.

9. Montessori, *Child in the Church*, 7.

10. Montessori, *Secret of Childhood*, 1–5.

11. Montessori, *The Absorbent Mind*, 286.

12. E. M. Standing, *Maria Montessori: Her Life and Work* (1957; reprinted, New York: Plume, 1998), ix. See also Angie Lillard, *Montessori: The Science Behind the Genius*. Lillard's research is particularly valuable due to its analysis of Montessori in light of modern theories of education and child psychology.

13. Montessori, *California Lectures* (Oxford: Clio Press, 1915), 70–71.

14. Montessori, *California Lectures* (Oxford: Clio Press, 1915), 70–71.

Montessori observed that "the difference is much deeper than most people think."[15] Montessori discusses the negative ramifications of the continual conflict between adults and children due to a lack of understanding the child's true nature. One of the areas of difficulty that faced children at the turn of the century was that they were too often treated as "little adults" who merely needed time to grow up.[16] Such is apparent even in children's clothing at the time. Perhaps such misunderstandings contributed to the abstract and cognitive method of children's catechesis prevalent at her time. "There are some of those who think the child's only value for humanity lies in the fact he will someday be an adult. In this way, they detract from the true value of childhood by shifting it only into the future." [17] Yet as Montessori observes, the child's secret lay "not in what he would become but in who he already is."[18]

Psychic Needs and Vital Exigencies

The physical needs of a person are obvious and therefore more readily addressed than his or her invisible psychic needs. Yet as psychologists have increasingly come to realize, the psychic needs of a person have a far greater urgency than even the physical needs.[19] At the time of Montessori's work, Jean-Martin Charcot and Sigmund Freud had made great discoveries in the realm of the subconscious, especially discovering that some psychosis can be linked to trauma during infancy.[20] But Montessori saw their work as "inadequate, [because] it remained in the realm of the abnormal."[21] For example, Freud deduced his psychological theories while treating people with mental illness. Given this, his theories do not always lead to a cure.[22] Montessori found it more productive to observe the non-disabled child and to find ways to *assist the psychic life of children.*[23]

The child's psychic needs, or *exigencies*, are not reactions to environment: they are inner sensibilities or ontological needs, such as the need to love, to belong, to work, to engage with reality, and to act independently.

---

15. Montessori, *Child in the Church*, 7.

16. See Montessori, "The Accused," ch. 2 in *Secret of Childhood*.

17. Montessori, *Child in the Church*, 7.

18. Montessori, *Child in the Church*, 7.

19. In recent years, clinical child psychologist and former parish catechetical leader Dr. Joseph White has done much to promote a faithful marriage between psychology and catechetics. White currently serves as a national catechetical consultant for Our Sunday Visitor Publishing and is the author of *The Way God Teaches: Catechesis and the Divine Pedagogy* (Huntington, IN: Our Sunday Visitor, 2015).

20. Montessori, *Secret of Childhood*, 9.

21. Montessori, *Secret of Childhood*, 9.

22. Montessori, *Secret of Childhood*, 9.

23. Montessori, *Secret of Childhood*, 9; emphasis mine.

Montessori calls these inner sensibilities "divine thoughts being elaborated within the intimacy of the living being" that assist the person in navigating the outer world.[24] The inner sensibilities are vital exigencies that give direction and protection to the child. When the child's psychic needs are met, he becomes interiorly integrated, and this in turn helps him to become socially integrated.[25]

Conversely, when a child's psychic needs are not met, he will suffer, sometimes gravely, from this deficiency. "The neglect of the child's psychic needs manifests itself in a variety of repercussions," Montessori observed. When the child's psychic needs are not addressed, various "deviations" occur.[26] Original sin notwithstanding, Montessori was so convinced of the integrity of the child's interior exigencies that she assessed a child's tantrum as "a manifestation of a nobler trait seeking to reveal itself."[27] Under normal circumstances, a child who displays frustration or contrariness does so out of an inner need for perhaps order or freedom or security. Sr. Anna Christi Solis, OP, shares an insightful story in this regard:

> One of my three-year-olds would finish a pasting work in the atrium and then cut it up. Before my training in Montessori's Method, I would have scolded her, I am sure. Instead, I wonder about her particular need to cut even her own work. With the help of my aide, I created a specific work for her to do during Atrium that allowed her to cut. After spending many hours cutting and sweeping up the small pieces of paper, I observed in her a kind of joy and satisfaction. When she was finished she put away her materials and never cut her CGS work again. It was a mystery to me but one that I reverenced to be sure.

Maria Montessori made it her life mission to help others recognize and appreciate the child's psychic needs rather than work against them. She believed that when these needs were met, the child would become "normalized," acting with dignity and self-direction.[28]

The Normalized Child

The normalized child is one who is able to think and choose according to the inner laws of his nature. Because the child's psychic needs are governed

---

24. Montessori, *Secret of Childhood*, 201.

25. Montessori, *Secret of Childhood*, 147.

26. Montessori, *Secret of Childhood*, ch. 23.

27. Montessori, *Secret of Childhood*, 109. See also Montessori, *To Educate the Human Potential* (1948; reprinted, Amsterdam, Netherlands: Montessori-Pierson Publishing, 2007).

28. Montessori, *Secret of Childhood*, 8–12.

by an inner law set by God the Creator, Montessori was convinced that to discover these laws governing the child's development was to "discover the spirit and wisdom of God who is at work within the child."[29] "Anyone who is responsible for the child's normal development," insisted Montessori, "should become acquainted with those laws. To turn away from them would mean to lose that direction which God, as the guide of the child, gives us."[30]

Following the success of her first *Casa dei Bambini*, Montessori was convinced that catechists, too, "must respect the objective needs of the child as something which God Himself has instructed us to satisfy."[31] This understanding of the child's psyche is so critical that Cavalletti and Gobbi insist that "before catechists [can] adequately help children in their relationship with God, they must first experience a change in their inner disposition and attitude regarding children."[32] Understanding the child's psyche is also recognizing that normalization to the atrium takes time and this requires great patience on the part of the CGS catechist.

Montessori has much to say about the need for adults to carefully aid the child in developing this power, maintaining that the normalized child will opt to engage in meaningful work when given the chance.[33] Sr. Anna Christi Solis, OP, shares another story of a three-year-old who took two years to normalize. He did not speak English and would only stay in the atrium for about ten to fifteen minutes and then would dart off to be with his mom. Every time he worked with the flower arrangement, he would pluck off every petal and blow them everywhere. As a trained Montessorian, Sister knew that his behavior was the manifestation of some deeper unfulfilled psychic need. She sought ways to redirect him and offered a variety of works that might encourage his normalization. She recounts, "When Gordon returned to the atrium at the age of five, I decided to give the Liturgical Calendar presentation to him. This was a gamble since the work has over forty pieces. It could have been very messy. It wasn't." Gordon remained absorbed for over thirty minutes. When he finished, this child, who would only ever run or skip through the atrium, walked with dignity and poise to return the Liturgical Calendar to its place on the shelf and then carefully pulled off another work.

29. Montessori, *Secret of Childhood*, 4.

30. Montessori, *Child in the Church*, 14.

31. Montessori, *Secret of Childhood*, 4.

32. Cavalletti, "And a Little Child Shall Lead Them . . . ," in *Journals 1984–1977* (Chicago: Catechesis of the Good Shepherd Publications, 1978), 167.

33. See Montessori, *The Secret of the Child*, especially ch. 26, "The Instinct to Work," 85–189.

"It took a long time," Sister recalls, "but when he was ready, it all clicked for him and he has moved with self-possession and freedom ever since."

Four Planes of Human Formation

Montessori identified four distinct planes or phases of human formation: infancy, childhood, adolescence, and maturity.[34] While these phases are commonly recognized today, they were not recognized at the turn of the century. Montessori was ahead of her time and was validly recognized by the field of educational psychology for her breakthroughs.[35] To speak of *the discovery of the child*, something for which Dr. Maria Montessori remains famous, is to recognize that each physiological phase possesses its own unique psychic (including religious) demarcation.

To appreciate Montessori's revolutionary insight into the child, it is helpful to present first the common view of formation. Figure 9.1, Stages of Development, depicts this common view.

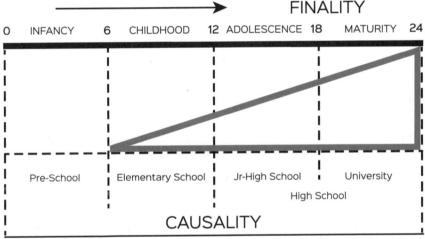

Fig. 9.1

The increasing slope of the triangle in figure 9.1 represents an increasing stage of development that simply progresses in quantity as the child grows older. Paralleling this physical growth is an educational program designed to simply increase in difficulty the same concepts that are studied in the younger ages. For example, as a child progresses through primary

---

34. Gobbi, *Listening to God*, 78.
35. See Lillard, *The Science behind the Genius*.

school to secondary school the subject of history tends to add more complexity to the same topics of American or World history.

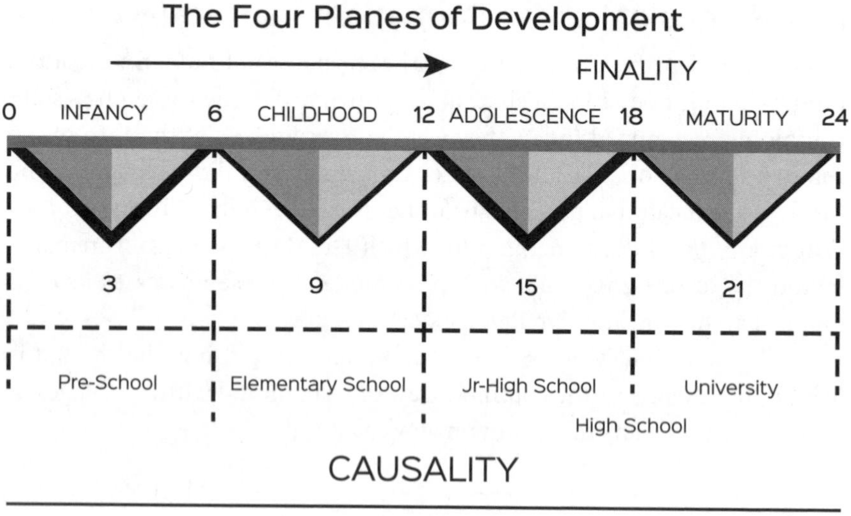

The Four Planes of Development

| 0 | INFANCY | 6 | CHILDHOOD | 12 | ADOLESCENCE | 18 | MATURITY | 24 |

FINALITY

3   9   15   21

Pre-School   Elementary School   Jr-High School   University

High School

CAUSALITY

Fig. 9.2

In contrast, figure 9.2, The Four Planes of Development, portrays the four planes of human growth observed by Montessori.[36] Gobbi explains that these phases—infancy, childhood, adolescence, and maturity—are differentiated by alternating screens of dark gray and light gray because "the [dark] gray screens represent sub-phases which are characterized by intense, constructive work." The dark gray sub-phases are followed by more tranquil and less creative light gray sub-phases "during which the earlier, intense work is being consolidated."[37]

Montessori intentionally chose a triangular form "to point out that there is a period of greater intensity during every phase of the life line [dark gray] which then decreases once a maximum is achieved [light gray]."[38] It is an inverted triangle to demonstrate that at each phase there is an incubation followed by a birth. In the life of a child there are no less than four births: first from the womb (0); another significant psychic birth occurs at 6 years, then at 12, 18, and finally 24. Surprisingly prophetic for our day, Montessori maintained that the child was not a mature adult until after the age of 24.

36. Replication mine.
37. Gobbi, *Listening*, 72.
38. Gobbi, *Listening*, 72.

| The Catechesis of the Good Shepherd

The chart at left identifies two mirrored stages of growth (set off with red lines 0–6 and 12–18). The child at these two stages experiences the greatest intensity of growth in mind and body and has a greater need for a physical experience of life. The 12–15 child, in particular, learns again his place in the world through the work of his hands. Montessori recommended that this child be apprenticed in some practical trade or work on a farm. Interpreting the diagram more fully, Gobbi writes:

> We can imagine the top line as a building being constructed floor by floor. Each floor is prepared for by the preceding one and, in turn, prepares for the next one. Obviously, one cannot begin a building with the second floor. Rather, it is necessary to start with the foundation if we want to construct a solid building that will last.[39]

In the first phase, the critical "foundations are laid for all the psychic characteristics that will accompany the child throughout life and will constitute the child's personality."[40] Gobbi's explanation is reminiscent of the Lord's admonition not to build your house on sand (see Matthew 7:24–27). Catechesis is the solidifying of the faith of one who has been evangelized (GDC, 63). Yet as many have recognized, too often the attempt is made to catechize the unevangelized, creating a spiritual edifice that is unstable and non-lasting (GDC, 63).

The CGS approach applies this understanding of the four planes of development in numerous ways. First, the CGS approach is built upon the foundational proclamation of the Gospel that God is love and he wants us to share in his love (see CCC, 221). The conceptual language for this teaching is "covenant" and it too lies at the heart—the foundation—of the CGS curriculum. What is more, the unique scope and sequence of the CGS curriculum ensures that certain doctrines are proclaimed only after the proclamation of necessary foundational doctrine is absorbed by the child. For example, the meaning of the seven petitions in the "Our Father" prayer is taught only after the child has discovered that the Kingdom of Heaven is a reality that dwells within her soul. When the child prays, "Thy Kingdom come," she recognizes that she is praying first for God to reign in her heart.

---

39. Gobbi, *Listening*, 71.
40. Gobbi, *Listening*, 72.

Sensitive Periods

Through her observations, which were definably scientific, Montessori recognized that the child has very specific interests at different times, which she called "sensitive periods."[41] E. M. Standing summarizes Montessori's insights thus:

> During the development of certain organisms there come periods of special sensibility. The periods of sensitivity are related to certain elements in the environment towards which the organism is directed with an irresistible impulse and a well-defined activity. These periods are transitory; and [they] serve the purpose of helping the organism to acquire certain functions, or determined characteristics. This aim accomplished, the special sensibility dies away, often to be replaced by another and quite different one.[42]

Montessori discusses the various sensitive periods and psychic needs of the child in her books *The Secret of Childhood* and *The Discovery of the Child*. Some of the sensitive periods include times of language acquisition and a time in which the child has an intense need for order. There is a period of intense interest in small objects and refinement of the senses when the child's five senses are highly engaged in his acquisition of knowledge. There are also sensitive periods of faith formation.[43] Recognizing the sensitive periods of faith formation of the child is critically important if we hope to offer proclamations of the Gospel that are meaningful.

Cavalletti shares an early experience of not appreciating the child's sensitive period. When she first presented the Parable of the Good Shepherd, Cavalletti included the wolf and the hireling, but the young children became distracted by the thought of the wolf going after the sheep and thus were not able to meditate on the image of the shepherd with his sheep. The more she pared down the parable, the more the smaller children became engaged. The

---

41. Montessori, *The Secret of Childhood*, 37–48. Montessori's work was inspired by the Dutch botanist and early geneticist Hugo de Vries (1848–1935), who studied the sensitive periods of development in animals.

42. E. M. Standing, *Maria Montessori*, 119.

43. Montessori, *Discovery of the Child*; see in particular ch. 22, "Religious Education." Much has been written on the topic of children's spiritual development and faith formation. I recommend to my reader only a sample of resources: James Fowler, *Stages of Faith: The Psychology of Human Development and the Quest for Meaning* (San Francisco: Harper & Row, 1981); Robert Coles, *The Spiritual Life of Children* (Boston: Houghton Mifflin, 1990); *Handbook of Spiritual Development in Childhood and Adolescence*, ed. Eugene Roehlkepartain et al. (Thousand Oaks, CA: Sage Publications, 2006); *Children's Spirituality: Christian Perspectives, Research, and Applications*, ed. Donald Ratcliff (Eugene, OR: Cascade Books, 2004); *Nurturing Children's Spirituality: Christian Perspectives and Best Practices*, ed. Holly Catterton Allen (Eugene, OR: Cascade Books, 2008).

child was deeply satisfied with the simple and essential proclamation: the Good Shepherd knows his sheep by name (see John 10:14).

Cavalletti and Gobbi recognized that the first level child falls in love with Jesus the Good Shepherd and simply needs to hear his voice. Only later, when he has reached the age of reason is the child ready to consider the wolf and the hireling. Even then, the first aim of this consideration is to simply relish the love of the Shepherd, who lays down his life for his sheep. At a third stage, the child comes to recognize that he, too, can return the Shepherd's love by laying down his life through following the Good Shepherd's commands. The gradual progression of the proclamation corresponds with the child's sensitive period.

Failure to recognize the child's sensitive periods can result in a deformation of the child's view of Jesus. One of my Sisters shares the story of a child in her atrium who had been prematurely introduced to the concepts of hell, the devil, and the final judgment.[44] When Sister proclaimed the parable of the True Vine (a parable that is primarily a proclamation of being intimately united to Jesus), this child became fixated with the vines that were cut off and burned. This is not the typical experience of children. In fact, another child in the same atrium was enamored by how many times Jesus used the word "I" in the passage: the True Vine was for him so personal, so loving. Yet for the previous child, the more foundational and beautiful meaning of the True Vine was lost. She was never able to appreciate the intimacy of being united to Jesus so intimately as to share his very life—his grace. She could only think about being cut off and being burned.

Failure to recognize the child's sensitive periods can exacerbate the frustrating task of trying to give answers to questions children are not asking, while ignoring the task of providing answers that they are desperate to receive. Thomas Groome once made a similar criticism, for which he is often vilified. As a new and inexperienced high school religion teacher, his concern over the disinterest of his students led him to put aside his lesson plan and follow instead their burning questions. While I take issue with Groome's method of Shared Christian Praxis, which he developed in response to his early angst as a high school religion teacher, I do support his desire to do something different. Unfortunately, Groome's desire to address the existential needs and questions of his students led him away from a faithful and

---

44. Sr. Theresa Anne Knuth, OP, is a CGS catechist trained in all three levels of the CGS. She serves as a Level I and II catechist and an adult formation leader for Level I. She resides in the Netherlands and has translated all of the CGS materials into Dutch.

systematic proclamation of Church teachings. This infidelity to Church teachings remains the fundamental problem with his method of Shared Christian Praxis. A catechesis that fails to proclaim the truth of the Gospel fails to offer a person the path to true freedom (see John 8:32). In the CGS approach, however, we have a model for achieving both fidelity to the Church *and* fidelity to the person. In fact, it was Cavalletti's and Gobbi's fidelity to God and to the Church that guaranteed fidelity to the child.

The Transcendent Child

It may surprise you that I refer to a child as being *transcendent*; it is, after all, such a lofty term, describing what is beyond or above normal human experience. Yet this is precisely what Montessori recognized in the child: that he is able to penetrate almost effortlessly beyond the veil of signs and "see with utmost facility their transcendent meaning, as if there were no barrier between the visible and the Invisible."[45] It was Montessori's discovery of the transcendent or metaphysical child that convinced Cavalletti and Gobbi that the gestures of the liturgy themselves can be intelligible and therefore instructive. The transcendent child really can peer through the gesture of the epiclesis and see the power of the Holy Spirit, transforming the bread and wine into the Body and Blood of Jesus, the Good Shepherd. The child's power of abstracting from reality the deeper meaning to which the sign points gives force to the CGS approach of focusing on the gestures and other symbolic elements of the Mass in order to teach the doctrines that underlie these gestures and symbols.

Cavalletti recounts a time when she wanted to help a group of children understand the gift of the Holy Spirit received in the sacrament of baptism. She began by holding a ring in her hand and opening her hand to allow the ring to fall into the hands of the children. She explained that this is the gesture she would make to give them a gift. She then went on to explain that this is the same gesture that the priest makes over the infant in the sacrament of baptism, yet "we do not see anything fall." "Why does he do this?" she asked. The children replied almost in chorus, "Because he is giving us the Holy Spirit."[46] This is one of many accounts wherein the children demonstrated that they can see an invisible reality.

Another time, a catechist was working with a group of children between the ages of six and seven. Together they were meditating upon

---

45. Cavalletti, *Religious Potential 1*, 15.
46. Cavalletti, *Religious Potential 1*, 15.

baptism as a participation in the life of the risen Christ. All the children were holding little candles that were lit from the paschal candle, the symbol of Christ. The catechist wanted to help the children's meditation and spoke about the beauty of the light they had received, but one child corrected her, saying: "It isn't light; it's goodness."[47] For that child, the reality of Christ's goodness was more visible than the light itself!

Cavalletti and Gobbi observed that when the young child is introduced to the parables of the Pearl of Great Price and the Hidden Treasure, his response is simply to delight in the magnificence of the pearl, which is a symbol of the Kingdom of Heaven. Unlike the adult, who very often hears in these parables the moral demands to give up everything, the young child is unhindered by what he should or should not do to obtain this pearl; he is content to simply enjoy its beauty.[48] The magnificence of the Kingdom is the greater reality and in truth we never can *merit* its glory.

It was their confidence in the child's ability to grasp the transcendent that enabled Cavalletti and Gobbi to trust that the particular words and gestures and materials used in the atrium would indeed "speak to the child," revealing God's inexhaustible mystery. The child—precisely because he is the transcendent child—is able to enter into those mysteries with an extraordinary facility, as children in the CGS atria all over the world have demonstrated. This is why Cavalletti considers the child as a model of Jesus' parable of the Kingdom of Heaven. Unlike the mustard seed (its littleness will become as great as the Kingdom of Heaven), the child already possesses this greatness in his littleness.[49]

The Essential Child

Children accept things that are simple and essential without any difficulty and, in fact, are only truly satisfied with *the essentials*.[50] A common mistake of adults is to respond to a child's question with more information than he requested or needed. When Cavalletti first began the CGS work on the Mass, she observed that when she presented the elements of the Rite in sequential order, beginning with the Introductory Rite, the children were disinterested and unaffected. Yet when she began with the essence of the Mass, the

---

47. Cavalletti, *Religious Potential 1*, 15.
48. Cavalletti, *Religious Potential 1*, 114.
49. Sofia Cavalletti, "An Adventure: The Catechesis of the Good Shepherd," trans. Patricia Coulter, in *The Way of Holy Joy* (Chicago: Catechesis of the Good Shepherd Publications, 2012), 10.
50. Cavalletti, "And a Little Child Shall Lead Them . . . ," 168.

Eucharistic prayer and the words of consecration, they became attentive and consequently interested in the other parts of the Mass.[51]

A number of my own religious Sisters have experienced this same phenomenon with their second-grade students. Sr. Imelda Garrison, OP, is a master teacher who has prepared countless children to receive their First Holy Communion. While the children were always excited to receive Jesus Christ in the sacrament, she confesses that she always struggled to excite their interest in the Mass. Her training as a CGS catechist revolutionized her approach, even though she remains in a traditional school setting. Now she begins instruction with the heart of the Mass, the words of consecration. The children are immediately engaged and their interest remains through her entire unit on the Mass.

In an interesting turn from traditional textbooks, the CGS approach makes no adaptation to the words of Scripture or the liturgy. Instead, the child is given the most substantial food of the Gospels and the liturgy, in their essential proclamation. As with milk from a nursing mother, the Gospels and liturgy provide the child with spiritual nourishment that is as substantial as it is essential. Though mother's milk lacks material complexity, it is the *most* substantial food for an infant. More importantly for our discussion, mother's milk satisfies the infant's physical and psychic needs. A piece of steak served on the proverbial silver platter could not do as much for an infant as the embrace of his lactating mother. On this point the 2020 *Directory* gives important guidance:

> We must not think that in catechesis the *kerygma* gives way to a sup-posedly more "solid" formation. Nothing is more solid, profound, secure, meaningful and wisdom-filled than the initial proclamation. All Christian formation consists of entering more deeply into the *kerygma*, which is reflected in and, constantly illumines, the work of catechesis, thereby enabling us to understand more fully the sig-nificance of every subject which the latter treats. It is the message capable of responding to the desire for the infinite which bides in every human heart. (DC, preface, 5–6)

It is not an easier catechesis that satisfies the child's appetite, but rather an *essential* catechesis—and this is not understood by every person engaged in catechesis. Mary Mirrione, national director of CGSUSA, shares an anecdote that illustrates this point. She was an invited participant at a

---

51. Cavalletti, *Religious Potential 1*, 50.

gathering of the USCCB bishops and representatives from the major religion textbook publishers. During the meeting, several bishops requested that more direct texts from the Gospel be included in the religion textbooks, rather than paraphrases. One textbook representative responded that the children were not able to understand the Gospel texts. Mirrione challenged this prevalent misunderstanding on the part of the publishers, explaining that the CGS approach uses the Bible text, reading directly from the Bible, for its proclamations.[52] Again, it is not the case that the child needs the proclamation to be easier; he simply wants it to be more *essential*.

The Religious Child

The question regarding the nature of children's religious education continues to challenge the approach to catechesis. The 2020 *Directory* rejects the notion that "catechesis per se" occurs before the age of six (DC, 239). At most the young child receives a "form of religious socialization" which serves as a preparation for the "development of the Christian moral conscience" (DC, 239). I think Montessori, Cavalletti, and Gobbi would ask for clarification of this assertion and perhaps respectfully disagree. All three women were deeply convinced that the young child's religious potential is real and has been largely neglected and unrealized for generations.

From start to finish, the work of Montessori was a religious pursuit. She writes, "Respect for the child's nature, which God Himself demands of us, compels us to search most carefully for those conditions in which children can abandon themselves most easily to God."[53] Appreciating the inherent link between God and the child was foremost in the work of Montessori (as well as that of Cavalletti and Gobbi). In her formation classes and lectures she would insist, "Religion is the greatest reality . . . it is the only truth for the religious human being . . . the fount, the support of the human's life."[54] If the purpose of education is to lead the person to his full potential, then an education in faith becomes intrinsically united to the formation of the whole person, since the destiny of every human person is to be with God. Montessori insisted that the child is not fully educated unless he possesses an adequate and lively knowledge of God.[55] It is for the child's sake that he is taught who God is.

---

52. In a personal conversation with this author on November 25, 2015.
53. Montessori, *Child in the Church*, 16.
54. Montessori, *1915 California Lectures*, 46.
55. See Montessori, *Child in the Church*, 14–18.

Cavalletti's *The Religious Potential of the Child* opens with an examination of the child's attraction to God. This attraction is so much more than mere socialization. Even the unbaptized child raised by atheistic parents has displayed an awareness of God. Cavalletti references a story told by Montessori of a child who, though he had received no religious education, nevertheless challenged the idea that life was formed by chance. When the boy was asked how life began, he responded with conviction: "It is God!" [56] In the same chapter, Cavalletti offers another example of a four-year-old boy, Lorenzo, who had not received any catechetical instruction or any religious formation. When asked to draw a picture of God, he first drew a small figure of a human in the bottom-left corner of the page. He then filled the page with a series of signs in which numbers could be recognized. When he was asked to explain his reason for all the numbers, he replied, "Because there are many." Lorenzo's intuition was that "God is infinite."[57]

Drawing from the writings of Maria Montessori and her own experiences, Cavalletti shares several examples of children who, though raised in atheistic homes, nevertheless demonstrated a profound awareness of the existence of God.[58] Reflecting on these observations Cavalletti notes that, "[B]efore [the] intellectual age, there exists a relationship between the child and God that is more deeply rooted than in the intellect alone."[59] The child's religious potential can only come to its full expression when catechists recognize that the child comes to God in his own unique way. Montessori writes,

> A deeper respect for the nature of the child in his education in the supernatural life will produce greater success. The educator who does not believe that children feel the truths of faith in a somewhat different manner from adults, and who does not realize that children need other ways than ours to express their hope and their love for God—such a one will not be able to guide the child in a manner suitable to his religious needs. . . . Even in the presence of God the child must remain a child. God Himself wants it that way and that is precisely why He created him as a child.[60]

---

56. Cavalletti, *Religious Potential 1*, 12.

57. Cavalletti, *Religious Potential 1*, 12.

58. The *CGS Journals* offer a number of examples. See, for example, Maria Christlieb, "Christ the Good Shepherd: From God and the Child Understand Each Other," in *Journals of the Catechesis of the Good Shepherd 2003–2008*, ed. Mary Fox, trans. Kathy Dahl-Brendine (Chicago: Catechesis of the Good Shepherd Publications, 2009), 48–51.

59. Cavalletti, *Religious Potential 1*, 2.

60. Montessori, *Child in the Church*, 15–16.

I am reminded of several pastors who shared with me their initial disappointment in the CGS approach because the First Communion class was not able to answer particular questions put to them. These same pastors confessed that when they began to spend time in the atrium, they discovered that it was not the case that the children lacked the right answers, Father simply asked the wrong questions. When asked to share what they believe or understand about a certain doctrinal proclamation, the children in a CGS atria reveal a very profound and even mature knowledge of the Faith.

Though the child's religious potential is clearly apparent even in the young child, Gobbi laments that "the Church still tends to wait until the child is six years of age to begin formal religious education. And, even then the focus is more on religious instruction than on religious formation."[61] The religious child is also a praying child and this aspect of his faith formation needs expression.

The Praying Child

The child has a tremendous capacity for prayer. Cavalletti remarks that the prayer of young children "is usually prayer of thanksgiving and praise [and we] can help their prayer correspond to and be an expression of their interior life."[62] Before being a response to God, prayer is first a listening and being aware of his presence (see CCC, 2567). My own encounter with the praying child is one I hope that I never forget.

Joey was not yet three years old when he came to an atrium in which I assisted. Initially, he was so unsure of the environment that his mother had to stand at the door until he engaged in a work, and even then, there was no guarantee that he would stay. Every now and again, he would glance toward the door to make sure she was there. I was asked to show him how to make a silence in the atrium.[63] The purpose of this presentation is to aid the child's prayer by helping him calm the mind and body. Joey's response to the moment of silence was nothing short of mystical. As he opened his eyes, I beheld a very deep serenity, as if he had found that place of Divine Indwelling within his soul. Quietly, I asked him if he would like to make a silence again. He smiled, nodding ever so slowly. This young child who could hardly be away from his mother's knee; whose language was still in formation, could rest in the Presence of God and speak God's language of silence.

---

61. Gobbi, *Listening*, 68.
62. Cavalletti, *Joyful Journey*, 10.
63. See Cavalletti, *Joyful Journey*, 90.

Cavalletti observes that "prayer has a special importance in the life of children, both because of their great capacity for prayer" and "because it is the way they nourish their baptismal life" until they are "able to participate fully in the Mass, the highest and most complete form of prayer." [64] The child prays in a great diversity of expressions, sometimes in words of praise or thanksgiving and at other times in silence and repose. Sometimes the child's prayer is expressed in his body with leaps of joy or even tears. Cavalletti is not the only CGS catechist to ever hear a child's prayer expressed in terms of "My body is happy."[65] The child's prayer also finds expression in his art. What is most important for catechists is to "step aside in order to allow the children to really express themselves and, if possible, to glean the secret of their prayer."[66]

The children's prayers often draw from expressions they hear in the various CGS presentations. For example, after the presentation on baptism, a child prayed, "Jesus, you are Light." After the presentation on the Good Shepherd, another child prayed, "You are so good." In the same fashion, the presentations on the liturgy evoke prayers such as, "Jesus, you are gift," and "Jesus, thank you for giving your whole self to us." Allowing the child to enjoy his own spontaneous expression of prayer does not mean that the Church's official prayers are unnecessary.

Often a criticism is levied against "rote prayer" as if the "Hail Mary" or the "Our Father" somehow lack true expression of the heart. This is not true for the child in the CGS atrium. Because these prayers are pondered within the context of the Scriptures and the whole mystery of Jesus, the children in the atrium find them most nourishing. Still, Cavalletti cautions her catechists against imposing words upon the child, as she makes the careful distinction between teaching prayers to a child and "helping the child's prayer."[67] Prayer is first and foremost a response to God and we must trust that when the child has encountered him, God will guide the child's expression.

Conclusion

Over a hundred years ago, Dr. Maria Montessori wrote, "The vision of the teacher should be at once precise like that of the scientist, and spiritual like

---

64. Cavalletti, *Religious Potential 1*, 89.
65. Cavalletti, *Religious Potential 1*, 89.
66. Cavalletti, *Religious Potential 1*, 89.
67. Cavalletti, *Joyful Journey* (first edition, 1995), 79.

that of the saint."[68] Some translations of the text use the term *mystic*, which I find more fitting. A scientist is one who observes reality with great precision, recording the truth of what he observes. He will check his experiment multiple times to ensure its validity. He will discuss his findings with colleagues, and when convinced that he has interpreted his observations correctly, his report has the potential to contribute to the improvement of any number of sectors. Likewise, a teacher should approach the child with the same care to avoid injecting her preconceived notions. The teacher must be a mystic, who approaches with reverence the child she is observing since before her truly is one to whom the Kingdom of Heaven has been promised.

Maria Montessori believed that more attention needed to be given to forming the spirit of a teacher than handing on specific techniques.[69] I believe her reasons are clear. One can learn and use a technique without ever internalizing why it works, causing the technique to become rigid, and with it the teacher. On the other hand, when we form the spirit of a teacher we form her to never stop peering into the mystery of the child and seeking ways to help that child reach his full potential.

As educators of the faith, we must strive to understand the nature of the child and minister to his particular physical, emotional, religious, and existential needs. The question is not "What do we need to teach children about God?" The question is, "What is the face of God that the child *can* see and *needs* to see?"[70] I am convinced that the Catechesis of the Good Shepherd approach reveals the face of God in the way that the child is best *able* to receive and delights in receiving, but this is only because the theologian and the master educator had the humility to observe the child and respect what they observed. The fruits of their observations are found in the CGS approach. The following chapter explores more particularly the manner in which the CGS approach corresponds with the unique nature of the child.

---

68. Montessori, *Discovery of the Child*, 137.

69. Montessori, *Discovery of the Child*, 5.

70. See Cavalletti, *Religious Potential 1*, 141.

Chapter 10

Responding to the Mystery of the Child

In chapter 9 we considered some of the overarching principles that Montessori discovered regarding the nature of the child. The child possesses psychic needs and vital exigencies that must be respected if we hope to bring the child to her fullest potential. Specifically, the nature of the child possesses a powerful, self-creative instinct; a love of order; a precocious intellect; an attachment to reality; a spontaneous self-discipline; and a desire for harmony with others. In this chapter, we will examine more deeply the child's unique features and how the CGS approach fits these features.

The catechetical work of CGS primarily unfolds in the first two planes of development, those of infancy and childhood.[1] Plane I corresponds with Level I of CGS; plane II encompasses both Level II and Level III of the CGS curriculum. Given the limitations of this book, my application cannot be exhaustive. Yet I hope to provide enough evidence to convince my reader that the CGS approach is a faithful *Christocentric* catechesis precisely because it is an authentic, *anthropological* catechesis. Through their encounter with Jesus, the Good Shepherd (both as parable and as Person), the children in CGS experience a deep delight that has lingering effects in their life: "Sometimes I feel happy, and there's no reason. Nothing special has happened. And then the Good Shepherd comes to mind."[2]

The Absorbing Child—Plane I (0–6 years)

The first phase of child development (0–6 years) is distinguished from all others by the distinctive quality of the child's intellect that Montessori

---

1. Gianna Gobbi, *Listening to God with Children: The Montessori Method Applied to the Catechesis of Children*, ed. and trans. Rebekah Rojcewicz (Loveland, OH: Treehaus Publications, 1998), 71.

2. Cavalletti, *Religious Potential 2*, 9.

referred to as "the absorbent mind."[3] We could also refer to this phase as the *absorbent self*, because the child's entire metaphysical being is developing: his mind, his emotions, his personality, his will, indeed, his very identity. In her book *Listening to God with Children*, Gianna Gobbi offers important interpretation of Montessori's insights. She writes, "The first phase marks the time of the greatest transformations in the child." The world of the 0–6 aged child is "full of surprises and wonder." Everything at this phase is an opportunity for knowledge, and yet the child needs little if any assistance by the adult. The child learns more by osmosis than he does from direct instruction. In fact, Montessori observed that "the adult cannot intervene in this work, but can only offer peripheral assistance."[4]

The absorbent child is passive, but not in a pejorative sense. On the contrary, he is highly sensitive to and engaged in his surroundings. The absorbent child is at the greatest level of openness to the wide horizons of life that surround him and at the greatest level of receptivity and learning. One example of this that educators have for some time recognized is the incomparable ease with which young children learn a second language; many preschool and kindergarten programs now include this component in their curriculum. Several characteristics of the absorbent child are uniquely addressed in the CGS approach.

. . . Needs to Experience Reality

Agreeing with Aristotle, St. Thomas Aquinas observed, "Nothing is in the human intellect, unless it comes first through the senses."[5] In observing the child, Montessori noticed that the child's sense of touch plays an essential role in the child's intellectual development, serving as something of a prehensile organ of the intellect.[6] In fact, "[t]he child *needs* to manipulate objects and to gain experience by touching and handling."[7] For the child, the hand is the instrument of intelligence. When a child is given the opportunity to experience and explore reality through the manipulation of his hands, his intellectual achievement is higher.[8]

There are many examples in Montessori's method that serve to illustrate how the hand serves the child in his acquisition of knowledge. One is the

---

3. Montessori, *The Absorbent Mind*.

4. Gobbi, *Listening*, 72–73.

5. *Praeterea, nihil est in intellectu quod non sit prius in sensu* (Aquinas, *De veritate*, q. 2, a. 3, arg. 19).

6. Montessori, *The Absorbent Mind*, 152.

7. Montessori, *The 1946 London Lectures*; emphasis mine.

8. Montessori, *The Absorbent Mind*, 152.

familiar exercise of teaching a child to read. For a small child or any illiterate person, the alphabet is a completely foreign set of lines and shapes. For this reason, the method of instruction must be approached with care. Montessori's method was to begin with having the child trace sandpaper letters while making the sound of the letter, thereby evoking a heightened sensorial encounter with the symbols of language. Only after the child's sensorial exploration of the alphabet does a direct instruction in reading begin. Montessori was successful in having children as young as four years of age read.

Similar experiments with mathematical concepts proved equally successful. Montessori filled her classroom with a variety of geometrical shapes and counting rods. The first stage of instruction allows the child ample and independent time for sensorial exploration of the materials; direct instruction on how to use the materials begins only after this period. Still, Montessori did not limit the stage of exploration of materials to the pre-literate or concrete thinking child. The child's use of material things remained valuable even at later stages of development because Montessori found that it deepened the child's powers of concentration.[9]

Unlike Montessori's mathematical materials, however, the purpose of the CGS materials is not to *teach* the child religious truth but to *facilitate* the child's meditation on religious truth.[10] The CGS materials provide concrete sensorial ways for the child to experience the truth proclaimed on a sensorial level that in turn promotes a religious experience. Gobbi was careful to insist that the CGS materials are not meant to convey abstract ideas or "the formulation of concepts," but to lead to "a vital encounter with a real Person."[11] Sr. Maria Teresita Rodkey, op, shares the story of a Level I child who, with spontaneous joy, exclaimed, "I've never been able to touch God before!"

In the CGS approach, the primary material used is the Word of God announced in Scripture and the liturgy. Most of the catechetical presentations (lessons) include sensorial materials that correspond with a specific doctrinal proclamation. For example, the materials that accompany the proclamation of the mystery of the Incarnation taken from Luke 1:26–38 include a figure of the Blessed Mother, a figure of the angel Gabriel, and a symbol of the Holy Spirit set within a box structure that resembles a house. As the catechist proclaims the Gospel passage, she moves these figures accordingly, though not dramatically. The focus of the presentation is not the figures, but

---

9. Lillard, *Science Behind the Genius*, 20.
10. Gobbi, *Listening*, 20.
11. Gobbi, *Listening*, 20.

the Gospel truth that is proclaimed. The purpose of the figures is to engage the child's sense of sight, heightening the already engaged sense of hearing. Following the presentation, the child is then invited to work with the materials, engaging her sense of touch. The child may work independently in prayerful silence or with another child, depending on the specific presentation. The structure of the atrium allows the child to work with these materials repeatedly throughout an atrium session and even throughout the year.

Often it is not until the child has worked with materials independently that she comes to understand and experience the doctrine proclaimed. By "experience," I simply mean that the child has been touched by God's grace, which gives the child a moment of peace, joy, and sometimes a sense of overwhelming warmth. By "understand," I simply mean that a truth arrives in her intellect, again through God's grace, and we perceive the "A-ha!" moment or even hear the shouts of glee from a child.

Sr. Imelda Garrison, OP, shares the story of Paul, one of her second graders who, even with a limited experience of the atrium, has spoken remarkable insights to Sister. One in particular followed the presentation on the Cenacle. She writes, "Paul with amazement in his voice proclaimed, 'The night before Jesus is going to die, he gives us the gift!' He just kept referring to 'the gift.'" Sister added, "Paul's mother has cancer." Through the interior work of the Holy Spirit, Paul was not only able to pierce the meaning of the Eucharist as Jesus' gift, he was also able to link death with this gift. In so doing, it is possible that Paul will come to embrace his mother's illness not as a punishment from God but somehow as gift bearing. No matter how hard Sister may have tried to help Paul grapple with his mother's illness, she could never and would not have dared to help this young boy see it as a gift, yet God was able to help Paul see it as such.

The beauty of the CGS pedagogy is that theological insights are not forced upon the child. In the course of any presentation, the CGS catechist does not directly tell the child all of the magnificent doctrinal connections inherent in the presentation; rather, in a true educative fashion the child is led to observe, question, and ponder those truths. For example, in the passage for the Annunciation, the catechist draws attention to certain words spoken by the angel: "What was the good news that the angel Gabriel gave to Mary?" "By whose power did the angel say that Mary would conceive?" "What does that tell us about Jesus? Is St. Joseph his father?" "I wonder what the presence of an angel might tell us about this baby that Mary is going to have?" The child is left to ponder the religious mystery on his own aided only by the materials and the Holy Spirit. The more the child engages with a particular work, the more its transcendent reality penetrates his whole being. The child's insights become increasingly deeper. All throughout the child's time in the atrium, she is led to see that Jesus is truly the Son of God and the Son of Mary. Yet this doctrine is taught in such a manner that the child comes to recognize and affirm this truth when she is ready.

While the full discussion on the value of sensory materials is reserved for chapters 11 and 12, on the nature of education and catechetical methodology, it is introduced here for their important correspondence with the child's way of receiving truth. The incarnational dimension of God's pedagogy referenced by the catechetical directories points not only to the Person of Jesus Christ, but also to his own manner of instructing his apostles through visible signs (GDC, 143; DC, 165). One of the key strengths of the CGS approach and one that sets it apart from other catechetical models is precisely its incarnational dimension that provides for the child a most fitting way to ponder, penetrate, and grasp the invisible realities of our faith. Two other approaches to children's catechesis that share similarities with the CGS approach are Jerome Berryman's *Godly Play* and the *Come Follow Me* program created by the Notre Dame de Vie community in France.

Berryman was trained in the CGS approach and used most of Cavalletti and Gobbi's ideas for his own *Godly Play*. In my estimation, his adaptations are concerning. For example, catechists who use Godly Play do not receive nearly the same amount of catechist formation as those formed in the CGS approach. We know that the success of any educational pedagogy relies on the teacher who is formed in both a knowledge of the subject matter and the proper skill in communicating that knowledge. In catechetical education, a third element is introduced; namely, a "knowing how to be with" *the child* (see DC, 140). The deepest aspect of catechist formation "has to do with *being* a catechist, even before *acting* as a catechist" (DC, 136).

The *Come Follow Me* program also incorporates sensorial elements and parallels the beautiful contemplative dimension of CGS. Unfortunately, the materials for this program are used primarily, and at times exclusively, by the catechist, relegating the child to the role of mere spectator during a catechetical presentation. The *Come Follow Me* program does not allow for the child's independent sensorial way of meditating upon the mysteries of faith to the same degree as CGS. While these other programs have much to offer, they simply cannot compare to CGS for its recognition of the child's need to see, hear, touch, and contemplate the mysteries of the faith. As with *Godly Play*, the *Come Follow Me* catechist receives only minimal training in the approach, leaving much to chance. Indeed, I have seen the approach work with children but only with catechists who themselves were already well formed.

. . . Needs to Do for Himself

In order to grow, the child of Phase I must be active in his tasks, and this means that where it is at all possible the child must be allowed to "do for self."[12] This psychic need is so vital that Montessori warns teachers and parents that "every useless help is an obstacle to his development."[13] Montessori observes, "[The child's] intelligence tells him what he can do and if people go to help the child, they act instead of him."[14] The more adults do for the child what is his own work, the more they frustrate his own nature and inhibit his own development. To illustrate her point, Montessori draws attention to the ordinary way of Mother Nature: the butterfly cannot be forced out of its cocoon prematurely, the chicken must peck his own way out of the shell or it does not survive, and the flower bud must open itself. The same is true for the child.

According to Montessori, a good teacher is one who, upon asking the child if he needs assistance, honors the child's honest response: "Personally, please do nothing. You can do nothing directly for me."[15] Here again, the radical nature of Montessori's understanding of the child, as well as the purpose of education, stands out in relief against the traditional model of teaching. Unlike the teacher in a traditional classroom, the role of the Montessori teacher is to direct the child's natural growth by creating a prepared environment that fosters a child's independent learning and to give guidance only as needed. Though Montessori's view is in stark contrast with a traditional model of catechesis, she is in agreement with Augustine and Aquinas—that "only God can teach interiorly and principally."[16] In chapter 11, we will examine more fully the nature of teaching and learning demonstrating how the teacher can only be an *instrumental cause* to the student's learning.

You may ask, "How does this need to 'do for self' compare with the work of catechesis?" After all, the Church clearly teaches that no person is the author of his own faith, but rather receives the Word that is preached to him (see GDC, 54, 105). Gobbi seems to have anticipated the question:

---

12. Montessori, *The Four Planes of Education* (1938; reprinted, Amsterdam: Association Montessori Internationale, 2004), 2–3.
13. Montessori, *Discovery of the Child*, 58.
14. Montessori, *Four Planes*, 4.
15. See Montessori, *Discovery of the Child*, 52–58.
16. Augustine, *De magistro*, XIV, 45. Aquinas, *De veritate*, q. 11, a. 1.

It is precisely in the field of religious education that we should most readily pursue the full actualization of the child's potential and free ourselves from the traditional conception of education as something the adult gives to the child. It is precisely in this religious sphere that educational practices must be freed from external causality and must, instead, follow the "constructive rhythms of Life" if we are convinced that life comes from God.[17]

As it is true that no one can give himself faith, it is equally true that, properly speaking, no one can give faith to another. Faith is a gift of God (CCC, 143).

So often, adults approach the work of catechesis as if the child is tabula rasa—a blank slate—that lacks any awareness of who God is. Yet as I have already recounted in chapter 9, the experience of Montessori, Cavalletti, and so many CGS catechists is that this is not true. Sr. Marie Celine Laird, OP, shares a story that illustrates this point:

> Early in the year, one of my three-year-old boys, we'll call him Johnny, asked me during prayer time, "Sister, where is Heaven?" We had only just begun in the Atrium and I was cognizant of not wanting to say something that would confuse or mislead him. So I replied, "I wonder if Jesus might tell you when you pray." Johnny seemed content with this response and closed his eyes as if to pray right then. When he opened his eyes, he said, "I didn't hear anything." I said, "That's okay. Jesus will speak to you. Just keep asking." I knew that we would be exploring the Kingdom parables soon and we could revisit his question. A week or so later, we were eating [a] snack and Johnny said to me, "Sister! Jesus told me where Heaven is! It went in my ear and down to my heart." Johnny touched his heart and continued, "He said, 'Heaven is in here.'" I was overwhelmed. It was clear that he got this insight from the Lord Himself. As the tears welled up in my eyes, Johnny's face became crestfallen. "Sister, what's wrong. Why are you crying?" "Oh, Johnny," I whispered. "What you said was just so beautiful, and yes, that is true. Jesus taught his apostles that the Kingdom of Heaven is within."

God is present to every person as the Creator who holds all things in existence. For the baptized person, his Presence dwells within through his created sanctifying grace. The baptized child has a relationship with God beyond compare. He does not require much by way of introduction; he asks

---

17. Gobbi, *Listening*, 69.

only that we help him come to know God better. In a very real sense, the child pleads, "Show me the path to God, but please, let me have my own dialogue with him."

The unique methodology of the CGS will be examined further in chapter 12, but here it is important to note that the CGS method flows from an understanding of the child's need to do for self and that it finds greater success through the use of fewer words, not more. This method embodies the divine pedagogy of grace wherein the Holy Spirit is given primacy of place in the catechetical session (GDC, 142). To honor the child's plea is nothing short of recognizing that the child has his own way of relating to God, and this must be understood and appreciated by the catechist.[18]

. . . Needs to Wonder, Investigate, and Contemplate

According to Aristotle, wonder is a dynamic value in a person who is "naturally curious and seek[s] to understand what [he does] not understand."[19] For the child especially, "everything is a source of wonder because everything is new" to his understanding.[20] "[W]onder is not an emotion of superficial people," Cavalletti points out.[21] She adds, "If we skim over things, we will never be surprised by them."[22] Only those persons who are "able to settle and rest in things," persons who are "capable of stopping and looking," are capable of wonder.[23] If Plato and Aristotle are correct in saying that the sense of wonder is the mark of the philosopher,[24] then it must be concluded that every child is inherently a *philosopher*!

Cavalletti observes that the child's capacity for wonder is at the source of so many of his activities, such as "the ability to observe, experiment and classify experience and information."[25] Wonder stimulates the child "to question the world in ways [that combine] the scientific and poetical frames of mind."[26] Wonder stimulates the child to question and to investigate, to

---

18. Gobbi, *Listening*, 70.

19. Aristotle, *Metaphysics*, Book I, chapter 1, trans. Richard Hope (Columbia University Press, 1952), 3.

20. Cavalletti, *Religious Potential 1*, 107.

21. Cavalletti, *Religious Potential 1,* 108.

22. Cavalletti, *Religious Potential 1*, 108.

23. Cavalletti, *Religious Potential 1*, 108.

24. Plato, *Theaetetus* 155c-d, trans. Benjamin Jowett, https://www.gutenberg.org/files/1726/1726-h/1726-h.htm.

25. Cavalletti, *Religious Potential 1*, 107. Cavalletti quotes directly from the 1972 United Nations Educational, Scientific, and Cultural Organization (UNESCO) report on education.

26. Cavalletti, *Religious Potential 1*, 107. I have taken the liberty to replace Cavalletti's "Man" with "child" because in this same section, Cavalletti ranks the child next to "poets, artists and old persons" as those who have "known how to live by beholding and contemplating the world surrounding [them]."

express himself and listen to others, to rearrange information and repeat activities. Indeed, the child "develops under the sign of wonder."[27]

In another sense, the child wonders because he has already perceived the depths of reality and is hungry to know more.[28] The child's wonder comes from a contemplative gaze at reality that has revealed itself in "ever widening horizons."[29] Wonder is thus the activity of the philosopher and the contemplative. We know that when a child's sense of wonder is engaged, he will remain with the same activity for hours. On the contrary, when he does not find an object that stimulates his desire for wonder, the desire is stifled, and the child becomes restless and bored. The child needs an object "whose frontiers are always expanding as the child slowly proceeds in the contemplation of it."[30]

From her many years of working with children, Cavalletti observed that time and time again it was the parables, especially the Parable of the Good Shepherd, that "enkindled that deep light in the children's eye" and nourished their deep hunger for God. The CGS approach uses the direct words of Scripture and prayers of the liturgy as its primary source of doctrine—never their paraphrase, as is so often found in religious textbooks. The direct words of Christ and the Church are objects so rich and so worthy of the child's contemplation. The parables, especially, provide the child with an opportunity for contemplating the inexhaustible mystery of God and his Kingdom.[31]

. . . Needs to Love and Be Loved

"The whole concern of doctrine and its teaching must be directed to the love that never ends" (CCC, 25). Hence, the driving question in catechesis, directing both catechetical content and method, ought to be, "How does *this* proclamation, *this* activity, *this* selected reading establish, foster, deepen the relationship of love between *this* person and God?" Cavalletti strongly links the goal of the CGS approach with the Church's catechetical goal of fostering in others "intimacy with Christ" (CT, 5). The CGS approach achieves this goal by providing clear evidence from God's revelation that he is love and that he has created and redeemed us so that we may come to participate in his eternal exchange of love (see CCC, 221).

---

27. Cavalletti, *Religious Potential 1*, 107.
28. Cavalletti, *Religious Potential 1*, 108.
29. Cavalletti, *Religious Potential 1*, 108.
30. Cavalletti, *Religious Potential 1*, 109.
31. Cavalletti, *Religious Potential 1*, 109.

The Level I child (3–6) is most attentive to love and seeks, first of all, relationship. This child has a limitless capacity for great love, and for this reason is drawn most especially to the Good Shepherd who knows his sheep and calls them by name (see John 10:14). He has a need for intimacy and is particularly drawn to the Good Shepherd, who carries his sheep around his neck. Cavalletti offers several accounts of children, some living under desperate circumstances of illness or poverty, who became quite peaceful and satiated upon learning that the Good Shepherd knew them by name.[32]

Anyone who has had sustained interaction with children knows that they possess a profound capacity for love—both to give and receive it. The child loves unconditionally—she forgives so readily and for this reason Cavalletti believed that the "necessary Partner" for the child was God. Anything less than God is quite unfulfilling for the child.[33] "There is a special rapport between young children and God," Cavalletti observes. "[In their] covenantal relationship with God, children find what is most precious in themselves: the capacity to love."[34] Cavalletti and Gobbi recognized that the child's deepest need is for relationship and this is the child's strength and gift. Very young children, in particular, easily fall in love with God: "It comes from the depth of their soul."[35] "If we start catechesis or religious education before the age of six," Cavalletti observed, "[then] we begin building on the actual foundation floor; helping the child to establish a relationship of *being in love* with God."[36] The genius of the CGS approach is that it recognizes and works with the child's lively predisposition for intimacy with God.

The doctrinal proclamations throughout the CGS curriculum are not focused on proving God's existence to the child, but instead, they strive to deepen the child's relationship with God by bringing into focus the face of God, who is *already* known and loved. All the doctrine comes together like spokes on a wheel around the one central doctrine of Jesus who reveals himself as "the *good* shepherd" (John 10:14, added emphasis) who gives his whole self to us and leads us to the heart of his Father.

During Level I, the foundation of the child's character is laid. The same is true about his psychic (including religious) development. It is therefore quite fitting that the CGS curriculum introduces the parable of the Good

---

32. Cavalletti, *Religious Potential 1*, 137.
33. Cavalletti, *Joyful Journey*, 12.
34. Cavalletti, *Joyful Journey*, 12.
35. Cavalletti, *Joyful Journey*, 11.
36. Cavalletti, *Joyful Journey*, 11; italics original.

Shepherd at this phase. The Parable of the Good Shepherd contains many doctrinal insights into the nature of Christ and the nature of discipleship. At this phase, the parable is limited to stress only the truth that the Good Shepherd knows his sheep by name. In this phase, the bond of trust and a sense of belonging are firmly established between Jesus and the child. Such spiritual formation is critical for the child's initial faith, as well as his continued growth in faith.

If the psychic foundation has been firmly laid down in Level I, the six-to-nine-year-old child is ready to be firm in the Lord and to follow him more faithfully. The firm foundation for subsequent catechesis is laid upon the child's secure knowledge and experience of being known and loved by Jesus. In Level II, most children celebrate the sacrament of penance and reconciliation for the first time. It is the most fitting time for moral formation, and for this reason, the moral parables spark the greatest interest, but the interest is interior. The child wants to know how he can best follow the Lord. He is not thinking globally. Appeal is made again to the Parable of the Good Shepherd, but now the focus is on the Shepherd who leads his sheep. The six-to-nine-year-old child seeks justice, fairness, and valor. He is particularly drawn to the heroism of the Good Shepherd who "lays down his life for the sheep" (John 10:11). In Level II, most children celebrate their First Holy Communion and they are drawn to the strong Eucharistic themes found in the Good Shepherd Parable. Finally, the six-to-nine-year-old child is most sensitive to the need for belonging and is therefore greatly attentive to the Shepherd who cares for his flock.

St. John the apostle proclaims, "[W]e have known and believe the love that God has for us. God is love, and those who abide in love abide in God and God abides in them" (1 John 4:16). John's proclamation stands at the heart of the Gospel as a kind of "summary of the Christian Life" (*Deus caritas est*, 1). The entire deposit of faith is expressed most succinctly and poetically in paragraph 221 of the *Catechism*: "God is the eternal exchange of love and he has destined us to share in that exchange." The eternal, unconditional exchange of love who is God, finds a most willing recipient of his love in the child.

The Consolidating Child—Plane II (6–12 years)

Whereas in the first phase of development, the child is in a critical stage of *absorbency*, in the second phase he is in the critical stage of reasoning and consolidation. Gobbi reminds us that even the child's body is undergoing a process of consolidation wherein "his bones and teeth [are all] solidifying." This phase of childhood is marked by a relatively quiet, stable period of development. During this time, the child assimilates all that was developed in the preceding phase, while not entirely putting aside all his earlier psychic needs.[37] The "Consolidating Child" still longs to be known and loved; still desires autonomy; still delights in discovery, wonder, and reasoning; and still learns best through direct contact with reality. Yet there are also new physical and psychic needs at this time. The Consolidating Child has a greater need for interior order, to belong to a community, to celebrate joyfully the milestones of life, to think for himself, to wonder and reason deeply.

The GDC speaks of catechesis as the work of solidifying the faith in others. "Starting with the 'initial' conversion of a person to the Lord, moved by the Holy Spirit through the primary proclamation of the Gospel, *catechesis seeks to solidify and mature this first adherence*" (GDC, 80).[38] Notwithstanding, to become "solid" does not necessarily mean to become more complex or more abstract, as the 2020 *Directory* points out. There can be nothing more solid than the *kerygma*. To be solid in the faith means to be committed to Christ with all that we are—our intellect, will, and passions. It is unfortunate that because children in the second phase of development are able to think more abstractly, catechesis has tended toward a more exclusively intellectual approach, often neglecting the formation of the will and the affective dimensions of faith. In a most preeminent manner, the CGS approach is able to engage the older child on both his intellectual and affective planes.

. . . Needs to Interiorize

While all children have need for exterior order, Cavalletti observed that the older child has a great need to order his *interior* life, and thus he begins to develop a remarkable interest in rules and right behavior. This, she says, is "rooted in a deep psychological and existential need and not merely a matter of curiosity."[39] "To provide children with moral norms," she writes, "is not to burden them with a collection of arbitrary rules; rather it is to help them enter deeply into reality."[40] Cavalletti observed that our Lord's parables of mercy and his maxims have particular appeal to the seven-to-nine-year-old child whose capacity for moral reasoning is emerging. The Gospel offers

37. Gobbi, *Listening*, 74.
38. Emphasis added.
39. Cavalletti, *Religious Potential 2*, 86.
40. Cavalletti, *Religious Potential 2*, 87.

"more space for the objective reflection necessary to arrive at a broader, more enlightened judgment."[41]

The older child is striving to establish a rule of standard within herself but seeks assistance from adults. We observe this in the child who innocently tattletales: it is as if she is asking of the adult, "Is that really the way we are supposed to act?" Often when second graders would demonstrate this behavior, a simple response of "No, it is not the way" suffices to redirect the child back to his or her work; she simply needed to be reassured. In proposing the moral law to children, our approach must correspond to the child's exigencies and imitate God's pedagogy.

In an essay entitled "Divine Pedagogy and Moral Formation in Catechesis," papal theologian Fr. Wojciech Giertych begins by asking, "How does *God* conduct the process of education leading to a moral formation?"[42] He answers by first examining St. Paul's treatment of the Old Law and the New Law. The Old Law was something of an external *paidogogos* (pedagogue) who was the slave that took children to school in the ancient Greek civilization. The New Law of the Gospel (and by New Law, Father Giertych means all of the saving events in the life of Christ) is more than external teaching."[43] The new law is in fact the gift—the grace—of the Holy Spirit "who dwells in the souls of Christians [and] moves them from within, animating not only their mind but also their wills and hearts." In keeping with the divine pedagogy, "[m]oral formation in the Church, therefore, consists primarily in such a direction of human action so that the grace of the Holy Spirit may flower within it."[44]

With regard to the moral law, God's pedagogy is always invitational and always works from within. "If you *wish* to be perfect," Jesus says to the Rich Young Man, "go sell your possessions . . . " (Matthew 19:1, emphasis added). He cannot say otherwise without violating his own principle of love as a gift freely given. God extends his grace always in an invitational manner.

Moral formation of a person is a delicate matter that requires more than merely telling him what is right (DC, 142): it requires the grace of an inner conversion. We read in the *Catechism*:

> Interior repentance is a radical reorientation of our whole life,
> a return, a conversion to God with all our heart, an end of sin, a

---

41. Cavalletti, *Religious Potential 2*, 91–92.
42. Wojciech Giertych, OP, "Divine Pedagogy and Moral Formation in Catechesis," in *Pedagogy of God*, 110. Father's essay is worthy of careful study by all catechists and parents.
43. Giertych, "Moral Formation," 112–113.
44. Giertych, "Moral Formation," 113.

turning away from evil, with repugnance toward the evil actions we have committed. At the same time, it entails the desire and resolution to change one's life, with hope in God's mercy and trust in the help of his grace. (CCC, 1431)

When there is no prior recognition of the moral law in a child's psyche, the sudden intrusion of rules upon a child can feel arbitrary and imposed.[45] A healthy formation of the moral conscience requires that the child be exposed first to what is morally good before giving him a yardstick with which to measure his own behavior. When this sequence is not followed, the child might obey the adult who demands moral behavior of him, but in the end, the correction rarely become interior.[46]

In the CGS approach, before the older child begins to question himself whether this or that action is good or bad, the moral parables are presented to him. Cavalletti recognized in the parables of Jesus the perfect pedagogy for presenting the moral law to children. She writes,

The parables open a door and invite us in; they invite us to a work of personal reflection, a work that leads us to a gradual comprehension of their meaning and enables us to feel more personally engaged in the mystery they proclaim.[47]

The parables of the Good Samaritan, the Pharisee and the Publican, the Insistent Friend, as well as the parables of mercy provide the child with an objective meditation on what is right and wrong according to what God would do. In his time of silent reflection on the moral parables, the child ponders God's actions and listens to the Holy Spirit's promptings to do likewise. The child relies on the strength of the moral parables to provide critical parameters for his behavior, yet this must be done in such a way that these parameters are internalized.

Finally, in the CGS approach, the child's conscience is formed always in the context of relationship.[48] Long before the challenge of our Lord's maxims are introduced to the older child, he has meditated repeatedly on the love of the Good Shepherd, who willingly lays down his life for his sheep (see John 10:11). Through repeated meditation on the parables, with the help of the Holy Spirit and with the careful guidance of the catechist, the child gradually begins to perceive a moral way of living that helps the child to remain

---

45. Cavalletti, *Religious Potential 1*, 120.
46. Cavalletti, *Religious Potential 1*, 120.
47. Cavalletti, *Religious Potential 2*, 89.
48. Cavalletti, *Religious Potential 1*, 120.

in God's friendship—remain on the True Vine—satisfying yet another vital exigency: *to belong to the community.*

. . . Needs to Socialize

The older child, though able to think for himself and do for himself, is no longer an isolated being but has become a social being. He now recognizes himself as part of a larger community. The child's horizons are expanding and he becomes curious about his place in his family, in the atrium, in the Church, and in the world. The themes of biblical geography and history that run throughout the CGS curriculum become increasingly attractive for the older child. The nine-to-twelve-year-old "cosmic child"[49] has discovered the world and beyond, and wonders about his place in that world.[50] This child is particularly concerned about societal issues and wants to talk about justice, authority, family, societal concerns, and unity among people. When this child hears the Parable of the Good Shepherd, he is drawn to the concept of the "other sheep" and the "one flock" (John 10:16). Already, he has encountered division in the world, in families, and in communities. He lingers on the idea of there being "one shepherd" who will bring the many sheep together, into one flock.

Finally, the nine-to-twelve-year-old child is beginning to see himself in relation to others and is drawn to the parables of mercy on a whole new level.[51] The spiritual and corporal works of mercy have significant appeal to the older child who longs to make his contribution to the community and the world at large. This child learns how to become part of the Kingdom of God and to spread that Kingdom. In a presentation entitled "The History of the Kingdom and My Place in It,"[52] the child is invited to reflect upon his unique contribution in the ongoing history of God's saving actions in the world.

To satisfy the vital need to belong, the Parable of the True Vine is introduced (John 15:1–17). In the image of the True Vine, the older child recognizes that the covenant entails multiple levels of belonging to Jesus and to the Church. This recognition serves as a foundational proclamation for a catechesis on grace, sin, and the sacrament of confession.[53] As in the parable

---

49. A term Montessori coined to describe the child's need to understand his natural world so as to understand himself.

50. Gobbi, *Listening*, 74.

51. Gobbi, *Listening*, 73–74.

52. See appendix C.

53. Cavalletti, *Religious Potential 2*, 52–53.

of the True Vine, the child discovers a deeper communion with God, and with his surrounding community in the Eucharistic liturgy. This communion is preeminently symbolized in the reception of Holy Communion but it is also symbolized in the gesture of the sign of peace.

Cavalletti observed that, as the child's hunger to belong in community increased, the gesture of peace takes on new meaning for him. He begins to see that it is not merely an invitation, but a growing imperative of Jesus, who is the True Vine.[54] The vertical union we have with Jesus is completed with the horizontal union we have with each other and this is recognized in the Rite of Peace. The priest extends to us the peace of Jesus: "Peace I give you." He then invites us to extend that peace with one another: "Let us offer one another the sign of peace."

. . . Needs to Celebrate

The need for celebration and ritual is not restricted to the child, nor to the religious world; indeed, psychologists have identified the negative effects in churches and cultures where there is "disdain for ritual."[55] In the biblical world, celebration takes the form of liturgy, serving "the same anthropological and social base," though with its own unique characteristics.[56] The place that liturgy occupies in the biblical world is extremely important, and for this reason, if the biblical message is to be understood by the child in "all its richness and concreteness," the child must be initiated into its liturgical form.[57] Israel did not merely celebrate the mighty deeds of God: they ritualized their memory, as commanded by God himself (see Deuteronomy 6:20–23 and 8:17–18). For us, salvation history would remain a thing of the past had not these events become liturgical celebrations.

Liturgical catechesis not only aids the child in his conceptual understanding of the saving events in salvation history, but it also inserts the child into an *experience* of those same events. The Church stresses the critical nature of liturgical catechesis when it teaches: "Catechesis is intrinsically linked with the whole of liturgical and sacramental activity, for it is in the sacraments, especially in the Eucharist, that Christ Jesus works in fullness for the transformation of human beings" (CT, 23). In the liturgy, the biblical message continues "to reverberate in the lives of believers and throughout western civilization." It is not enough to "merely bring the child into contact

---

54. Cavalletti, *Religious Potential 2*, 115.
55. Cavalletti, *Religious Potential 2*, 57.
56. Cavalletti, *Religious Potential 2*, 58.
57. Cavalletti, *Religious Potential 2*, 58.

with the scriptures," the child must come into contact with "the living experience of the [Scripture's] source." Cavalletti explains that this source is the Christian community (the Church), which has lived and celebrated a particular interpretation of the Scriptures throughout the ages.[58]

All throughout the Levels, the Mass is central in the CGS, but in Level III, every aspect of its richness is studied, especially its Biblical origins. This study is accompanied by the child's copying his own missal just as the monks would do of ages past. It is a rich contemplative work that provides the child time to reflect more deeply on the words that are prayed during Mass. The missal becomes his own aid to prayer during the celebration of Mass.

. . . Needs to Reason and Explore

The older child begins to experience the great dignity of being human: he reasons. Montessori expressed delighted surprise at this child's intelligence, observing that "when the child is placed in certain conditions that favor him, he manifests an extraordinary activity."[59] The older child has an insatiable hunger for knowledge and his horizons continue to expand even beyond the cosmos. Montessori recognized that at this age, the child requires a "cosmic education" or "expansive education." Cavalletti recognized that this child requires even more than the created universe; this child must search the heavens. He is a metaphysical child, whose hunger for truth stretches him beyond even the nature of creation to the nature of God's re-creation of humanity through the events of Salvation History.

Not in all my years as a Catholic school teacher, not in any of the grades, 1–12, that I have taught, have I found a curriculum of comparable "expansiveness" as to what I find in Level III of CGS. A sample of presentations under the heading "The Plan of God" include: the Peoples of God and the People of God (think "*Lumen gentium* for eleven-year-olds"), the Holy Bible and the Sacraments (think "*Sacrosanctum concillium* for ten-year-olds), and the History of the Kingdom of God in the Holy Bible (think "Introduction to Biblical Studies for twelve-year-olds"). Presentations under the heading "Old Testament Typology Studies" include: creation, sin, the flood, Abraham, and Moses/Exodus/Gift of the Law. These presentations draw from the Church's richest theological insights regarding typology.

Francesca Cocchini, one of Cavalletti's and Gobbi's atria *bambini* and now chair of the international CGS board, recalls how Cavalletti taught her

---

58. Cavalletti, *Religious Potential 2*, 58–59.
59. Montessori, *From Childhood to Adolescence*, 10.

to read the Sacred Scriptures in the same manner as the rabbis and the Fathers of the Church. She writes,

> I learned that in scripture actually "no word of the text is superfluous and without meaning" that "scripture is interpreted with scripture," and that the Word of God is like a chisel which, chipping away at a rock, makes lots of sparks. In fact, "every word that comes from the mouth of the Holy One"—as the school of Rabbi Ishmael teaches—"is translated into 70 languages and is capable of 70 interpretations." Seated next to Sofia, while reading the Bible I learned how to read the Bible. And later, as a grown-up, when I studied the Fathers of the Church and became familiar with their writings, I discovered in them that same hermeneutic method that has been for me, and continues to be, a source of great joy, a guarantee of truth and faithfulness.[60]

The work of the nine-to-twelve-year-old child is often on a high level of synthesis and critical thinking while no less stimulating in prayer. I'll never forget one of my early experiences of serving in a Level III atrium. Two eleven-year-old boys were invited to evaluate a maxim of choice in light one of the parables of choice. One of the boys brought the maxim: "Do to others as you would have them do to you" (Matthew 7:12). The parable he chose as a counter reference was the Ten Bridesmaids. This young man wrestled deeply with bringing together these two teachings of Jesus. He was really struggling. "I can't accept that the five wise bridesmaids would not share their oil. They would have wanted help if they were the ones who ran out of oil." We spent a good part of the time in atrium digging into the words of both the maxim and the parable, probing their meaning, evaluating the juxtaposition, challenging our own desire for the Kingdom and our preparedness to enter. He was only eleven years old, but he was wrestling with God's Word on a level that most adults rarely ever do.

Conclusion

The particular understanding of the child that Cavalletti and Gobbi brought to the work of catechesis was shaped by Montessori's "positive vision of the child and of the potentiality of childhood. It was a vision based on direct

---

60. Francesca Cocchini, "A Big Girl Who Helps Sofia," ed. Tina Lillig, *Catechesis of the Good Shepherd: Essential Realities* (Chicago: Catechesis of the Good Shepherd Publications, 2004), 33.

experiences and not on theories."[61] However, this chapter focuses primarily on the nature of the child. The child possesses a unique nature that has for its own a religious potential, vital *exigencies*, and specific phases of development, all which are served in a unique fashion by the CGS approach.

Though heavily influenced by the pedagogical and anthropological insights of Dr. Maria Montessori, Cavalletti and Gobbi conducted their own fifty-year experiment, which garnered its own insights into the nature of the child and, importantly, into the nature of the relationship between the child and God. For this reason, though greatly indebted to Montessori, the work of Cavalletti and Gobbi stands on its own merit.

In the view of Fr. Mongillo, the CGS approach works not because it has stumbled upon a new methodology as a substitute for others, nor even because it has hit upon just the right parable. The CGS approach *works* because it has discovered the mystery of the child and his communion with God. He writes:

> We are not dealing with a new methodology as a substitute for others. Its "newness" is the inspiration from which it originates: it is in the light of this inspiration that the forms into which it has been translated and expressed should be read. Should one attempt to ascribe its effectiveness to having hit upon just the "right" parable, we should recall the truth so often reiterated by Augustine and Thomas: even the letter of the Gospel would kill if the Spirit did not speak to the heart. Should one be led to maintain that [the CGS approach] is centered in that space reserved for the child's "creativity," we should point out that the best fruit of this "journey" is not a more intense inventiveness, but rather the peace, the profound joy of the encounter with Jesus, the opening of the child to listening, the delicacy of the relationship established with the Father, and the capacity to love.[62]

Fr. Mongillo's insight is particularly important as we move into the next chapter, which discusses the methodological component of the CGS approach. To discover the unique hermeneutic for its method, it is necessary to be purified of the preconceived notion that methodology is a particular technique. Fr. Mongillo warns against such a reduction. The CGS approach is an altogether new *pedagogy* that recognizes the inexhaustible nature of

---

61. Cavalletti, "Maria Montessori and the Catechesis of the Good Shepherd," in *Commemorative Journal: Sofia Cavalletti, 1917–2011* (Chicago: Catechesis of the Good Shepherd Publications, 2012), 21.
62. Mongillo, "Preface," 18–19.

God and the unique nature of the child and strives to bring them together. The CGS approach, therefore, is a unique catechetical *pedagogy* of bringing together the mystery of God and the mystery of the child.

Chapter 11

Educating in Christ

Introduction

The various catechetical directories have consistently referred to the work of catechesis in educational terms. The 1971 *Directory* spoke of catechesis as "catechetical education" (GCD, 41) and formation of the child's heart as an "interior education" (GCD, 79). The 1997 *Directory* asked catechists to envision catechesis as a "school of faith" and to recognize that it serves "the simple objective of educating others in the faith" (GDC, 148). The 2020 *Directory* (DC) likewise draws attention to the educational nature of catechesis that draws its inspiration from the "great educational work of God" (DC, 157). The *Catechism of the Catholic Church* gives highest authority to the particular insight of the 1977 Synod on Catechesis affirming that "catechesis is an education in the faith of children, young people and adults which includes especially the teaching of Christian doctrine imparted, generally speaking, in an organic and systematic way, with a view to initiating the hearers into the fullness of Christian life" (CCC, 5, citing CT, 18). In other words, catechesis is definitively the task of *educating others in Christ*.[1]

This raises a question. If education is the key to forming others in faith, then why do so many people, even those who attended Catholic schools, leave the Church after years of catechetical instruction? Cavalletti herself promoted a "de-schooling of catechesis."[2] Though I am convinced her protest was a reaction to schools that worked against the child's God-given nature, nevertheless, her prejudices and those of others must be addressed before we can move forward in our effort *to evangelize by*

---

1. In his book *Educating in Christ*, CGS catechist and Catholic schoolteacher Gerard O'Shea properly identifies the educational nature of catechesis.

2. Sofia Cavalletti, "Characteristics of the Good Shepherd," trans. Patricia Coulter, in *Journals of the Catechesis of the Good Shepherd 1984–1997*, ed. Victoria Tufano (Chicago: Catechesis of the Good Shepherd Publications, 1998), 25. I substantiate my interpretation later in this chapter.

educating and educate by evangelizing (see DC, 179; original emphasis). Even if school were a positive experience, care must be taken in applying educational concepts to catechesis, because faith is not gained through the discursive power of the intellect. At the same time, faith is not a blind impulse of the mind; nor is it mere sentiment. While I dare not simplify the matter, I am convinced that the crisis in catechesis is related to an impoverished understanding of the nature of faith, knowledge, teaching, and learning. The imperative remains: as catechists, we must adopt God's own *educative* pedagogy if we hope to faithfully lead children to the sources of his revelation, recognize his voice, understand his teachings, and fall in love with all that they discover.

The sub-headings of this chapter serve as a kind of pedagogy for leading you along the path of recognizing and appreciating the CGS as a superior model for catechetical education. We begin first with the meaning of faith and what it means to believe. In a chapter dedicated to education and knowledge, it is critical to establish an understanding of the proper relationship between faith and reason. Only then will I be free to examine the nature of knowledge and education without my reader thinking that we actually have control over the faith life of another. We do not. Still, the grace of faith does reside in the intellect, and for this reason we should give due consideration to the noble work of the intellect and to the noble role that teachers have in aiding its work.

Second, in order that we might appreciate fully the genius of the CGS approach to catechetical education, and thus its choice of methodology, we need to have at least a fundamental understanding of how the intellect comes to know truth. Cavalletti and Gobbi built the CGS approach upon Maria Montessori's philosophy of education. Montessori was schooled in the epistemology (theory of knowledge) of St. Thomas Aquinas, who in turn was influenced by Aristotle. I will not attempt to provide a scholarly treatment of their various epistemologies, though I do hope to show how the CGS approach provides a masterful education precisely because of its epistemological groundings. This includes the need for sensory materials and the critical role that wonder, contemplation, imagination, and the emotions have in the work of education. Finally, the chapter concludes with a few salient insights from Cavalletti on the nature of "Hebrew Pedagogy," which she penned in an Italian anthology on education.[3]

---

3. Cavalletti, "L'Educazione Ebraica" (Hebrew Pedagogy), 11–62.

Faith

Faith "is a personal adherence of the *whole* man to God who reveals himself. It involves an assent of the intellect and will to the self-revelation God has made through his deeds and words" (CCC, 176). The *Catechism of the Catholic Church* provides multiple characteristics of faith, all of which are helpful in formulating an accurate concept of what it means to *educate* another *in faith*. Faith is a grace (153). It is a human act (154). Faith requires understanding and freedom (156, 160). Faith is necessary (161) and requires nurturing (162). Finally, faith is the beginning of eternal life here on earth (163). In speaking of faith as a grace, the *Catechism* reaffirms the Church's ancient teaching that God is the sole source of faith. We can neither give faith to another, nor arrive at faith through our own power of reason.[4]

From beginning to end, faith is a gift from God. God infuses in a soul the theological virtue of faith so that contact may take place between him and the believer. It is only through this habit of the soul that a person is able to have direct contact with God, hence the necessity of faith. By faith, we possess in a very real way the God for whom we long and hope to be with forever in heaven. Thus faith is the beginning of eternal life. Indeed, it is "the assurance of things hoped for, the conviction of things not seen" (Hebrews 11:1).

Without diminishing the primacy of God's grace, the Church teaches with equal insistence that faith is a free, human act that requires the assent of the intellect. In the next section of this chapter, we will examine more fully what it means to know, but suffice it to say, to know a thing is to intellectually grasp the truth of its essence and existence. We can easily appreciate that our finite intellect is simply incapable of comprehending the essence of the infinite God.[5] Nevertheless, faith is in no way a "blind impulse of the mind" (CCC, 156). Through the supernatural prophetic light of faith, the intellect is able to give assent to a reality that is greater than its cognitive capacity. Faith is God's adaptation to the mind that provides the intellect with the evidence or substance it needs to give assent (see Hebrews 11:1).

Like Jacob who wrestled with the angel of the Lord, the person of faith never ceases to wrestle in his mind with what he believes. This is not doubt. Intellectual doubt stops the inquiry altogether; but faith never ceases to seek understanding (CCC, 158). St. Thomas Aquinas points out that, with knowledge, the intellect comes to a latent rest in what it now possesses, where with

---

4. Aquinas, ST II, q. 6, a. 1.
5. Aquinas, ST I, q. 12, a. 7.

faith, the intellect is never at rest, even when it gives firm assent. While grace has enabled the intellect to assent, it still cannot see the terminus (God), and for this reason, there remains in the believer a lingering "mental unrest."[6]

Cavalletti and Gobbi understood faith's mental unrest and created a unique catechetical approach that anticipates the child's desire to explore ever more deeply God's inexhaustible mystery. In the CGS approach there exists a symphonic collaboration between doctrine, materials, and manner of presentation that stimulates in the child a sense of wonder. It is the child's wonder that leads to knowledge, which furthers belief.

Knowledge

What does it mean "to know"? Philosophers and educators have wrestled with this question since before the time of Plato. Their answers vary significantly. Aristotle, Aquinas, and Montessori all teach that real things exist outside of the mind and that the intellect is capable of knowing such things through sense experience. In fact, they insist that there is nothing in the intellect that is not first in the senses.[7] From the senses, to the imagination, to the intellect, the process by which a person moves through the stages of experiencing reality is natural even in the smallest child, as Maria Montessori observes,

> There are indeed moments of sudden intellectual expansion in the lives of these tiny scholars when one can almost see the "*intellectus agens*" abstracting the "*species intelligibilis*" from the "*phantasmata*" which the children have gained through contact with the material.[8]

Montessori's language is characteristically Thomistic and perhaps unfamiliar. To illustrate what she means, here is an example from the atrium.

The Epiclesis is a presentation given in Level I (three-to-six-year-olds). The aim of this presentation is to introduce to the child the liturgical gesture of the epiclesis, to foster in the child greater attentiveness at Mass, and to set afire in her heart a love for the liturgy. The method of presenting is as follows:

---

6. Aquinas, *De veritate*, q. 14, a.1, ad 4.

7. Aristotle, *The Metaphysics* I. 1, 980a, trans. Richard Hope (New York: Columbia University Press, 1952). Richard McKeon (Chicago: University of Chicago Press, 1973). Aquinas, ST I, q. 84, a. 6; *De veritate*, q. 2, a. 3, ad 19. Montessori, *The Secret of Childhood*, 60–70.

8. Mortimer Standing, "Montessori Practice and Thomist Principles," *Blackfriars* 17, no. 192 (1936): 210.

I invite Evie (3 years old) to sit beside me at a small table which has on it the model paten with a paper host and the model chalice. I begin: "In the atrium we have learned that a gesture is something we make with our body." I then make the Sign of the Cross. I pause before continuing, "When you go to Mass, you notice that Father makes gestures. There is a very special gesture that Father makes while standing at the altar." I then proceed to stand and make the gesture of the epiclesis carefully raising my forearms above the altar while joining my open hands together side-by-side before gently lowering my hands to hover close to the paten and chalice. "Have you seen Father make this gesture?" I repeat the gesture. "This gesture is called the epiclesis." I repeat the gesture and then repeat, "Epiclesis." Brief pause. I ask, "I wonder why Father makes this gesture. What could this gesture mean?" Another brief pause. "When you go to Mass, you can watch carefully to notice when Father makes the epiclesis." Following another brief pause, Evie is invited to either practice the gesture herself or to work with another material.[9]

Using the terms of Montessori and Aquinas, let me describe what is happening intellectually and affectively within Evie during this presentation.

First, at the moment of my invitation to join me at the model altar, Evie has most likely experienced an emotional spark of curiosity. This is a critical starting place for all knowledge. Evie hears my voice and the sound sparks within her a series of intellectual and volitional movements. The words are intelligible to her. She has already experienced the joy of other presentations. Like most typical children her age, Evie is by nature inquisitive. My invitation reminds her of other pleasant moments of learning new things in the atrium. With each new presentation of the materials in the atrium, Evie gains more freedom. She can work with any material that has been presented to her. Of course my invitation could have sparked an emotion of disappointment. If Evie's interest was already fixed on another work in the atrium, she may prefer to continue her work. This is why the CGS catechist must discipline herself to be observant of the child. If the child's body and soul is engaged in meaningful work, it is best to leave her alone. Yet even if I were mistakenly to interrupt Evie, the nature of my invitation, as opposed to a command, provides her with an opportunity to strengthen her will by making a free choice to set aside what might be one preference

---

9. CGS Album page (lesson plan) on the epiclesis. Each CGS presentation includes a direct aim and an indirect aim. See glossary of terms for further explanation.

for another. Yet we are focusing on the intellect so I will continue with that exploration.

Second, once Evie kneels beside me, she sees the paten and the chalice on the altar. These items have already been presented to her and her memory is engaged. Evie has in her imagination an image (*phantasm*) of a chalice and paten, and she knows that these items are related to the Mass. If the first presentation left an impression, she will have a word in her memory that corresponds with the image in her memory. Evie might rename the item, "chalice." In so doing, she is returning in her mind to that moment when her experience of seeing the chalice was given particular meaning by hearing its name. However, the direct aim of my new presentation is not to review, but to introduce something new within the context of what is already familiar. It is time to give her a new experience, a new word, a new image, a new knowing, and a new memory.

In this new presentation, Evie hears that a new gesture is going to be shown to her, yet it is one that she has already seen the priest do at Mass. At this moment again, her imagination is engaged. If she goes to Mass, she wonders about the things she has seen Father do. If she doesn't go to Mass, she may wonder about what she is missing. I once asked a child whom I knew was not being taken to Mass, "Would you like to see this gesture that Father makes?" Her emphatic nodding of the head caused me to smile. Children are so hungry for religious experience. Either way, the child's interest is piqued.[10]

As I perform the gesture, Evie is engaged on all levels of her being. She is sensing, imagining, thinking, desiring. Her eyes observe and her sense of sight (one of the five exterior senses) collaborates with a set of inner senses, which Aristotle identifies as the common sense, imagination, memory, and cogitative senses. These inner senses form a sense image from which the intellect abstracts what is intelligible—what is able to be understood. It stands to reason that the greater the sense experience, the more sense data is received by which the inner senses can form a more refined phantasm. Through the whole process, which happens in the blink of an eye, Evie is getting to the essence of my gesture. Though she does not yet comprehend its meaning in the context of the Mass, she knows that something is happening that has meaning. Evie now has a specific image attached to a specific

---

10. The neurological studies of Dr. Mary Helen Immordino-Yang give evidence that a heightened arousal of emotions during the course of sense-data, especially emotions of curiosity and joy, spike activity in the brain. See Mary Helen Immordino-Yang, *Emotions, Learning, and the Brain: Exploring the Educational Implications of Affective Neuroscience* (New York: Norton, 2016).

moment that she can return to again and again, even after the immediate experience is over. By giving the gesture a term, *epiclesis*, I give Evie a word whereby the image can be more firmly fixed in her memory. The term provides Evie with the specific ability to pick out a specific moment on the continuum of her sensing, imagining, thinking, and desiring. Without the rich sense experience, it is unlikely that the term *epiclesis* would be intelligible for Evie, and yet without the term it is unlikely that she would retain the image in her memory. I think this is precisely what Canon Drinkwater and Cavalletti were hoping to achieve in proposing catechetical language that is intelligible to the child.

Before continuing to the section on the nature of education, I would like to draw particular attention to the role of the imagination. Aquinas observed that it is impossible for the human intellect to understand anything without some reference to sensation and imagination.[11] Cavalletti likewise draws our attention to the role of the imagination when she writes, "to pierce the meaning of the parable, we must work with our imagination and our intuition."[12] When we have an experience, a sense image is impressed upon our imagination and remains there ready for our intellect to use at any time and in a variety of ways.[13]

The imagination is a great gift that serves as a bridge between previous knowledge and new knowledge. For example, we can have in our imagination an image of gold and an image of a mountain and put these two images together to form a new image of a golden mountain. Images help the intellect rise from the material world to understand the divine truths and abstract concepts of the immaterial world.[14] A good teacher—and a good *catechist*—is one who can use images and illustrations effectively to assist the child's understanding. It is because the child has in his mind the images of a mustard seed and a full-grown mustard bush that he is able to imagine the expansiveness of God's Kingdom (see Matthew 13:31).

Because the imagination stores images and indiscriminately presents them to the intellect, sometimes we find ourselves thinking about things at

---

11. ST I, q. 84, a. 7.

12. Cavalletti, *Religious Potential 1*, 128.

13. Aquinas, ST I, q. 79, aa. 4, 6; q. 84, aa. 1, 3, 6; q. 86, a. 4. See also Aquinas, *De memoria et reminiscentia* (MR), 450 a. 27, in *Commentaries on Aristotle's "On Sense and What Is Sensed" and "On Memory and Recollection" (Thomas Aquinas in Translation)*, trans. Kevin White and Edward M. Macierowski (Washington, DC: Catholic University of America Press, 2005), 196.

14. Aquinas, *Division and Methods of the Sciences: Questions V and VI of His Commentary on the "De Trinitate" of Boethius*, trans. Armand A Maurer (Armand Augustine) (Toronto: Pontifical Institute of Mediaeval Studies, 1986), 74.

the most inappropriate time; for example, while at Mass we might reflect on a recent movie that we watched. There is, in fact, a continuous coming and going between the imagination and the intellect. For this reason, we need the virtues and gifts of the Holy Spirit to choose when it is appropriate to engage the imagination and to recognize when to leave it alone. More germane to my thesis, however, is the imagination's role in aiding the child's faith. As I hope to demonstrate in chapter 12, the CGS approach capitalizes on the use of images to convey the deepest religious truths to the child.

Teaching and Learning

Cavalletti would often make appeal to St. Augustine's maxim *"Ego numquam possum docere"* (I can never teach).[15] But what is meant by this statement? Relying on St. Thomas Aquinas's seminal work *De veritate* (On Truth), Cavalletti herself directs us to a proper understanding: "Through teaching, the mind is stimulated to know; but the one who stimulates the other to know is not capable of *making* the other know, just as the person who stimulates the eye to see is incapable of making the eye see."[16] The teacher's task is that of the person who "proposes aids and tools."[17] In his book *Aquinas*, Vivian Boland, OP, provides a useful exposition of the various texts in which St. Thomas Aquinas develops his view on the nature of teaching and learning.[18] For those of us engaged in faithful catechetical education, Aquinas' insights will prove to be beneficial.

According to Aquinas, one work of the intellect is to relate things to each other, and to identify different kinds of relation between things.[19] Some objects and concepts are immediately intelligible and thus the child is able to arrive at knowledge on his own. Other things are more difficult and can only be identified and related with the assistance of a teacher who leads (*educens*) the student through the intellect's natural discursive process.[20] Agreeing with St. Augustine, St. Thomas comments that a teacher is like "someone who uses his finger to point something out."[21] Boland expounds,

---

15. Cavalletti, *Religious Potential 1*, 64.
16. Cavalletti, *Religious Potential 1*, 24; emphasis mine. See also Aquinas, *De veritate*, q. 11, a. 12.
17. Cavalletti, *Religious Potential 1*, 24, citing ST I, q. 17, a. 1.
18. Vivian Boland, OP, *St. Thomas Aquinas* (London: Bloomsbury, 2014).
19. Aquinas, ST I, q. 85.
20. Boland, *Aquinas*, 44.
21. Augustine, *De doctrina christiana*, § 3; Aquinas, *II Sentences* 28, 1, 5, ad 3, cited in Boland, *Aquinas*, 44.

One person is said to teach another when the discourse of reason which the mind can naturally do for itself is expressed for the learner through signs, *per signa*, so that the natural reason of the student comes to know something it did not know before through the aids, *instrumenta*, that are thus proposed to it.[22]

While a teacher cannot give the power of sight to a student, she can point something out for the student to see. Boland explains, "The teacher proposes signs of intelligible things from which the student receives intelligible intentions."[23] By pointing out relationships between signs, especially between what the student already knows and the new concept to be understood, the teacher provides necessary assistance.[24] Cavalletti speaks of this work of the teacher as providing an "education to the reading of signs."[25] A good teacher knows exactly how much assistance is necessary. As Cavalletti so aptly understood, the task of the teacher is to excite in the pupil's mind a real movement from potential knowledge (*not knowing*) to actual knowledge (*knowing*).[26] Hence, the deeper meaning of "to educate" is to cause—by way of stimulation—the movement of another's intellect from *not knowing to knowing*.[27] Good educational pedagogy is thus *the art—and science—of knowing how to lead the child to knowledge*.

According to St. Thomas Aquinas, teaching involves both the presentation of the concept and providing an interior illumination by which it comes to be understood.[28] A human teacher can announce truths, but properly speaking, only God can teach the truth interiorly: understanding and wisdom come from God.[29] This is the true meaning of the oft quoted "only God can teach."[30] Yet before this insight can be misconstrued, St. Thomas makes an important distinction. Insofar as they present the object to be understood and, as needed, direct the student's sense perception, which augments the interior light, humans may indeed be called "teacher" because God permits them to participate in his pedagogy as *instrumental* causes of knowledge.[31]

---

22. Boland, *Aquinas*, 48.
23. Boland, *Aquinas*, 49.
24. Boland, *Aquinas*, 44.
25. Cavalletti, *Religious Potential 1*, 130.
26. Aquinas, *De veritate*, q. 11, a. 1, ad 12, cited in Boland, *Aquinas*, 50.
27. Boland, *Aquinas*, 50.
28. Boland, *Aquinas*, 43.
29. Aquinas, *De veritate*, q. 11, a. 1, ad 1.
30. Augustine, *De magistro*, XIV, 45. Aquinas, *De veritate*, q. 11, a. 1, ad 1.
31. Boland, *Aquinas*, 43–44.

Recognizing the dignity of the child, and indeed the true nature of education, a good teacher knows what the child needs to do for himself. Think back to chapter 9: a good teacher never does for a child what he can do for himself. By way of analogy, recognizing the dignity of the child, and indeed the true nature of education, a good teacher does not merely tell a child about orange juice or even show him pictures. Nor does she simply hand the child a glass of orange juice. Rather, she leads the child to the orange grove and, if assistance is needed, lifts the child, or gives him a ladder, so that he can pick an orange himself. A good teacher allows the child to start the peeling process, again, giving help only as needed. From the experience of walking through an orange grove, climbing an orange tree, picking and then peeling an orange, the child comes to an entirely new level of knowing the taste of orange juice. Anyone who has served the education of children knows firsthand the difference between a child who is told about reality and a child who experiences it for himself.

In the unique pedagogy of the CGS, we do not merely tell the child about God or show beautiful pictures (though we certainly do both). We *lead* (*educens*) the child to God through God's sources of revelation. We lift up for the child particular aspects of that revelation that uniquely satisfy the child's religious hunger. By way of careful question, we point out for the child particular aspects of God's revelation but allow the child to make connections on his own. In other words, we pull back the veil to God's mystery only as much as the child requires, allowing him to continue on his own journey, led by the Holy Spirit to the heart of the Trinity. In this way, the CGS approach serves the true nature of the child and the true nature of education.

Wonder

In chapter 10, we considered the child's innate sense of wonder. From their many years of working with children, Cavalletti and Gobbi were convinced that an education in the faith was most importantly *an "education to wonder."*[32] *Wonder* is the key to a catechetical pedagogy that engages the mind and the heart. Cavalletti writes, "Wonder sparks within the religious person sentiments of praise and admiration" and "confers a religious character to our whole life, forming a consciousness of being plunged into an unfathomable and incommensurable reality."[33] Wonder is "fulfilled in a deepened

---

32. Cavalletti, *Religious Potential 1*, 107.
33. Cavalletti, *Religious Potential 1*, 108.

sense of mystery . . . [an] ever-flowing, unfathomable, and inexhaustible" mystery.[34] Wonder acts like a magnet "situated ahead of us and attracts us with irresistible force toward the object of our astonishment."[35] For this reason, a catechetical education that encourages wonder is an "education that helps [the child] to go always more deeply into reality."[36]

St. Thomas defines wonder (*admiratio*) as a "kind of desire for knowledge; a desire which comes to man when he sees an effect of which the cause either is unknown to him, or surpasses his knowledge or faculty of understanding."[37] Without a developed sense of wonder, a person is not able to penetrate the meaning of things and because of this he is tragically not able to find the Creator of all things. As a result, the deeper mysteries of life and of faith go unnoticed and unappreciated. It is only because of wonder that we are drawn deeper and deeper into "the contemplation of something that exceeds us."[38] It is the gift of wonder that prompts the child to probe and ponder always more deeply the inexhaustible mystery of God's reality.

As keen observers of the child, Cavalletti and Gobbi recognized that a child's wonder is a delicate matter needing an appropriate stimulus, but not too much. Cavalletti writes, "It is the educator's task . . . to offer the child's wonder an object capable of taking [him] always farther and deeper into the awareness of reality, an object whose frontiers are always expanding as [he] slowly proceeds in the contemplation of it."[39]

In my estimation, Cavalletti and Gobbi were catechetical educators of the highest regard. Throughout their long catechetical experiment, they continuously grappled with finding the right balance of spiritual food that would nourish, but not overwhelm, the child's wonder. So highly did they esteem this God-given exigency, that many of their early catechetical materials, which were painstakingly hand-crafted, were banished to the work closet because they failed to engage the child's wonder. Many other materials and presentations were adjusted based on the way the child wondered about their inexhaustible doctrine. Over the years, Cavalletti and Gobbi recognized

34. Josef Pieper, *Leisure: The Basis of Culture*, trans. Gerald Malsbary (South Bend, IN: St. Augustine's Press, 1998), 121.

35. Cavalletti, *Religious Potential 1*, 107.

36. Cavalletti, *Religious Potential 1*, 108.

37. Thomas Aquinas, *Summa theologica*, trans. Fathers of the English Dominican Province (New York: Benziger Brothers, 1911–1925), ST I-II, q. 32, a. 8.

38. Cavalletti, *Religious Potential 1*, 107.

39. Cavalletti, *Religious Potential 1*, 109.

that the religious themes (doctrines) that sparked the greatest wonder in the child were the parables, especially those of the Kingdom of God.[40]

The 2020 *Directory* recognizes the important role of wonder within its considerations on the role of beauty. Beauty does not merely refer to the sacred images that we are called to use in catechetical methodology; because it is true and good, the eloquent St. Chrysostom reminds us that doctrine is beautiful (DC, 13)! Jesus spoke "*beautiful words* that with their efficacy heal the depths of the soul" and "performed *beautiful actions*" (DC, 107; original emphasis). This beauty flowed from the inner source: Jesus is the *beautiful one*. His words and actions recorded in the Scriptures and continued through the Church's liturgy are more than enough to sustain a child's wonder.

I am reminded of an exchange that a friend of mine had several years ago with his Eminence Christoph Cardinal Schönborn, Archbishop of Vienna and general editor of the *Catechism of the Catholic Church*. My friend was a new catechist in the cardinal's diocese and, wanting to assist with a much-needed catechetical renewal, she asked him where to begin. His Eminence could have proposed any number of catechetical initiatives. His reply was quintessentially Thomistic: "Teach them to wonder."

Memory

One of the distinctive features of the CGS approach—and a problematic one for some catechetical theorists—is the absence of tests and textbooks, such as what one might find in a traditional school setting. I hope that my reader has figured out by this point how the CGS method actually strengthens the memory by punctuating the child's experience more intentionally with rich sensorial experiences. I can assure you that CGS does not fall into that pernicious category of a "memory-less catechesis" (CT, 55).

St. Thomas teaches the key to memory is meditation.[41] Echoing Aquinas's insight, the *Catechism of the Catholic Church* recognizes that

> [m]editation engages thought, imagination, emotion, and desire. This mobilization of faculties is necessary in order to deepen our convictions of faith, prompt the conversion of our heart, and strengthen our will to follow Christ. (CCC, 2708)

---

40. Cavalletti, *Religious Potential 1*, 109.

41. Vivian Boland, OP, "St. Thomas's Sermon *Puer Iesus*: A Neglected Source for His Understanding of Teaching and Learning," in *New Blackfriars* 88, no. 1016 (July 2007): 468.

As food needs to be digested in order to nourish the body, truth needs to be pondered in order to nourish the soul.[42] CGS uses a "spiral method," by which doctrines are presented, revisited, and expanded upon throughout the year and indeed throughout all three levels. There is no such thing as "one and done" in the CGS approach. The repetition is always with a new aspect of pondering the doctrine at a deeper level of inquiry, which serves both the child's wonder, his memory, and his plane of development.

We want to form children who can ponder the Word of God as did Our Lady and the great mystics of the Church. The practice of pondering doctrine not only impresses the doctrine more firmly upon the intellect, but it also allows the will to savor the doctrine's goodness, thereby strengthening the child's desire to know and follow God more and more. By affording the child the time and materials to ponder the doctrines proclaimed, the CGS pedagogy offers the best opportunity for doctrine to penetrate deep into the child's memory and imagination, giving rise to faith.

The educational principles of CGS are governed by its own unique Montessorian-Hebraic pedagogy. Following Montessori's principles of education, the texts used in CGS catechetical education are primary resources: Scripture and the Roman Missal. In a Level III atrium, where the child has become a "researcher" (to use Montessori's term), supplementary texts may include the *Catechism of the Catholic Church*, writings from the Fathers of the Church, encyclopedias, and books on the history and culture of ancient peoples.

In keeping with Montessori's philosophy of education, the children in the atrium are not tested on their knowledge; they are observed. The educational method serves the educational goal. If the goal of catechesis is more than the mastery of religious data (and it is!), then we must stop the method of testing and move to a model of assessment that relinquishes all superficial control of the child's faith development. As a teacher and catechist for over thirty years, I know: just because a child passes a test doesn't mean she has been evangelized.

The Latin root for *assess* is *assidēre*, which means "to sit beside." This is exactly what we do in the CGS atrium. The catechist's assessment is by way of observation, sitting beside the child to see if those physical and spiritual exigencies, which we looked at in chapters 9 and 10, are being met. She watches carefully to capture the right time to give a presentation, waiting for the child's physical, intellectual, spiritual, and emotional readiness.

---

42. Boland, "*Puer Iesus*," 468.

She observes the child at work, noting how often he returns to a particular presentation and the manner in which he engages with the materials, and she remains in conversation with the child about his work. She notices if a child needs a re-presentation of a doctrine or if he is ready for a new presentation. The CGS *Journals* contain many accounts of the tender experiences of God that children have had while in the atrium. There are also accounts of the profound theological insights that children have shared with their catechists. Such stories have been recounted throughout this book as well. These anecdotes demonstrate that, through the method of observation and dialogue, catechists are able to assess the child's growth better than any test could.

Strictly speaking, it is the catechist who is accountable in the atrium. She is accountable for knowing the content of the faith (DC, 143) and for writing good album pages (think "lesson plans"). She is responsible for knowing how to give a presentation (DC, 148) and for "perfecting" the manner of presenting. She is responsible for keeping records of the presentations each child receives and how the child lives and works in the atrium. She is responsible for creating the specific conditions so that the relationship between God and the child can be deepened.[43] To ensure that she can fulfill her responsibilities, the CGS catechist receives a tremendous amount of initial formation and ongoing support from the CGS community. Each Level of CGS requires approximately 90 hours (150 hours for Level III) of catechist formation in the CGS pedagogy. Many more hours are spent making materials and writing album pages. On a regular basis, a CGS catechist assesses herself as she strives, like Cavalletti and Gobbi, to become more and more faithful to God and to the child through being faithful to the CGS pedagogy.

Learning How to Listen

Already in chapter 8, I mentioned Cavalletti's essay on the nature of Jewish pedagogy. Her insights bear further consideration in this chapter on the nature of education. Formed by her studies of Semitic language as well as her exposure to the Jewish culture, Cavalletti came to appreciate that the Jewish people have much to teach us.[44] "The creed of the Jew," she points out, is "Hear, O Israel." Thus, the world of the ancient Jews "can be defined as the

---

43. Cavalletti, *Religious Potential 1*, 24.
44. Cavalletti, *Way of Holy Joy*, 66–67.

world of listening." The Jewish prophet was the one who turned his ear "to the Word of God, in order to deliver it to men."[45]

The Hebrew word *dābār* can be translated as "word" but more precisely it means "to speak." It is an action of God. Scripture scholar Caroll Stuhlmueller explains,

> When a prophet announced: "Hear the word of God," he was more than a teacher arranging his thoughts in logical sequence, so as to elucidate a doctrine or truth; he was a herald of divine presence. God was *there* in those words, irresistibly "pushing" or "driving forward" the action which his words uttered.[46]

God's word *is* God himself acting upon the listener.[47] There is a consistency about God; he is trustworthy. Knowledge is imparted by his actions, but the knowledge itself acts upon man.[48] It is a knowledge which is life because it extends God's personal concern to every segment of the person's being.[49] During each moment of the Jewish people's life, God revealed himself by love and care and as the Jews experienced this "word" of protection, they came to know the mystery of God.

Cavalletti and Stulmueller's insight are all the more fascinating when we consider that the word *catechesis* comes from the Greek *katechein* which means "to echo." The 2020 *Directory* draws our attention repeatedly to the *kerygmatic* nature of catechesis, which is at all stages an announcement of the Gospel (DC, preface). The announcement of the kerygma has a unique quality in that it is both a proclamation and an action. "Evangelizing is not, in the first place, the delivery of doctrine; but rather, making present and announcing Jesus Christ" (DC, 29). Of course, after our study of knowledge, we understand that the delivery of doctrine *does* in fact carry the presence of Jesus, but only with the accompanying method of wonder, whereby a person is led to contemplate the face of God, whose features are accentuated by the Church's doctrine. Echoing St. Thomas' insight on the nature of truth, Cavalletti writes, "Knowledge does not arise through domination but through attentiveness to the object. Such attentiveness conforms the knower

---

45. Cavalletti, "Hebrew Pedagogy," 13.

46. Carroll Stuhlmueller, "The Prophet and the Word of God," *The Thomist: A Speculative Quarterly Review* 28, no. 2 (April 1964): 138.

47. Stuhlmueller, "The Prophet," 138.

48. Stuhlmueller, "The Prophet," 139.

49. Stuhlmueller, "The Prophet," 146.

to what is known rather than the other way around."[50] We possess truth when our intellect is in conformity with reality.

The intellect has an indispensable role in faith; yet our posture toward God matters. The posture taken in the CGS atrium is one of receptivity, like that of a beggar where hearts, minds, and hands remain ready to receive. It is the posture of the Son of God, who did not deem equality with God something to be grasped at. It is the posture of our Mother Mary who even in her questioning of the angel remained the lowly handmaid of the Lord. "It is an error as common as it is fateful—to think that truth can be approached without homage."[51] The great scholastic theologians St. Thomas and St. Bonaventure probed the mysteries of the faith in the most humble manner; not seeking to master the God that they came to know, but to fall in love with him whom their hearts sought. As catechists, we are called to imitate their method of investigation and cogitation—a method fitting for faith's mystery.

We live and catechize in an age when most of the public wants to create its own truth. It is the logical result of epistemological skepticism. When doubt is cast against the intellect's power to know, then universal agreement about truth is unattainable. We see this not only in society, but sadly within in the Body of Christ as well. Opposing views of Church teachings reveal a people of God who can no longer listen and hear his voice. Cavalletti saw the important work of education as that of "disposing [the child] to listen to reality in all of its vastness." [52] "To be educated is to learn how to listen," Cavalletti insists. "Without this incessant listening to the order [of reality] established by God man is lost."[53]

An education to listen has possibilities in catechetical education that are truly "Copernican." The Jewish people pursued God in love because they *already* knew themselves to be loved by him. They sought to know God precisely because they *already* knew him. God had entered into their lives *already*. In other words, while the Greeks pursued truth, the Jews were *pursued by* Truth. The goal of catechetical education is not a mastery of religious data; the goal is to help others discover that they are *already* immeasurably loved by God—that they *already* belong to him. No one pursues God until they have *already* come to believe to some degree that he loves them. One

---

50. Cavalletti, "Hebrew Pedagogy," 13.

51. Newman, "Faith and Reason," (Oxford University Sermons, 1880), 198.

52. Cavalletti, "Hebrew Pedagogy," 14.

53. Cavalletti, "Hebrew Pedagogy," 13.

wonders: how might Cavalletti's Copernican view affect the way we approach catechesis?

The whole catechetical project of the CGS approach has the character of an education to listen—an education to relationship. When the child is introduced to the CGS atrium, he is told: "There is a Voice that speaks to us, God's Voice, and I can help you to hear his Voice." The child in the atrium is primarily formed to listen to the Voice of the Good Shepherd—to listen and "to wait for the Lord" (Isaiah 40:31).

Conclusion

A story about the great Dominican theologian Reginald Garrigou-Lagrange (1877–1964) continues to be told at the Angelicum in Rome.[54] I heard the story from Fr. Joseph Henchey, css, who was present the day it happened. One day, Fr. Reginald approached his podium to begin a lecture for a course on Trinitarian theology. He began, "God." This was followed by a long silence and gaze at the seminarians sitting before him. Fr. Reginald composed himself and began again, "God." This too was followed by an even longer silence and a long glance down at his notes. After several moments, Fr. Reginald tried a third time pronouncing the single word: "God." He could say no more. The esteemed Dominican quietly collected his notes, bowed his head to the seminarians and left the room. Fr. Henchey told me, "It was the best lecture on the Trinity I ever heard."

True, the *Catechism* honors the human intellect's capacity to know, by the natural power and light of reason, that God *exists* (CCC, 37); but this is not to have him mastered by any kind of a *knowledge* of his essence. God is the quintessential, unfathomable, and inexhaustible mystery. His *essence* is beyond what our finite intellect can abstract. To paraphrase the esteemed author of *De trinitate*: "If you comprehend, it is not *God*."[55] It is only by the gift of faith that the human intellect can assent to what it is incapable of understanding. As such, when we teach the Church's doctrine, we must always do so in a manner that, while confident in its veracity, nevertheless, continues to inspire in others the desire to seek the Face of God more and more.

The Church has consistently called catechists *to evangelize by educating and educate by evangelizing* (see DC, 179; original emphasis). This means

---

54. Father Garrigou-Lagrange helped to navigate the Church's theology through the Modernist heresy. He authored numerous theological and spiritual books and taught St. John Paul II.

55. Augustine of Hippo, Sermon 52, 16, in *The Works of Saint Augustine: A Translation for the 21st Century*, trans. Edmund Hill, op, ed. John E. Rotelle, osa (Brooklyn, NY: New City Press, 1990), 57.

that there can be no opposition between religious knowledge and religious experience. Catechesis seeks to form the whole person: mind and heart, body and soul. This requires a clear intention on the part of the catechist to form the child in a knowledge of the faith. We are called to faithfully proclaim the kerygma with clarity and confidence (DC, 163). Cavalletti would say, "We cannot teach another the Mystery of God, we can only help them seek Him."[56] We must teach children how to seek the face of God, to listen for his voice, to wonder at his majesty, and when he reveals himself, to rest in his Truth, Beauty, and Goodness.

This chapter examined the nature of education in the Judeo-Christian-Thomistic-Montessorian heritage. We now must finish our examination of the pedagogy of the CGS by considering the specific method that Cavalletti and Gobbi recognized as the best means for giving children an authentic *catechetical education in Christ*.

---

56. Cavalletti, "Characteristics of the Good Shepherd," in *Journals of the Catechesis of the Good Shepherd 1984–1997*, trans. Patricia Coulter (Chicago: Catechesis of the Good Shepherd Publications, 1998), 28.

Chapter 12
A Method for the Mystery

Introduction

Often the term *methodology* is used interchangeably with the term *pedagogy*, and this is misleading because methodology serves pedagogy. Merriam-Webster defines methodology as "(1) a body of methods, rules, and postulates employed by a discipline: a particular procedure or set of procedures; (2) the analysis of the principles or procedures in a particular field."[1] Methodology refers to *the system of concrete steps that apply a pedagogical theory, or the steps used to reach a desired goal.* Other words that serve as synonyms for methodology include *approach, fashion, manner, strategy, style, technique.* Thus we can say, an *educational method* is the particular strategy that a teacher uses to help *lead* a student to knowledge. A good teacher recognizes that a sound educational method is determined by the particular concept the teacher is trying to teach *and* the capacity of the student who is trying to learn.[2]

Reflecting on the nature of educational methodology, Cavalletti observed that the "educational method is determined by the educational setting (context)."[3] More recently, Pope Francis has highlighted that faith "needs a setting in which it can be witnessed to and communicated, a means which is suitable and proportionate to what is communicated" (*Lumen fidei*, 40). The subject matter in catechesis is the inexhaustible mystery of God's revelation, which is both his person and his teaching. Following the principle of "fidelity to God and fidelity to man" set forth by the Church, the choice of catechetical method must take into consideration both the nature of the content *and* the nature of its recipient (see GDC, 145, and DC, 194).

---

1. Merriam-Webster, s.v. "methodology," https://www.merriam-webster.com /dictionary/methodology.
2. See Boland's treatment of Aquinas's commentary on *De Trinitate, caput 2* in *Aquinas*, 75–78.
3. Cavalletti, "Hebrew Pedagogy," 15.

Expressed in terms of CGS, catechetical methodology must serve both the *Mystery of God* and *the mystery of the child*. Throughout this book, we have been considering the nature of the CGS pedagogy identifying the unique nature of its catechetical content as well as its appreciation for the unique nature of the child. We can anticipate, therefore, that the CGS approach uses a unique catechetical method in its robust *catechetical education*. This chapter will finish the discussion by examining the method of CGS, which is inspired by its pedagogical goal.

Importance of Catechetical Method

The importance of sound catechetical methodology cannot be overemphasized. It is how catechesis achieves its pedagogical goal (DC, 194). As noted in chapter 2, history demonstrates that an impoverished catechetical method contributes to an impoverished formation as a disciple of Christ. Likewise, as noted in chapter 4, the failure to use a method that instructs another in the teachings of Christ and his Church results in a failure to provide a knowledge of the faith (DC, 80). The goal of catechesis has "the twofold objective of maturing the initial faith and of educating the true disciple of Christ, by means of a deeper and more systematic knowledge of the person and the message of our Lord Jesus Christ" (DC, preface). Thus, the pedagogical goal of catechesis should be animated by an all-encompassing *paideia* (program of education) that seeks to form the whole person in every dimension of Christian discipleship.

Recognizing the diversity of age, culture, intellectual development, and "many other personal circumstances," the Church, in her wisdom, does not specify one method or another, provided that the methods used are not "contrary to the Gospel" (GDC, 148; DC, 195). Catechists are entrusted with the responsibility to discern their choice of methods in light of the pedagogy of God (GDC, 148) and the educational goal of catechesis (DC, 194). Dr. Caroline Farey observes, "The closer and more fully a method follows God's pedagogy, the richer and more effective the catechesis will be in nurturing and encouraging a true experience of the Faith and thus a filial encounter with God."[4] Cavalletti observed that, in the catechetical setting,

---

4. Caroline Farey, "Methodological Principles," in *The Pedagogy of God: Its Centrality in Catechesis and Catechist Formation*, ed. Caroline Farey, Waltraud Linnig, and Sr. M. Johanna Paruch (Steubenville, OH: Emmaus Road Pub, 2011), 164.

"method is not like an empty box that can be filled with anything whatsoever"; the method has a soul, and this soul should correlate to the content that is being transmitted through the method. Between method and content there should be a profound accord, an affinity of nature; otherwise there is a risk of distorting the content.[5]

For Cavalletti, the best method for conveying the inexhaustible nature of God is *the method of signs*.[6] She explains why. Signs point out the "unfathomable reality of the Kingdom of God through elements of everyday life (bread, wine, water, etc.) and in this way they propose to us an object of meditation that can be continuous."[7]

The "connection between the sign and its content is not extrinsic; rather, they are linked at the very level of being even though the container is smaller than the content."[8] A sign is not open to any or all interpretations. The sign bears an ontological likeness to the thing signified.[9] For example, the image or sign of the vine and the branches does indeed point to the reality of how grace operates in the soul; the mustard seed "*is* in some way a bearer of the reality of the kingdom."[10]

The Choice of Language

The question of method is not only linked to content; it is also linked to language (DC, 204–217). Indeed, of the many conundrums that challenged catechetical theorists throughout the twentieth century, perhaps the most difficult had to do with the linguistic form of the catechetical proclamation. During the three historical phases of catechesis, the form of the proclamation went through a transformation from concise statements in a catechism, to stories in the Bible, to the story of one's own life.[11] The catechetical proclamation must echo the teachings of Jesus and the catechist knows that her task is the faithful proclamation of his teachings in all their "rigor and vigor" (CT, 30). The question remains however: "What *linguistic* form is best for this catechetical proclamation?" I have argued throughout this book that the best form is the one that is faithful to the mystery of God *and* faithful to

---

5. Cavalletti, *Religious Potential 1*, 125.
6. Cavalletti, *Religious Potential 1*, 125.
7. Cavalletti, *Religious Potential 1*, 127.
8. Cavalletti, "ABCs of Christianity," 2.
9. Cavalletti, *Religious Potential 1*, 128.
10. Cavalletti, *Religious Potential 1*, 128; original emphasis.
11. These phases in catechesis and the nature of the catechetical proclamation are examined in chapter 1.

the mystery of the child. In other words, our catechetical proclamations must be simultaneously *intelligible* and *inspiring*.

There can be no question—no challenge—that the doctrinal language of the Church has a necessary place in catechesis (DC, 204–205). The Church insists that catechesis has a particular "language of the faith" (DC, 204) that includes, among other things, "the writings of the Fathers, Creeds, [and] formulations of the Magisterium" (DC, 205). Notwithstanding, the choice of language must be guided by pedagogical principles, for example, the child's receptivity (see DC, 206). This has been a repeated theme throughout the book. The CGS approach possesses a unique catechetical pedagogy that is animated by the *perichoretic* relationship between content, method, *and* the child. Every decision made by Cavalletti and Gobbi redounds to this relationship. In other words, CGS proclaims *this* content in *this* manner because of *this* child. Though I have touched upon this matter already in the book, it may be helpful to give further examination to their decision to restrict the language of the atrium to the language of the Scriptures and the liturgy.

The Language of the Catechism

In his essay "Handing on the Faith and the Sources of Faith," Cardinal Ratzinger takes issue with theologians and catechetical theorists who use the Scriptures as a source of doctrine without any appeal to the Church's tradition. He writes:

> [N]ow there is an attempt to lead people to Christianity by means of direct dialogue between present-day experience and the biblical message. . . . Dogma was not denied for the most part in this development, but it declined in importance to become a sort of external frame of reference that no longer had much significance for the structure of catechesis or for its contents. Behind this was a certain embarrassment with regard to dogma.[12]

Already, in chapter 7, I have noted that Cavalletti recognized that the Church's magisterial teachings were a rich source of the deposit of faith. In *Religious Potential of the Child 1*, Cavalletti makes a rather alarming remark that seems contradictory, validating Ratzinger's concern. Quoting her biblical professor Alonso Schoeckel, sj, she writes:

---

12. Ratzinger, "Handing on the Faith and the Sources of Faith," in *Handing on the Faith in an Age of Disbelief*, 22.

The difficulty does not come from the fact, let us note, that the formulation is erroneous; it resides in the very fact of the use of formula. We should not complain to ourselves that the reasoning is poorly constructed or that it must be improved, but rather that the pedagogical preoccupation with formula tends to restrict and distort the Scriptural text.[13]

Before offering an interpretation of why I think Cavalletti is sympathetic to Schoeckel's view, I must make a corrective remark regarding her comment that doctrinal formulations tend "to restrict and distort the Scriptural text."

Since the second century, the Church has had to clarify misinterpretations of the Scriptures. One thinks of Marcion's distortion of Jesus' teachings on marriage and the kingdom.[14] One thinks as well of Tertullian (160–220), who, though a great Scripture scholar, became entangled in the Montanist heresy, all the while disdaining the positive influences of Greek philosophy. And then, there is Bishop Arius, whose misinterpretation of Scripture led to his denial that Jesus was true God and true man. The list continues even to our day.

The Church does not always give a dogmatic interpretation of Scripture, but when she does, it is to proclaim an insight given by the Holy Spirit and, at times, to correct false interpretations that compromise God's revelation and thus jeopardize our salvation. The formula that defines the *hypostatic union* might not ignite in most people a deep love of Jesus, but the dogmatic teaching that the two natures of God and man are joined in the one divine person of Jesus Christ does inspire us to live in hope that one day we might become "participants of the divine nature" (2 Peter 1:3–4).

In promulgating the 1994 *Catechism of the Catholic Church*, the Church provides catechists with a clarity and uniformity regarding doctrine that is necessary. The *Catechism* brings into focus the truths of revelation in an unsurpassed way, reflecting the beautiful "symphony of faith."[15] The unity of doctrine provides a unity of language as well as an authoritative—inspired—interpretation of Scripture. Certainly, the *Catechism* does not (nor can it) represent the final word on the inexhaustible mystery of God, who has revealed himself in Christ Jesus. But this does not mean that what is

---

13. Cavalletti, *Religious Potential 1*, 125–126. The quote is from Alonso Schoekel, *Il dinamismo della tradizione* (Brescia, Italy: Paidea, 1970), 265ff.

14. Marcion baptized only those who were not living in matrimony: virgins, widows, celibates, and eunuchs; all others remained catechumens.

15. *Fidei depositum*, 2.

expressed fails to capture the reality. Allow me to be repetitive. While doctrinal formulations are not the material object of our faith, they nevertheless serve as valid portals to God, who is the object of our faith (CCC, 170, 143, 150). Doctrine feeds the mind of the believer, and when the mind rests on truth, the will is moved to pursue it as goodness. The statements of the *Catechism* are quintessentially true, and for this reason, when they are grasped by the intellect, likewise, the will is drawn to God's goodness.

Those who knew Cavalletti personally knew of her love for the Church and for the Church's teachings. Cavalletti herself gives testimony to her love for the Church and reflects on Gobbi's and her life's work:

> The *Catechesis of the Good Shepherd* is based on two pillars: the richness of the creature of God when, in his smallness, he opens to Him, and the power of the Word. When these two "poles" meet each other, a marvelous spark is lit. It is this spark—which we believe we have glimpsed in this little fragment of the Church in which we live and work—that, with the wonder and the joy of the gift received, we wish to offer Mother Church the catechesis as gift.[16]

Given their fidelity to the Church on all other matters, I maintain that Cavalletti's and Gobbi's resistance to "formula" is *pedagogical*.

The Language of the Child

Let us remember that the choice to exclude a formulaic catechism was not an initial decision on the part of Cavalletti and Gobbi. Rather, it was one that developed organically as they observed the children and responded to their unique exigencies. Cavalletti recounts in a CGS article, "Prehistory and History,"

> We noticed that one of the boys was completely indifferent; he hardly studied the definitions, and whatever he had studied went over his head without leaving a trace. In this instance, as in many other cases, we had chosen a course of action before we were able to justify to ourselves or others why we had done so. The first indications came neither from books or our own making, but rather *from what the child appeared to be asking of us.*[17]

---

16. Cavalletti, "The Catechesis of the Good Shepherd as Gift," in *Commemorative Journal: Sofia Cavalletti 1917–2011*, trans. Maureen Armas (Chicago: Catechesis of the Good Shepherd Publications, 2012), 15.
17. Cavalletti, "Prehistory and History," 69. Emphasis mine.

I see two principles of education behind Cavalletti and Gobbi's decision to follow the child in this regard. The first relates to what we examined in chapter 11 on the nature of knowledge. Knowledge requires intelligible signs.[18] According to St. Thomas, the words of a teacher offer the most intelligible sign.[19] Yet for the child the words must be intelligible so that he can form concepts and construct his own understanding. This does not mean that the child constructs his own truth; truth is objective. But in its process of abstraction and judgment, the intellect comes to possess the truth contained in the reality.[20] In other words, while the intellect does not *make* truth, it does make truth *its own*. Cavalletti and Gobbi spent over fifty years working with children, observing their religious habits, dialoging with them about religious truths. The children communicated in multiple ways that they were grasping the most profound theological truths but in their own manner.

Second, the child wants, needs, and has a right to the greatest and most essential realities.[21] The untimely introduction of doctrinal formulas, prior to an adequate presentation of the Scriptures and the liturgy, tends to inhibit the child's sense of wonder and exploration. If learning is sparked by wonder—and it is—then our catechetical language must possess a quality that excites in the child a sense of wonder. Cavalletti and Gobbi observed that a child's intellect is greatly excited and nourished by the imagery in the Scriptures and by liturgical symbols and gestures which provide provocative objects of wonder.

The language of the *Catechism* is indispensible for the Church and for the catechist, but ordinarily its complexity does not spark wonder in the child (or the childlike). On the other hand, the language of imagery, such as what Jesus spoke, not only sparks wonder, it also serves as a foundational communication for the child who needs a simple expression that is intelligible. The images that Jesus uses to reveal to us the mystery of God and the mystery of his Kingdom are "fundamental sounds" of God's Word. [22]

"Just as in giving the alphabet, we offer [to the child] only the most fundamental, rather than all the nuances, of the sounds, so too for the [ABCs of catechesis]."[23] A child sees a vine and its branches—touches it, even. From

---

18. Boland, *Aquinas*, 44.
19. *De veritate*, q. 11, a. 1, ad 11.
20. ST I, q. 16, a. 1.
21. Cavalletti, *Religious Potential 1*, 21–23.
22. Cavalletti, "ABCs of Christianity," 3.
23. Cavalletti, "ABCs of Christianity," 3.

this experience of reality, he is better able to comprehend the unfathomable mystery of a number of doctrines: the life of grace in the soul; the intimate union between Jesus and his Church; the effects of sin on our relationship with Jesus and other members of the Church. Jesus teaches the meaning of allusive doctrines such as grace, sin, eternal life, and death through images such as sheep, seeds, soil, weeds, and wheat. These are images that a child comprehends.

God's Word "surpasses man as heaven surpasses the earth," Cavalletti writes. Hence, when speaking about God, "[h]uman language is always an approximation."[24] "Our human words always fall short of the mystery of God" (CCC, 42). The Eastern Church especially recognizes that whatever we can say that God is, we are always more precise when we say what he is *not*. In the Divine Liturgy of St. John Chrysostom, perhaps the most eloquent preacher of the early Church, the Church prays to "the inexpressible . . . the incomprehensible . . . the invisible . . . the ungraspable" God.[25]

In the writings of St. Thomas Aquinas, we have the unsurpassable theological heritage of the Western Church; yet even St. Thomas testified in the end to his fellow Dominican, Brother Reginald, "All I have written seems as straw."[26] As the receiver of God's mystery, the child requires a language that is both intelligible and nourishing to him. Cavalletti proposed that the language "by which we [may] draw near to the Mystery" can be none other than an "allusive language of signs."[27]

The Language of Signs

St. Thomas explores the question on the use of imagery (metaphors) in the Holy Scriptures concluding that "God provides for everything according to the capacity of its nature." Since it is "natural to [the human person] to attain to intellectual truths through sensible objects," it is fitting that "spiritual truths [are] taught under the likeness of material things."[28] In the Old Testament, God's immanence is the breeze in the evening (Genesis 3:8), while his transcendence surpasses the highest heavens (Psalm 103:11). He is simultaneously a flash of fire (Ezekiel 1:4) and silence (1 Kings 19:12). He is a mother who can never forget her nursing child (Isaiah 49:15–16). Jesus, the perfect image and Word of God, tells us that he is the Good Shepherd, the

---

24. Cavalletti, *Religious Potential 1*, 132.
25. St. John Chrysostom, *The Anaphora*.
26. Josef Pieper, *The Silence of St. Thomas*, trans. Daniel O'Connor (London: Faber & Faber, 1957), 52.
27. Cavalletti, "ABCs of Christianity," 2.
28. Aquinas, ST I, q. 1, a. 9.

Vine, the Lamb, a mother hen. The Kingdom of God that we all seek is the Pearl of Great Price (see John 10; John 15; Matthew 13) and the smallest of seeds (Matthew 13:31).

Recall from chapter 2 that at the start of the catechetical renewal in the early 1900s, England's Canon Francis Drinkwater addressed the issue of catechetical language forthrightly. In an essay entitled "The Use of Words," Drinkwater takes issue with the language of a "Denzinger catechism," because he found it to be "too scientific" for the typical catechetical setting.[29] According to Drinkwater, even simple words, such as *divine* or *grace*, require careful theological explication. Inevitably, the heart that seeks understanding and encounter can become lost in all the attention given to explanation. At the time of his writing, Drinkwater was accused of contradicting the Church's pedagogy and of seeking an emotional appeal in catechesis. But this was not the case. "Nobody could possibly believe more than I do in definition, in its right place," he countered.[30] "All I am doing is calling the reader's attention to a fact: namely, that if you want to reach people's hearts, Scientific language is not going to do it; even Scientific-simple language will not do it.'[31] The heart demands a "Poetic-simple language [sic] used by Our Lord [such as] 'I am the Vine and you are the Branches.'"[32]

The Method of Signs

As mentioned, one person is said to teach another when the discourse of reason, which the mind can naturally do for itself, is expressed for the learner through intelligible signs.[33] A sign is anything that represents to a knowing subject something other than itself. In the words of St. Augustine, "You see one thing, you understand another from it."[34] The sign is composed of "concrete elements—visual, tangible, as well as audible—which refer us to a content that exceeds the realm known by the senses."[35] The sign is rich in meaning, able to open the door "to ever wider horizons moving from the visible to the Invisible."[36] Cavalletti maintained that catechetical education requires a catechetical language and method that does not give the

29. Drinkwater, "The Use of Words: A Problem of Both Content and Method," in *Shaping the Christian Message: Essays in Religious Education*, ed. Gerald Sloyan (New York: MacMillian, 1959), 264.
30. Drinkwater, "The Use of Words," 274.
31. Drinkwater, "The Use of Words," 276.
32. Drinkwater, "The Use of Words," 274.
33. Boland, *Aquinas*, 49.
34. Cavalletti, *Religious Potential 1*, 126.
35. Cavalletti, "ABCs of Christianity," 2.
36. Cavalletti, *Religious Potential 1*, 126.

impression that "everything has already been researched and resolved" and thus it requires a language that "does not enclose or restrict."[37] It requires a method of signs.

An "education of signs is extremely dynamic," Cavalletti observes.[38] The method of signs "creates space for the individual's personal work of absorption."[39] With such a method of signs, the child "cannot stop learning and be satisfied with that which has been given to him, but needs to allow the received teaching to ferment in him."[40] To help illustrate how the method of signs works, Cavalletti provides two figures:

Figure 12.1 demonstrates how the signs serve as *signposts* that lead the child deeper and deeper into the vital nucleus of the mystery.[41] The sign becomes the starting point [for] further and more thorough search of the meaning.[42] Once given the proper sign and its accompanying proclamation of the *kerygma*, the child is given the opportunity to engage the mystery "personally and wholly."[43] The child returns repeatedly to the work provided, "making [it] an ever new object of his meditation and dialogue with the interior Master, and he will reach a high degree of penetration into the parables."[44]

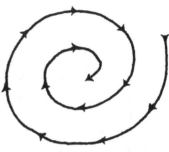

Figure 12.1

Cavalletti and Gobbi always considered the child's joy or serene peace as evidence that the desired interiority actually occurred. Once while observing children in a Level II atrium, I came upon a child who was creating an illuminated manuscript of Psalm 23. I observed in silence the child's deep and prolonged recollection. The art that surrounded the text was bright and beautiful, and as she worked she sang in a soft whisper a simple, repetitive song. The peace and joy indicated to me that the child was internalizing the Good Shepherd's love.

---

37. Cavalletti, *Religious Potential 1*, 126.
38. Cavalletti, "Hebrew Pedagogy,"16.
39. Cavalletti, *Religious Potential 1*, 132.
40. Cavalletti, "Hebrew Pedagogy," 16.
41. Cavalletti, *Religious Potential 1*, 131
42. Cavalletti, *Religious Potential 1*, 131.
43. Cavalletti, *Religious Potential 1*, 131.
44. Cavalletti, *Religious Potential 1*, 131.

Figure 12.2 demonstrates how, once having arrived at the nucleus, "the sign becomes the instrument" for greater understanding of the mystery proposed, and its global significance.[45] For example, meditating upon the dynamic nature of the mustard seed, which though the smallest of seeds becomes the largest of shrubs, the child begins to see the dynamic nature of the ever expansive Kingdom of God even unto the Parousia.

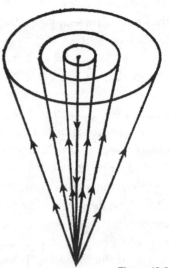

Figure 12.2

The method of signs of CGS promotes a contemplative approach to the mystery of God. It fosters a sense of wonder and investigation, and this stirs the heart's desire to seek God all the more. At the same time, it respects the mystery of the child who comes to God on his own terms, at his own pace. In implementing an allusive method of signs, the CGS approach gives the child an instrument that is peripheral, so to speak, leaving the child the work of reaching the vital nucleus. Though the entire Bible speaks through sign, "the method of signs finds one of its highest expressions in the parable."[46]

Parabolic Signs

Our Lord used parables to reveal the most profound truths regarding himself and the mystery of the Kingdom of Heaven. His own method was intentionally allusive: I speak in parable, so that "they may indeed look, but not perceive, and may indeed listen, but not understand" (Mark 4:11–12). Cavalletti recognized in Jesus' use of the parable a methodological importance. She explains,

> [T]he parable does not explain, clarify, or "define"; [but instead] offers an element for meditation. [T]o pierce the meaning of the parable we must work with our *imagination* and our *intuition*.[47]

---

45. Cavalletti, *Religious Potential 1*, 131.

46. Cavalletti, "ABCs of Christianity," 3.

47. Cavalletti, *Religious Potential 1*, 128; emphasis mine. Cavalletti's use of intuition aligns with Father Thomas Flynn's explanation of the soul's cogitative power. See Thomas Flynn, OP, "The Cogitative Power," in *The Thomist: A Speculative Quarterly Review* 16, no. 4 (October 1953): 542–563.

Cavalletti compares the parable to a nut enclosed in its shell or a jewel encased in a box. Like the shell or the box, the parable makes its hearers work rather than enjoy its "savory or precious contents right away."[48] She writes,

> The parables open a door and invite us in; they invite us to a work of personal reflection, a work that leads us to a gradual comprehension of their meaning and enables us to feel more personally engaged in the mystery they proclaim.[49]

The work required to discover its meaning increases the child's joy. Here is another application of Montessori's principles regarding the child's need *to do for self*, which was discussed in chapter 10. Allowing the child to contemplate the word of Scripture, along with the words and signs of the liturgy, is to give the child the space within which to wrestle, like Jacob, with the Holy Spirit who is the true interior teacher.[50]

In various places of the *Summa*, St. Thomas explores the relationship between joy and desire.[51] Desire increases with delayed satisfaction. The greater the desire, the greater one's joy when the object is finally obtained. Though it may sound counterintuitive, it seems to me that a method of catechesis that delays instant and superficial understanding—one that makes the child work—actually increases the child's desire to seek the face of God and to delight even more in finding him. Like the pearls not meant to be thrown under the feet of the swine (Matthew 7:6), the parable is not meant to be casually considered; it is truth, carefully weighed and appropriately prepared for presentation, which is why some parables are returned to each year from age three to twelve.

The child's personal engagement with the parable—his wrestling with its meaning—provides an opportunity for personal acceptance. One can see how the parable method fosters the personal response. Even when a moral exhortation is very strong in a parable, it also contains a *kerygmatic* element. For example, the parable of the Prodigal Son contains a powerful exhortation to conversion while, at the same time, "it reveals to us the scope of the father's tenderness, which does not wane in the face of his son's negative behavior." Some parables are difficult to hear, such as the Wedding Banquet, the Ten Virgins, or the Workers in the Vineyard, yet these also reveal something profound regarding the nature of God's covenant with us. Even when

---

48. Cavalletti, *Religious Potential 1*, 128.
49. Cavalletti, *Religious Potential 2*, 89.
50. Cavalletti, *Religious Potential 1*, 24.
51. See Aquinas, ST I-II, q. 11, a. 4; q. 25, a. 2; q. 32, a. 3.

the parables are less explicit in their moral exhortation "to do as God does," they teach us how to think and act by showing us "how God thinks, how God views certain matters."[52]

Liturgical Signs

The CGS curriculum dedicates a considerable amount of time to the presentation of the various liturgical signs used by the Church. As with the parables, the materials used for liturgical instruction were the result of much patience, trial and error, and purification as Cavalletti and Gobbi sought to discover the most essential signs for helping the child penetrate the deepest mysteries. Cavalletti notes that "the Church has always spoken through 'signs,' particularly in her sacraments."[53] "Liturgical signs recount for us the action of God and help us to be involved in it."[54] Ordinary elements such as water, oil, vows, and bread speak of the greater reality of God's grace, and they become a privileged place of encounter with his grace. For this reason, the Church instructs catechists to be mindful of the intrinsic link between catechesis and liturgy for "it is in the liturgy Christ acts most fully for the total transformation of the human person" (CT, 23).

The signs themselves belong to the Church, but they need a way to be presented to the child so that the child can receive the fullness of the sign's meaning. Mark Searle points out that what liturgical catechesis needs most "is not interpretation of signs but a mode of presenting the sign-signifier in such a way that the participants are enabled to leap from the seen to the unseen."[55] As previously described, Cavalletti recounts a story shared with her by a catechist who was giving a lesson on baptism using the Baptismal Candle to guide the child's reflection on Christ who is the light of the world. The child corrected the catechist saying, "It's not light . . . it is goodness."[56] The child was able to penetrate the sign of light and find God's goodness as well.

Conclusion

While this chapter identifies a particular method for catechesis that fits the mystery of God and the mystery of the child, Cavalletti and Gobbi never referred to the CGS as a method, but rather as an approach. Their reasons

---

52. Cavalletti, *Religious Potential 2*, 90–91.
53. Cavalletti, *Religious Potential 1*, 126.
54. Cavalletti, "ABCs of Christianity," 3.
55. Cavalletti, *Religious Potential 1*, xxi.
56. Cavalletti, *Religious Potential 1*, 15.

for this choice are indicative of their understanding of the nature of catechesis. Method often denotes a foolproof procedure that easily reproduces identical results. But catechesis itself cannot be reduced to a method; it can only ever be an *approach* to the mystery of God and the mystery of the child. It is, properly speaking, a unique *pedagogy*.

The specific methodological choices that Cavalletti and Gobbi made were for the sake of achieving its pedagogical goal of leading the child to know and delight in God's unfathomable mystery. Their choices were based on what they understood about God and what they understood about the child. The choice of language was for the sake of the inexhaustible mystery of God and the child's way of receiving his mystery. Likewise, their choice of parables and liturgical gestures were the result of the child's ability to be transcendent and his need for essentiality.

Over the course of their years working with children, Cavalletti and Gobbi formed a unique understanding of how to approach the mystery of the child and facilitate his encounter with the mystery of God. Their unique approach is a kind of *pedagogy for children's catechesis—a perichoretic pedagogy*—with its own overarching principles regarding content, method, and the child. Chapter 13 provides an overview of these principles that keep the CGS approach faithful to God, faithful to the child, and faithful to the Church.

Chapter 13

Pedagogical Principles

Introduction

CGS is a unique approach to children's catechesis due to its unique synthesis of the three essential components of catechesis—namely, content, child, and method. After giving due consideration to the principles regarding each of these three main components, it is time to consider their unique expression in the CGS pedagogy. The CGS approach has been in practice since 1954 with positive results in the faith formation of children. Nevertheless, it is important to discern the specific pedagogical traits that contribute to its success in order to preserve and strengthen them because, as it has been repeatedly noted, unless a catechesis imitates God's pedagogy, it will not achieve the desired goal of faith in the person being catechized.

This chapter investigates various elements of the CGS approach, in light of the guiding traits of God's original pedagogy of faith set forth in the 2020 *Directory*. The specific elements in the CGS approach to be examined are: the environment, timeframe, catechist formation, materials used, method of presentation, the choice of doctrinal content and its progressive proclamation, and the goal toward which all these elements are directed, namely the child's participation in the liturgy. These pedagogical elements can be conceptualized as the two movements of gift and response. God's self-revelation is gift, the *fides quae creditur* (the faith *that* is believed). The reception of this gift, on the part of the believer, evokes in turn a response to God, the *fides qua creditur* (the faith *by which* we believe). The pedagogy of the CGS approach likewise has these two movements of *gift* and *response*.

The Pedagogy of the Environment

The 2020 *Directory* invites catechists to give due consideration to the particular space where their catechesis takes place and to rethink the traditional "school building" model (DC, 222). The 2020 *Directory* draws attention to the special significance that the Church has placed on spaces that foster the religious life of her members—spaces adequate for welcoming the faithful, celebrating the divine mysteries, promoting fraternal sharing, and handing on the faith (see DC, 221).

Cavalletti and Gobbi have always insisted that the atrium is not so much a place of *religious instruction* (as in a school classroom) as it is a place for *religious life*.[1] At the same time, "[e]verything that is placed in the atrium is an instrument of education, specifically an education in the faith."[2] Cavalletti and Gobbi were quite insistent on this point recognizing that, by its very nature, catechesis is an educational activity. The atrium "resembles a classroom in that it is a place of work and study," but in the atrium, "work and study become colloquy with God, and therefore it is already a place of worship in some sense."[3]

The Creation account in Genesis demonstrates how God prepared a fitting environment within which he revealed himself. The Garden of Eden is beautiful and all things created are good and for the sake of Adam and Eve. The garden is God's gift and it serves the purpose of a space within which God offers Adam and Eve the gift of his friendship. Scripture's poetic image of God walking with Adam and Eve "at the time of the evening breeze" (Genesis 3:8), expresses this gift of intimacy between Creator and creature. Similarly, the CGS approach creates an environment—a *miniature cosmos*—for the sake of the child, that he may encounter God and receive his revelation. This environment is called the *atrium*.

The atrium is a beautifully and carefully prepared environment. It is a place fit for the child, where the child feels at home. The chairs, desks, and shelves are all her size. All materials are within her reach. The atrium belongs to the child, who has the freedom to move about in a manner that is self-directing. All the spaces within the atrium serve as a potential means of encounter with God and for this reason all are good for the child. When the child enters the atrium, she experiences an immediate, and at times overwhelming, recognition that she belongs in the atrium. Sr. Maria Teresita, OP, shares the story of a three-year-old girl who walked around the atrium on her first day, talking to herself and saying things like, "Oh, look at that

---

1. Cavalletti, *Way of Holy Joy*, 41; original emphasis.
2. Gianna Gobbi, "The Meaning, Importance and Limitations of Our Catechetical Materials," trans. Rebekah Rojcewicz, in *Journals of the Catechesis of the Good Shepherd 1998–2002* (Chicago: Catechesis of the Good Shepherd Publications, 2003), 100.
3. Cavalletti, *Way of Holy Joy*, 41.

flower! God is with us." This same little girl stood before the well-known picture of Jesus knocking on the door and said, "Oh yes. He opened the doors to heaven for us!" I myself have observed a number of children who stand speechless in the doorway of the atrium, their eyes full of wonder— their faces full of expectant joy.

The atrium is a little like the Garden of Eden. It is a place for being with God and where work "becomes conversation with God."[4] The atrium is designed to be a place "where the child comes to know the great realities of his life as a Christian . . . [and] begins to live these realities in meditation and prayer." It is "already a place of worship according to its own rhythm." It is like a "retreat house" that "facilitates recollection and silence."[5] Several CGS catechists that I know personally invite each child into the atrium for the first day with an introduction to its purpose: "Here in this place God speaks to us and we listen." The catechist then introduces her role as one who can help the child hear God's voice. The child is invited to accompany the catechist on a tour of the atrium, during which he becomes more and more acclimated to his new surroundings. The child learns how to move in the atrium in a manner that is free and self-controlled.

Since the work of the CGS is directed toward aiding the child's full participation in the liturgy, Cavalletti instructs her catechists that the atrium itself should be "Mass-centered." In the arrangement of the furnishings, "special prominence is awarded to the materials relative to the Mass."[6] In so doing, the room itself catechizes the child on the centrality of the Mass in their life of faith. They come to recognize that the Mass is the place of greatest encounter with the Good Shepherd; the Mass is where Jesus feeds his sheep and lays down his life for them.

The Pedagogy of the Materials

The materials used in the CGS approach emphasize the incarnational dimension of our Faith. Throughout history, God has spoken to humanity and has manifested his presence in both word and deed. In the person of Jesus Christ, God walked this earth at a particular time and in a particular place. He said particular things and performed particular acts. The purpose of the CGS materials is to provide the child with access to the words and works of God

---

4. Cavalletti, *Religious Potential 1*, 27.
5. Cavalletti, *Religious Potential 1*, 27.
6. Cavalletti, *Religious Potential 1*, 27.

throughout history but in a particular way through his Son, Jesus Christ. Given their catechetical purpose and importance, the materials in the atrium

> must be attractive but "sober" and must strictly adhere to the theme being presented. In making the material, the catechist refrains from adding superficial embellishments which would distract the child from the essentials of the theme being presented. In other words, the material must be simple, essential, and "poor" in order to allow the richness of the theme's content to shine through.[7]

Materials used in the atrium include a globe, maps of the Holy Land, items in creation, two- and three-dimensional figures depicting various Scripture passages, and model items related to the Mass.

Because the atrium is a place designed for catechesis, newcomers are often surprised that practical life activities also take place there: polishing brass, pouring beans, or cutting and arranging flowers. These activities serve a twofold purpose. First, they prepare the child for later works, which may require refined movement and coordination. Secondly, they prepare the child to receive the Word of God by helping the child calm his body, which in turn quiets his soul, so that he can learn how to listen for God's voice.

Contrary to traditional teaching techniques, the CGS materials are not meant to help the catechist teach but rather to help the child contemplate the mysteries of the faith proclaimed to him. The primary aim of the materials is "to aid meditation and prayer, while also honoring the vital needs and ways of learning that correspond to the child in his . . . particular stage of development."[8] Pedagogically, the materials become a means by which the child is able to engage personally with the doctrine and thus dispose him to receive the inspirations of the Holy Spirit, who is the primary teacher. During the child's orientation to the atrium, the catechist points out the various materials and explains their purpose: "These materials are for your use and I will show you how to use them to listen to God's voice." Thus, the materials allow the adult to be a true servant of the child and the Gospel. That is, the catechist becomes one who does what is necessary to "assist the child's encounter with God, and then steps aside once it has begun."[9]

The materials serve one purpose: to aid the child's reflection on the specific doctrines proclaimed and to serve as portals to the inexhaustible mystery of God. Cavalletti and Gobbi were so committed to the principle

---

7. Point #12 from the CGS 32 Points of Reflection. www.cgsusa.org/the-32-points-of-reflection/
8. Gobbi, "Meaning," 103.
9. Cavalletti, "And a Little Child Shall Lead Them . . . ," 167.

that the CGS materials serve the child, that any material that did not engage the child's continued work, regardless of how lovely it was or how long it took them to create it, was removed from the atrium. Longtime coworker and CGS catechist formation leader Patricia Coulter explains,

> Gradually a series of catechetical materials was developed. It was the children who guided this process. Through careful observation of their reactions, it was seen that some biblical or liturgical theme would draw forth a peaceful attitude in the child and an interest in using certain materials again and again. When a theme or material evoked this quality of response, they knew a vital need had been nurtured in the child. When a material proved its value to engage the child's desire and ability for prayer and meditation it was kept; otherwise, it was discarded.[1]

CGS has maintained this practice. The materials used in CGS are in constant review by the *Consiglio*, an international committee formed by Cavalletti to help guide the work and to make appropriate adaptations as needed. The *Consiglio* has been especially helpful in working on the curriculum and materials for the Level III (nine-to-twelve-year-old) atrium. Cavalletti and Gobbi died before this level.

Just as the catechist is trained to keep her words to the essentials, the materials too must be essential in order to isolate the theology of the presentation and provide appropriate control to the proclamation. For example, the presentation on the Annunciation only has Mary, the angel Gabriel, and a small dove or flame. These three materials, when coupled with the proclamation of Luke's Gospel, isolate the theology of the Incarnation. CGS catechists are strongly discouraged from adding any extra decorations to the formal works, such as tables, chairs, or buckets of water. Such adaptations distract the child from the essence of the mystical encounter that Mary has with the Holy Spirit.[2]

Another unique aspect of the CGS approach is the requirement that each catechist commit to making her own materials. Though today, there are companies that have begun to craft the larger materials, such as the altar and the sacred vessels cabinet, Cavalletti and Gobbi offer insightful reasons

---

1. Cavalletti, *Joyful Journey*, 103.
2. On this matter of essentiality, I recommend Linda Kaiel's article "The Essentials of Material Making," in *Journals of the Catechesis of the Good Shepherd 1984–1997*, ed. Victoria Tufano (Chicago: Catechesis of the Good Shepherd Publications, 1998), 284.

why the CGS catechist should make most of her own materials.[3] Cavalletti explains that "the preparation of the material and environment is an integral and vital part of the catechist's task; in manual activity, the catechist finds an instrument for indirect service to children in their relationship with God." She further cautions, "making the materials and preparing the environment cannot and must not be viewed as secondary activity, one that we casually delegate to others."[4]

Sr. Maria Teresita, OP, provides testimony to the importance of CGS catechists making their own materials:

> I have been amazed at how often children in the atrium ask: "Did you make this?" In my experience as a Montessori teacher, the children never asked that question about materials for math, language, history, or the sciences even when I did make many of the materials they used. I think it indicates a fundamental difference between the work in a Montessori classroom presenting created truths and the work in an atrium presenting to the child truth Himself who is Himself gift. It is as if the children expect that the materials also would be gifts.

Sister followed this account with her own conviction that she did not always relish the thought of making "all those materials," but after the children's responses, she now values the need for her to do her own "work" in and for the atrium.

Making the CGS materials takes a great deal of time—indeed a great sacrifice of time. The sacrifice of time involved in making the materials also serves as a purification of intention. Becoming a CGS catechist is a labor of love: love of God and love of the child. The time spent, however, becomes an opportunity to contemplate the doctrine of each lesson and to make it her own. Indeed, through the prayerful construction of the CGS materials, the CGS catechist continues to be formed as a contemplative catechist. The catechist, laboring to build a miniature city of Jerusalem, meditates more deeply on the events of Our Lord's Passion internalizing their significance in her own life. This personal reflection and encounter with the Lord's sacrificial love is communicated to the child throughout the lesson as they together grow in appreciation of his love.

---

3. See Cavalletti, "Let's Make the Material with Our Own Hands," and Gobbi, "The Experience of Making One's Own Material," in *Journals of the Catechesis of the Good Shepherd 1984–1997*, ed. Victoria Tufano (Chicago: Catechesis of the Good Shepherd Publications, 1998), 282–283.
4. Cavalletti, "And a Little Child Shall Lead Them . . . ," 167.

The Pedagogy of the Catechist

Like all aspects of the CGS approach, the CGS catechist possesses a unique pedagogy that fosters the meeting of the two mysteries in catechesis: God and the child. Indeed, the catechist herself has pedagogical value. Cavalletti describes many key insights into the nature of the work, what the CGS catechists must do, and more importantly, who she must *be*, for this approach to fulfill its purpose.[5] What the catechist says and how she says it, what she does and how she does it, even what she refrains from saying or doing, is all pedagogical. Gobbi explains that the CGS catechist must know how to faithfully "draw from the heritage of culture and tradition, selecting and presenting what is most appropriate according to the developmental stage of the child."[6]

The CGS catechist undergoes a lengthy and thorough formation. To my knowledge, no other catechist formation program requires a comparable amount of time and work. By the time a Level III catechist finishes her formation she will have spent over 300 hours in formation with a certified CGS formator.[7] It is also strongly urged that the CGS catechist spend several hours observing a Montessori classroom as part of her formation. Added to this, is time spent practicing the CGS presentations, as well as planning and observing the child's immersion and emergence in faith. An experienced CGS catechist shared with me that they spent over 300 hours creating materials for a Level I atrium and another 100 hours setting it up.

It is easy to see why the *Godly Play* and *Come Follow Me* programs have such appeal to catechists—simply put, the formation is much easier. Yet we know intuitively and the Church emphatically reminds us that the personal formation of the catechist is one of the most significant factors to the success of any catechetical program. A catechist simply cannot give what she does not possess. Again, Cavalletti and Gobbi were a prophetic voice anticipating by more than fifty years the 2020 *Directory*'s exhortation for better catechist formation (DC, 130–150).

Notwithstanding, the formation of a CGS catechist is not the mere instruction in a technique. She is formed in *a way of being with children* in the catechetical setting (DC, 140). Primarily, Cavalletti wants the CGS catechist to see her place beside the child as one who also is listening to God

---

5. See Cavalletti, "And a Little Child Shall Lead Them . . . ," 167.

6. Gobbi, "Meaning," 100.

7. Levels I and II courses require 90 hours of direct formation. Level III requires 150 hours. This does not include an approximate 20–30 hours to complete the assigned readings.

still and discovering anew the truth and beauty of his self-revelation. She writes, "If I were to graphically depict the difference between catechism and catechesis, for catechism I would draw a very small figure (for the child) and a very large figure (for the adult), with the large figure holding a small book. Catechesis would then be depicted by two figures (an adult and a child) of equal stature, holding between them a large book."[8] What Cavalletti means by this is that the CGS catechist does not pretend to have all of the answers (or even all of the questions) related to God that she will then simply tell the child. The catechist is not the primary protagonist in the atrium: *God is.* The child does not seek answers in her: he seeks answers in God. In the atrium, the catechist is a *co-seeker,* a *co-listener* to God.

Becoming a CGS catechist is a formation of the mind and the heart. Patricia Coulter observed that catechists who completed formation in the CGS approach grew not only in their conceptual knowledge of the Church's teachings, but grew in their relationship with God.[9] The Church has always emphasized the need for catechists to give personal witness of their love for God, and some would suggest that the deep personal conversion of catechists would be sufficient alone to spark a renewal in catechesis. The recent emphasis on catechist formation that the 2020 *Directory* gives is significant. The personal encounter with God experienced by the CGS catechist serves as a powerful witness to the child. When all else fails, the presence of the Holy Spirit in the catechist unites with the presence of the Holy Spirit in the child whereby *heart* speaks to *Heart.*[10]

The Pedagogy of the Presentation

With each presentation in CGS, a discernible pedagogy emerges, one that simulates the *gift* and *response* of God's own pedagogy of revelation. Each presentation follows the same pattern of proclamation of the doctrine, guided reflection upon the proclamation, prayerful silence, and an invitation to respond. First, the catechist invites the child to receive a particular proclamation. The introduction to the presentations vary but ordinarily it begins with the catechist saying to a child something along these lines: "I would like to give you a presentation. Would you like me to show you this work?" The presentation is punctuated with intentional moments of silence

---

8. Cavalletti, "From Catechism to Catechesis," *Searching among Memories, Foglietto,* no. 18.
9. Patricia Coulter, "A Way of Being with Children."
10. A reference to John Henry Newman's cardinalate coat of arms, which primarily means our heart speaking to God's heart but is interpreted here as a unique grace that occurs in faithful catechesis.

providing "space" for the Holy Spirit to enlighten the child's intellect. The spoken proclamation is often accompanied by a careful demonstration of how to use the materials, according to their designed purpose. During the time of directed reflection, the catechist asks questions that draw attention to specific aspects of the presentation and spark wonder. While the child may be responding to God interiorly all throughout the presentation the final movement in the presentation specifically invites the child to respond either with a prayer, or a song, or a simple moment of silence. After the presentation, the catechist invites the child to use the materials independently for further reflection and prayer.

A critical pedagogical component of the presentation, and one that I find particularly valuable in the CGS approach, is its unique manner of using questions to engage the child in the educative process. While there may be some level of basic recall regarding the material presented, the catechist is formed to ask questions that foster dialogue between the child and God (see GDC, 143). Such questions spark theological investigation of the doctrine proclaimed and allow for profound insight on the part of the child. The CGS *Journals* recount numerous anecdotes to substantiate this claim. I offer here a sample from a CGS catechist in St. Louis, MO:

> After presenting the Mystery of Life and Death, I asked if anyone could recall another time in the Bible where we had read about "bearing fruit." These children had not yet had the presentation on the True Vine. Sampson replied, "Of course, in the Hail Mary prayer: 'blessed is the fruit of your womb.'" To which he then added, as if asking himself a question, "I wonder if Jesus knew he was the fruit when he said that 'unless a grain of wheat falls into the earth and dies [it will not bear fruit]. But if it does it bears much fruit.'"[11]

Another pedagogical value of the CGS presentations is the unconventional response that the catechist seeks from the child. In a traditional catechetical setting, the catechist asks specific questions of the children and seek specific "correct" answers. In the CGS approach, the child is invited to freely choose his response. He is free to respond to the doctrine proclaimed by singing a song, drawing a picture, writing a prayer, joining a procession, or remaining silent. Sometimes the child's response (invited or not) is a dance of joy. Most importantly, the invitation remains on a level that is not forced, or calculated, or measured.

---

11. See *The Catechesis of the Good Shepherd Journal*, no. 30 (2015), 10.

The Pedagogy of the Language

The catechetical language of the CGS approach has intrinsic pedagogical value as well. Cavalletti and Gobbi favored the language of the Scriptures and liturgy as a pedagogical choice. The Scriptures and liturgy remain primary sources for God's revelation and serve as an inexhaustible wellspring for religious knowledge and religious experience. Yet the more fundamentally pedagogical reason for using the Scriptures and the liturgy has to do with the child. The child requires language that is intelligible and nourishing. The child needs a language that is simple, yet substantial; concrete, yet allusive; expansive, yet on his own mental level.

Parents whose children are formed in the atrium provide the greatest evidence that the language of the CGS resonates in the mind and heart of the children. Sr. Marie Celine Laird, OP, shared the following email from the parent of Sarah. Three-year-old Sarah was able to relay to her mother the entire presentation on the nomenclature of the articles used at Mass. The mom writes,

> During lunch, [Sarah] said to me, "Mommy do you know what you call the special plate that is used at Mass to put the body of Jesus on?" I honestly couldn't name it and so I hesitantly replied, "the chalice?" [Sarah] replied, "No, mommy. The chalice is the special cup that holds the Blood of Jesus. Can you say 'chalice' mommy?" I repeated the word 'chalice' to her satisfaction. Then she continued, "Mommy, the paten is the special plate that is used to put the Body of Jesus on at Mass. Can you say 'paten' mommy?" I was blown away. She was so sincere about the entire matter that I could only try to respond with similar sincerity, "paten." "Yes, mommy, 'paten.'"

Even words such as *parousia* remain in the child's heart and mind. I once saw a video of girls in Level III who had written and performed a song about the *parousia*. It was a joyful proclamation of Jesus' Second Coming.

The Pedagogy of the Context

There is in the CGS approach a kind of *pedagogy of context*. The CGS catechesis is set within the larger context of the needs of the child and the corresponding pedagogy of God's revelation, as well as the Church's pedagogy of the liturgical year. In the Scriptures and the liturgical calendar, there is a discernible rhythm to the gift of revelation and the response of faith. There is likewise a rhythm to the child's desire for God. The CGS approach sets the child's faith formation within this rhythm of life and faith.

The CGS approach follows the Church's liturgical calendar, gradually inserting the child into the narrative of salvation. The instructional year for each level begins with a selective and progressive proclamation of the Messianic prophecies found in the Old Testament. This is followed by the Infancy Narratives and then the Paschal Mystery and the Parousia. Each year the child returns to these main doctrinal proclamations, reflecting more deeply on their theological meaning and their importance in his life.

The child also possesses a natural rhythm of desiring to know God more and to ponder the mysteries of the faith that are proclaimed to him. The CGS approach addresses this natural rhythm by allowing the child to return to any presentation throughout the year and level. In a traditional catechetical approach, a particular mystery of the faith is presented but then put aside as the teacher continues to move through her textbook and curriculum in a very linear fashion. However, in the atrium, none of the mysteries proclaimed are ever "put away" so that a child is free to return to a presentation as often as his spiritual hunger prompts him.

The Pedagogy of Gradual Progression (The Spiral Method)

One of the principles of God's pedagogy is that it is "gradual and progressive" (GDC, 143). This is likewise a principle of the CGS approach. Throughout the curriculum, the child is introduced to the truths of the faith gradually, with simple and essential proclamations. As I examined in chapter 12, the method of presentations follows a spiral pattern, such that any given proclamation of doctrine is revisited repeatedly throughout the child's years in the atrium. Each time the doctrine is revisited, another layer of teaching is added, another insight gained.

For example, the child first hears the prophecies of the Messiah, then he learns about the Infancy Narratives and how they fulfill the prophecy. The presentations on the Mass follow the presentations on the Parable of the Good Shepherd. With such a progression, the child learns first that Jesus, the Good Shepherd, knows and cares for his sheep (see John 10:4–5) and then that this means he "lays down his life for the sheep" (John 10:11). After these presentations, the child learns that the primary place where this happens is at the Mass, where "Jesus, the Good Shepherd, gives his whole self for us."[12]

---

12. This is how the catechist is encouraged to explain the essence of the sacrifice of the Mass.

The critical value of the CGS pedagogy of content progression—and its unique contribution to catechesis—is seen especially in the child's moral formation. In the CGS approach all moral catechesis follows what I call a "catechesis of encounter," a term that I believe best expresses the principle of God's pedagogy: "Truly, to help a person to encounter God, which is the task of the catechist, means to emphasize above all the relationship that the person has with God so that he can make it his own and allow himself to be guided by God" (GDC, 140). Initially, the child hears the parable of the Good Shepherd. At this first stage, the child is invited to ponder God's intimate love and to express delight in that love. The child's existential desire to be known and to be loved by God is satisfied, as he is given ample time to delight in the Shepherd's love for him and to fall in love with the Shepherd. Only after the child is taught how to listen and to trust the Good Shepherd's voice is he formed in the specific ways of following the Shepherd. This pattern of first *kerygma* and then *parenesis* is a particularly Dominican approach to moral catechesis and shows the early influence of Fr. Dalmazio Mongillo, OP.

The content and method of the CGS approach converge in the child's full participation in the Holy Sacrifice of the Mass, wherein the Good Shepherd lays down his life for the sheep and feeds them with his own Body and Blood. In the words of a six-year-old who had internalized the Eucharistic Presence of the Good Shepherd: "So, *that's* why we go to church every Sunday!"[13]

The Pedagogy of Time

On average, catechesis in a school setting consists of five twenty-to-forty-minute sessions per week. Sunday catechesis generally lasts one hour. Cavalletti and Gobbi recommended that an atrium session last two (or at least one and a half) full hours. For school catechists, this may seem insufficient or impractical. For catechists in a parish religious education program, it may seem too long. Why the insistence of this unique timeframe?

Personal relationships take time to develop. The same is true with faith formation. In the ordinary realm, the stages of faith follow something of a natural pattern of introduction, dialogue, intimacy, and the testing of hearts. The physical space between the head and the heart is all of twelve inches, but the spiritual gap is much greater. The path from knowledge about God to love for him is the exclusive work of the Holy Spirit, animating a

---

13. Story shared by Sr. Maria Teresita, OP.

person's intellect and will and passions, and while he can do this instantaneously, in most souls the Holy Spirit's operation is gradual.

If the object of catechesis was merely the transmission of information, the catechist would only need as much time as necessary to state the information and, if some level of understanding is desired, to explain the meaning of the words. But if the object of catechesis is an intimate relationship with the Lord, then there must be sufficient time for the child to encounter God and engage in dialogue with him. Faithful proclamation of doctrine in fact guarantees that the child is conversing with the one true God and not merely a figment of his imagination. Yet without sufficient time to ponder these truths, the child is rarely (if ever) able to reach Truth Himself.

It is important to point out that the pedagogical aspect of time in the CGS approach is indeed a matter of *sufficiency*. The soul needs sufficient time to become still to enter deeply into contemplation of the mysteries proclaimed. Cavalletti points out that often, when a child is prodded for a response too quickly, or if the child responds too quickly, this may indicate that "what has been communicated has stayed on the surface, that the child has repeated mechanically what he has heard without any personal participation."[14]

A personal response to God who reveals himself "is to be sought within the depths of oneself; this requires time."[15] The time needed to ponder deeply the mystery of God and the mysteries of our faith cannot be underestimated. Sr. Theresa Anne Knuth, OP, shares a story of a child for whom it took three years before a critical aspect of the Good Shepherd parable was understood:

> We are cautioned to not proceed with the Eucharistic Presence II presentation until the child has made the connection that he is one of the sheep who is known and loved by the Good Shepherd. Susan had been in the atrium for three years and was nearing six years old and she still had not identified herself as one of the Good Shepherd's sheep. It was the end of the year and I thought I would give the presentation to her one more time. As I proclaimed the parable and moved the figures, I prayed that the Holy Spirit would show [Susan] that she was a sheep. Then I asked the question that I had asked every time before, "I wonder, who might the sheep be?" There was a moment of silence. Susan looked at the sheep gathered around the tiny altar and at the Good Shepherd on top of the altar. Silence. I asked, "[Susan] who do we see at Mass each week?" She said,

---

14. Cavalletti, *Religious Potential 1*, 65.

15. Cavalletti, *Religious Potential 1*, 65.

"people." I nodded my head. "Yes, people." I prayed again. Then as fast as lightning strikes Sarah erupted with joy, "I'm the sheep!" Her face was illuminated with joy!

It took Susan and the Holy Spirit three years to make the connection that she was one of the Good Shepherd's beloved sheep, but once Susan received this truth, it was hers at the depth of her being. The story also reveals how a good teacher can aid a child's observation so that they might be able to make connections on their own.

For the older child, the need for sufficient time is even more critical, given the nature of the Level III materials, which are often referred to as "big works." On average, the amount of time needed to set up the materials, perform the specified work, and then put the material away is thirty minutes. Add to this the desired time for personal prayer and reflective practice, and the time needed stretches to forty minutes or more. Several catechists have shared with me that when the time for atrium is less than the recommended time, the children fail to engage in these large works, exhibit frustration, and can become disheartened, losing energy for their tasks. When I asked several of my religious Sisters to comment on the time frame of the atrium, their universal response was that the children often say to them, "Sister, atrium is too short."

The Pedagogy of the "Work"

The theology of revelation espoused by the CGS approach highlights the two-fold movement of gift and response. In the atrium, the gift is the proclamation of doctrine; the child's response of faith is expressed in and through work that she does during her time in the atrium (LG, 104). The child's work is a free personal response that bubbles up from within her soul and manifests the interior movements of the Holy Spirit. Following each presentation, the child is invited either independently or collectively to ponder the doctrine proclaimed. For example, following the lesson on the Grain of Wheat, she might plant her own grain and wait for its growth. Following the lesson on the Parts of the Mass, she may make her own missal. Following the lesson on the Preparation of the Chalice, she might return and practice the ritual herself.

The child's work in the atrium has an anthropological importance as well. Created in the image and likeness of God, the human person is invited to share in God's work of creation. The mandate to be stewards of the earth ennobles the human person, raising him beyond the status of mere consumer to one of coworker. In his catechesis on the dignity of work, Pope John Paul II identified man's work as a participation in the creative work of God. As such, work itself is not a curse, but the natural activity of one made in the image and likeness of God (*Laborem exercens*, 4–6). Noble work serves as means by which a person's humanity is fully realized (LE, 6). The child is no less in need of noble work that will help bring him to his full potential.

Maria Montessori observed a remarkable and intimate bond between the child and his environment. The child takes possession of his environment with his hand, and guided by his intelligence, he transforms it. Thus he completes his mission in the universe.[16] Montessori recognized this existential need in the child and responded accordingly by creating materials that attract the child's work during his time in the atrium. Cavalletti and Gobbi adopted most of Montessori's works and added others that correspond to the needs of the child. The child's need to use the CGS materials and the interior satisfaction that he derives from doing so is apparent in his self-motivation and sustained attention in the activity he has chosen.[17]

The works in the atrium take on a deeper theological meaning as well, when they are examined in relation to the central purpose of the CGS approach—namely, helping the child experience an authentic encounter with God in the liturgy. In the Christian tradition, the word *liturgy* refers to the participation of the People of God in the "work of God" (CCC, 1067). God's "work" is our salvation through the paschal mystery of Jesus Christ. The Church celebrates this mystery of faith in the liturgy (CCC, 1067). "The Eucharist is central to the life of the atrium at every level." It serves as a place wherein the child and the adult strive "to penetrate the mystery of the liturgical celebration."[18]

The Pedagogy of the Silence

A negative legacy of late scholasticism (1400–1600) has been the over reliance on *disputatio* during the catechetical session, to the neglect of *contemplatio*. This is particularly damaging when a catechist employs the standard teaching procedure of peppering a lesson with rapid questions that require only

---

16. See Montessori, *The Absorbent Mind*, 144–145.

17. While this claim is true, it is not without exception. I have observed children who do not fully engage in the work of the atrium. However, I would argue that such children are on the continuum of developing their power of free choice, having been wounded in their natural developmental expression of autonomy, either at home or in school.

18. Cavalletti et al., "Characteristics of the Catechesis of the Good Shepherd," in *Journals of the Catechesis of the Good Shepherd 1998–2002* (Chicago: Catechesis of the God Shepherd Publications, 2003), 5–8.

basic recall knowledge.[19] Cavalletti challenges such a method which creates a superficiality in the child's faith because "what has been communicated has stayed on the surface."[20] Indeed, though the child "may very easily repeat things he has heard about God . . . does this in fact mean that he is conscious of God's presence in his life?"[21]

Inherited from Dr. Maria Montessori is the often-repeated admonition to CGS catechists to "count your words."[22] When the catechist makes proper use of the catechetical signs in the CGS approach, a multiplication of words is actually unnecessary, since the sign already speaks to the child the essential doctrine being proclaimed. The child is satisfied with the essentials and wearies quickly when too much is said. Cavalletti illustrates this pedagogical principle when she describes the child's reaction to her initial mistakes in saying too much during a presentation. The children began to turn their attention away with body language that said, "Thank you. You have said enough."[23]

Silence and prayer are indispensable in the work of catechesis. Indeed, they are qualities of God's own pedagogy. Cavalletti recognizes that the catechist serves as a true mediator for the Gospel proclamation, but she warns, "The adult's function . . . should not be overvalued."[24] She challenges the CGS catechist to let go of the need to control the child's faith and to embrace, with courage, that the work of catechesis is something that is *not* of our doing. "The catechist who does not know when to stop, who does not know how to keep silent, is one who is not conscious of one's limits and, after all, is lacking in faith, because on the practical level at least, one is not convinced that it is God and his creative Word that are active in the religious event."[25] It is like the mustard seed whose "mysterious growth happens of itself while the sower knows not how."[26]

---

19. Bloom's taxonomy of cognition identifies seven levels of cognition with recall being the most basic and synthesis being the highest level.

20. Cavalletti, *Religious Potential 1*, 65.

21. Cavalletti, *Religious Potential 1*, 65.

22. Cavalletti, *Religious Potential 1*, 23.

23. Cavalletti, "How We Present Biblical Texts," in *Journals of the Catechesis of the Good Shepherd 1998–2002*, trans. Rebekah Rojcewicz (Chicago: Catechesis of the Good Shepherd Publications, 2003), 148.

24. Cavalletti, *Religious Potential 1*, 23.

25. Cavalletti, *Religious Potential 1*, 24.

26. Cavalletti, *Religious Potential 1*, 65.

Conclusion

As a true *catechetical pedagogy*, the CGS approach achieves the goal of leading the child to a knowledge and love of God. Every element of the CGS pedagogy is directed toward assisting the child's authentic encounter with God's incarnational, sacrificial, and inexhaustible Love through his Sacred Word and liturgy. In true imitation of the original pedagogy of faith, every component of the CGS pedagogy is designed to provide *God* with the greatest opportunity to lead the child to himself. There is, in the CGS pedagogy, a faithful and prophetic echo of his words to Hosea:

> Yet it was I who taught Ephraim to walk, I took them up in my arms; but they did not know that I healed them. I led them with cords of human kindness, with bands of love. I was to them like those who lift infants to their cheeks. I bent down to them and fed them. (Hosea 11:3–4)[27]

As a miniature cosmos, the atrium becomes a place where the child can begin to recognize his own purpose for having been created, while offering his own contribution of work. The rhythm of the atrium becomes the child's rhythm of life and prayer. All things come from God and return to God in a natural cycle of gift and response. The extended *chronos* in the atrium provides an opportunity for the child to experience God's *kairos*.[28] The materials become a vehicle for the transcendent God to become immanent to the child. Like the prophets of old, the catechist gives voice to God's word and models his patience, awaiting a free response in faith. The silence provides interior space in the mind and heart for the Holy Spirit and fosters a true dialogue between the child and God. The progression of content in the CGS pedagogy imitates God's own careful unveiling of his mystery. Through the unique pedagogy of the CGS approach, the child begins to comprehend with all the saints what is the length and breadth, height and depth of God's mystery and his love (see Ephesians 3:18).

---

27. These verses are cited in the GDC as a preface to the section entitled "The Pedagogy of the Faith."
28. *Chronos* refers to earth's measure of time while *kairos* refers to God's timelessness. In the CGS approach, children are blessed to experience the peace and joy of God's timelessness.

Chapter 14

And a Little Child Shall Lead Them (Isaiah 11:6)

As I conclude this book on the pedagogy of the Good Shepherd, I find the adage to be true that "the best has been the enemy of the good." Indeed, the book is long overdue. It is as St. Augustine once described: the utterance of my mind has been slow, unable to give justice to the vision of what has been illuminated.[1] I have tried in earnest to explain how and why the approach works, so that my reader might come to see it as a valid catechetical education for catechesis in our time. I have spent the greater part of ten years trying to explain to non-CGS catechists that this approach is exactly what the Church is asking its catechetical education to be. During those same years, I have tried to give CGS catechists the catechetical language needed to aid their dialogue with pastors, bishops, and diocesan leaders. I have tried to include enough anecdotes in this book to help non-CGS readers see what I see in the CGS approach, and I have argued as convincingly as possible that the pedagogical principles of the CGS make it what it is, and for this reason, we must be careful to preserve these principles even whilst making necessary adaptations to this approach.

This book that explores the *perichoretic* relationship between the theological, methodological, and anthropological components of catechesis is the first of its kind. I pray also that this is not the last book on the subject, because I know that there are many insights left unexplained, many stories left untold, many challenges in the work left unaddressed. My aim was to start a serious conversation about the nature of catechetical education and point to one approach whose pedagogy seems most aligned with God's. I believe that the Church desperately needs such a unitive approach in catechesis and I pray that this book encourages catechetical theorists to con-

---

1. Augustine, *De catechezandis rudibus*, 2.3.

sider the CGS approach as a model for all catechesis, but especially for children's catechesis. For the sake of the children, please, let us continue the conversation.

I mentioned in the introduction that too often it is the case that people are not converted to the CGS approach because of argument—no matter how researched it is—but because they have experienced it firsthand. Allow me to conclude with two conversion stories about the CGS approach. The first conversion happened through research: it is my own story. The second one happened through firsthand experience: it is that of one of my religious Sisters. It is my hope that, together, they bear witness to the truth: God has a *pedagogy* of forming his children in faith and the *Good Shepherd* knows that way. Let us be open to His Voice and follow.

Led by the Research

My first story illustrates my own conversion from a traditional approach to catechetics to the CGS *perichoretic* approach during the course of my doctoral research. I have taught "children" from the ages of three to ninety-three in a variety of catechetical settings. I even served as the director of the Office of Catechetics at Aquinas College in Nashville, where I was responsible for cocreating and implementing the college's Catechetical Formation Program. As I shared in the introduction, I received a solid faith formation from my mother, which was substantially strengthened by theology professors at Christendom College. My already substantial intellectual formation in the faith has been intensified throughout my thirty plus years of study as a Dominican Sister of St. Cecilia.

When I began to teach religion to children, I was sure that the best approach was to give them the same treasures that I had received, namely a rigorous knowledge of the teachings of the Church. My last eighth grade class would tease: "Sister, your quizzes are like tests, your tests are like exams, and your exams are like dissertations." Of course, we had fun in religion class— but by golly, we studied! There were, after all, still too many heresies "out there" that could lead my students astray. Many of my students have stayed in touch with me over the years and several have been honest enough to tell me that they no longer go to church. Others have shared that Jesus is no longer a part of their daily life. Regardless of the reasons for their choices, the revelation that all that doctrine has not stuck with them has weighed heavily on my heart and mind. I ask myself, "Was there something different I should have done?" I am not the only Sister to ask questions regarding the traditional approach to catechesis or, in our situation, "religion class."

When in 2008, my Mother Superior asked me to continue my studies, I requested if I could concentrate it in the field of catechetics. I wanted to find a better way. As I shared in the introduction, my postgraduate studies at the Franciscan University of Steubenville afforded me time to study deeply the Church's documents and to wrestle with the past and present situation of catechesis. In 2010, I attended an international gathering of catechists in Rome that probed the question of how a catechetical approach inspired by God's divine pedagogy might look. I was enthralled by the discussions and healthy debates. At that time, my doctoral question was just taking shape but I knew I wanted to research the manner in which both the head and the heart could be formed in catechesis.

About this same time, my religious community began to offer formation in the CGS approach. As it was explained to me, CGS was an approach to catechesis that involved "a more contemplative dimension." All full of my new knowledge about the Church's teachings regarding the nature of catechesis, I attended a Level I course training being offered at the college to see how it measured up. I remember saying to my thesis director, a prominent catechetical theorist at the Maryvale Institute in England, "We need to research this approach. I think it has what we are all looking for." And thus, I continued for six more years researching the history of the catechetical movements, going down proverbial "rabbit holes" as to what went wrong in the late scholastic period and what was the issue regarding divine revelation that seems to be the turning point.

I interviewed numerous CGS catechists, desperate to glean from their experience of working with the children. Everyone knew that something was different about CGS, but no one could quite tell me what or why. They would point to one aspect of the approach or another, unaware of catechetical history or polemic debates. They were unaware of the theological and catechetical milieu in which this approach was worked out and how that impacted the choices of Cavalletti and Gobbi. To me, it all mattered. The more I came to study the CGS approach and observe the children in the atrium, the more convinced I became that the approach is precisely God's way of forming his children. It was not until I actually tested this "new" approach that everything in me shifted.

Dominic

I was in my final year of writing the dissertation when I was invited to assist in an atrium that served all three levels. I was asked to sit beside seven-year-old Dominic and assist as he had need. In the course of our time together, Dominic asked me a question about the Blessed Trinity, causing a real existential crisis within me. Do I try to explain in the manner that I always have, shamrock and all? Or do I follow the CGS approach?

Dominic and I were sitting together at the presentation of the Origin of the Eucharist. The lead catechist had asked me to simply sit with him and assist in any way that he needed. I asked him to tell me about his work, which he did. Then he looked up at me and said, "Sister, you know what I don't get?" "No, Dominic. What don't you get?" "I don't get how Jesus is God and the Father is God. Isn't that two Gods?" My eyebrows went up and I took a deep breath. CGS does not teach directly the nature of the Trinity and here was a child asking precisely that question. I had studied Augustine and Aquinas and had taught Trinitarian theology to adults. Perhaps I really could make use of all that apophatic and cataphatic theology to make the mystery of God accessible to children. Before I could attempt a reply, Dominic began again, "You know what else I don't get?" He didn't wait for my response this time, and continued, "I don't get how Jesus could give us his Body at the Last Supper and how we can have it at Mass too." It was clear that this little fellow had been having some serious internal dialogue during all the atrium silence. The thought came to me, "Do it, Sr. Mary Michael. Do it the way Sofia and Gianna would. Trust the research."

And so I began, "Dominic, your questions are very big and very deep. Have you asked the Holy Spirit to tell you how this all works? Let's ask him now." We paused to pray. Then I began again, "What does Jesus say in the Scriptures about this?" He still had his hands on the Mass materials, more or less engaged in that work. I had my Bible in my hand and opened up to John 10:30, a passage I just happened to have bookmarked. "Jesus says here in the Gospel of St. John, 'The Father and I are one.' Elsewhere in the Gospel of John, at the Last Supper, Jesus prays to the Father. Do you remember that passage? In fact, there are a few places in Scripture where Jesus prays to the Father." I stop to see if Dominic's query remained. He paused and looked at me questioningly. "So if Jesus prays to the Father, he can't be the Father, right?" I ask. "Right," Dominic agrees. I say, "But then Jesus says, 'The Father and I are one.' Dominic, this is a very deep mystery and one that many saints, like St. Augustine and St. Thomas Aquinas, have asked." I pause again to see if the little fellow is still with me. I'm starting to panic because I remember

Sofia's admonition to "count your words" and I'm sure my count is up. But Dominic's body and his face convey to me that he is still very much listening—taking it all in—and so I concluded the reflection, "This much we know from what Jesus teaches us: Jesus is God and He and the Father are one. And the Holy Spirit is God but there are not three Gods. We have one God, Father, Son, and Holy Spirit." Dominic looked up and then went back to his work while I remained silent asking the Holy Spirit to help. Then Dominic lifted his head and looked right into my eyes and said, "So *that's* how he does it. That's how he gives us his Body at Mass."

I was not completely sure of the doctrinal *quiddity* of Dominic's insight but I was sure that the Holy Spirit had given an important insight related to Jesus, the Father, and the Holy Spirit being one God and that insight furthered another for Dominic so that he could put together for himself how the Mass is a timeless gift of Jesus. I simply nodded and affirmed, *"Yes. That's how he does it."*

Led by the Child

Sr. Anna Christi Solis, OP, was a Catholic school elementary teacher for several years prior to being trained as a Montessori teacher and a CGS catechist. She was one of our first Sisters to establish a mission in Scotland, where she now serves as a CGS catechist and a CGS Level I formator for catechists in Scotland, Ireland, England, and France. For many years, she has challenged the conventional view of education and especially catechesis, but it was not until her Montessori and CGS training that she began to see that the fundamental shift that has to happen in both Catholic schools and catechesis is for a new understanding of the nature of the child. She shares her story here in hopes that it might inspire others to evaluate their own prejudices against the child.

> I had been an elementary teacher for six years and was constantly seeking to improve the art and science of teaching. A few questions constantly burned in my heart as learned theories of education met with the practical experience of teaching real children:
>
> • I had learned to phrase all my lesson plans with "The student will . . . " But what do you do when the student *won't*?
>
> • How could I introduce children to the grand, overarching vision of God's plan of creation, showing how all knowledge, sacred and secular, is connected to its one creating Source?

• I began to notice how patterns of meaning consistently emerged from literature and history and certain signs, symbols, and stories could powerfully communicate these patterns to children of this age. Had anyone else ever noticed this too?

Several sisters began introducing me to the term *sacramental imagination* and its implications. This resonated with me and I sought to develop lessons that would spark and nurture children's sacramental imagination so as to see the Lord in everything around them, from liturgy and Scripture, to arts and sciences, to daily human interaction.

As a teenager, I had come across a horse trainer who had studied the nature of the horse and developed a method of training consistent with that nature (author's note: the story of Buck Brannaman). The efficacy of this method as I trained my own horse astounded me, and I always wondered if someone had done this same thing for children. Had someone studied the nature of the child and discovered key principles, lessons, and methods that would form children to reach their highest human—natural and supernatural—potential? That summer, as I experienced Catechesis of the Good Shepherd for the first time, my excitement and enthusiasm grew. *Here* was the method.

The Montessori method began by observing the nature of the child and then respecting and following each individual child in the classroom. If the "student won't," the first thing to do is not to judge and seek remedies, but to *observe*: the child, the environment, one's own emotional reactions as a teacher. What is the child's behavior revealing about his human and developmental needs, about the classroom environment and task he's being asked to undertake, about the adult's own needs to appear successful or competent or in control? This method was causing me to see these questions in a new light— and providing answers I had not encountered before.

The *Fettucia* was the work that "smote" me and sold me on the method.[1] As a millennial American in her twenties, I was still discovering my own sense of identity and wondering about my role in God's

---

1. *La Fetuccia* (literally "the ribbon") is a presentation that tells the overview of salvation history beginning with creation and continuing to the Parousia. The ribbon used in this presentation stretches 54 yards, and as the ribbon is stretched out, the catechist tells the Church's story of salvation. The full presentation can last an hour, yet in my experience, the children have never grown weary. It is a deeply satisfying experience of God's providential love for both the children and the catechist.

kingdom with my given history, skills, and personality. The *Fettucia* showed me that everything has been carefully planned and orchestrated by God and that each of us has a unique role to play: from the tiniest trilobite to the greatest world figures. "He has a good plan for me!" I experienced in that presentation a deep personal conviction of being known and loved and called by name to participate with God in writing the "blank page" of today's history. That realization opened up new horizons of confidence and purpose for which I will always be grateful. I couldn't wait to share this presentation with others.

This method, as none other I had encountered, explained and utilized the "method of signs," which I knew to be such a powerful way to reach children's hearts and minds. The only fly in my ointment was the prepared environment. As a poor religious, I had no personal funds, materials, or space to create an atrium. As one of our older sisters gifted me with two prayer cards, "Amen" and "Alleluia," I looked at them through tearful eyes, thinking this would be about all I'd ever have to create an atrium myself. "If I ever have an atrium, I'll call it the Mustard Seed Atrium because these two paper prayer cards are all I've got to start with." I had not yet discovered the vital power of the mustard seed. But the subsequent years have time and again fostered my faith, which is about the size of it!

Fast forward over a decade and that mustard seed grew into a Montessori elementary guide certification, several years of tiny in-class atria in various elementary classrooms in America, then it crossed the ocean to Scotland. There, with the help of my sisters and benefactors, I was able to begin a bona fide 3–6 atrium for the first time: the first for me and the first for that country. I'll never forget when the door rang with the first three-year-old. As I put my hand to the handle, terror gripped my soul, "What if this doesn't work?" Within minutes, I was pleasantly amazed. It *does* work. All the materials and methods actually meet the needs of the three-year-old child. The Level I atrium has consistently been my "happy place" where the children every week astound me with their love, reverence, and growth.

The children have led me to a new place as an adult as well. Following the child through observation, essentiality, and respect, combined with listening to God with children, has been a transformative experience. In my early years as a teacher, I had the idea that I was supposed to be in control of the children. The Montessori Method has taught me that I only have control of myself. God has placed into the child all that he or she needs to develop into an adult; and by the grace of baptism he has called that child into communion with Himself. As the adult in the room, my job is to prepare the environment, observe the child and his or her needs with intelligence and love, and then to be matchmaker between the child and the environment so that the one true teacher, Christ, may do His work both in the child and in me.

This new way of being with children reminds me of something a child once said during the presentation of the Hidden Treasure parable. Responding to my wondering, "Why do you think that man buried the treasure again?" with shining eyes the boy responded, "So someone else could find it!" By controlling my own impulse to over-explain or add my own interpretation to the parable, I had "hidden the treasure" so that he could discover the joy of finding it too!

As other adults come into the room to observe the children, I increasingly notice how their responses reflect attitudes and judgements that I myself once held before discovering the child. Once, a child was cutting all her paper works in half after finishing them. Asking my newly arrived assistant to share her observations of that day with me, I became aware of her judgement of the child's "naughtiness" at cutting the paper. I countered, "I see that the child has a great desire to cut. She doesn't know the importance of her paper so much as her burning inner need to learn how to cut at this stage of her development. So let's make available the cutting work next week so she can meet that need." Sure enough, the next week the child spent over half an hour using the cutting material and then learned how to clean up her work before dancingly putting it away. Her joy testified that we had match-made well. It also opened up the eyes of my assistant, "I am becoming a better person for being here and a better mother. Now I know why my children love to come here." A little child shall lead them.

That same week, a four-year-old who had been in the atrium for over a year finally "normalized." He had come at the age of three with no experience of English or group learning. He required a lot of strong direction during the time he was in the room, which wasn't long because he always insisted on leaving after about half an hour. Rather than wrestle him back, I decided he was probably right: he would eventually come to know and love the atrium as each material opened up to him bit by bit. (This trust in the child and in the method gives a deep peace when I make decisions like this and this trust has never been misplaced, even when I feel embarrassed when a child walks out of the room or the presentation before it would be considered socially acceptable to do so!)

A year later, he was still exhibiting his highly energetic and often disruptive behavior. One day, it occurred to me through observation that, though it would be a year early in the suggested timeframe, I would present the "liturgical calendar" to him. This work became the "key" to the entire atrium for him. After spending a half hour carefully and meticulously manipulating the pieces of that work, he deliberately and carefully walked to the shelf to get materials to make a paper copy of it. Then he set up the model altar and put it away. After that, he worked with the chasubles in the liturgical colors work. The next week, he spent almost 45 minutes with the City of Jerusalem. When he was finished, he copied the paper model and drew a large dragon around it with a cross both on Golgotha and in the center of the city. "Tell me about this picture," I asked this creative child. "The dragon is evil that is trying to destroy the city of Jerusalem. But Jesus on his cross defeated it forever!" Where did this child get all this? This little boy taught me the importance of "following the child," and not making every child conform to a preconceived norm. While not allowing him to destroy the materials or hurt other children during his long year of settling in, he was allowed a certain freedom and respect which has flowered into a joyful and productive encounter with Christ each week in the atrium. All this from a child whom various visiting adults, who had not yet learned to see, labelled as "strange," "troubled," "disruptive," or "a problem."

The CGS approach has changed the way I approach the Lord, the child, and life itself. As I develop initiatives for the new evangelization in my mission in Scotland, including those not related to CGS, I am rooted in the hope founded on the parable of the mustard seed and in the conviction that my role is to prepare the environment and to *match-make* but never to attempt to control. When my prioress general had said to me several years ago, "Sister, I *need* you to learn Catechesis of the Good Shepherd," little did I know then in how many ways it would be true to reply, "Mother, *I* need to learn it."

Led by the Church

Allow me to end where I began. For more than a hundred years, the Church has been engaged in catechetical renewal and for good reason: catechesis is integral to the identity, mission, and vibrancy of the Church herself. The Church exists to evangelize *and to catechize* (see DC, 31). The primary mission of the Church is to make disciples of all nations (Matthew 28:19–20) who know, love, and serve God, and neighbor, with all their heart, mind, soul, and strength (Matthew 22:36–40). Catechesis is not a matter of simply keeping the Church pews full—it's about filling heaven! To paraphrase St. Paul: How are people to be saved if they do not call upon the name of the Lord? (Romans 10:13). And how are they to call upon the Lord if no one teaches who he is?

As we have learned from the history of modern catechesis, not every catechetical approach has proven effective in making true disciples. Some approaches failed to appreciate the true nature of catechetical content, reducing it to religious data while other approaches failed to accept that divine revelation does indeed possess objective doctrine. Still other approaches failed to recognize the true nature of the child, ignoring his or her God-given exigencies that actually serve the child's religious formation.

As I consider the various catechetical initiatives of the past one hundred years and even contemporary ones, I see that there exists in the Catechesis of the Good Shepherd a necessary perichoretic relationship among the theological (content), methodological (method), and anthropological (the child) components of catechesis. The genius of the CGS approach that I have tried to show you throughout this book is that it integrates all three components in a unitive manner. The CGS approach teaches (in the true sense of the word) a particular content to the child, in a particular manner, because the child seeks a particular face of God at particular moments in his or her development. The catechetical triad of the CGS approach is simple: we offer this content using this method because of this child.

With the promulgation of the 2020 *Directory*, the Church continues her efforts to renew catechesis by offering to us a dynamic representation and at times reinterpretation of the nature and goal of catechesis (DC, preface). Catechesis still has only one purpose: to make disciples of our Lord Jesus Christ. For a person to become a disciple of Jesus, she must know him and know his teachings. Such knowledge, when it is truly possessed, necessarily bears fruit in love for Jesus and a willingness to follow his teachings. Knowledge of God and love of God are inseparable—yet the unity of mind and heart will be reached only when catechesis becomes an evangelizing education of the faith. There is a way to catechize others for discipleship—God has shown us the way. God's pedagogy offers to us the principles for an evangelizing education that sparks a desire to know and love him in a manner that fits our nature. The CGS approach demonstrates for us an effective and faithful application of these principles. It is my hope and prayer that this book will help catechists to expand their view of religious knowledge and religious experience; expand their view of the mystery of God and the mystery of the child; expand their view of education, teaching, and learning, so as to embrace a catechetical pedagogy that leads children (and the childlike) to a fullness of life in God's Kingdom.

ACKNOWLEDGMENTS

Though this book bears my name and is indeed my work, I am keenly aware that it would not have come to fruition without the generous contribution of many others who share a similar passion for catechesis, and in particular, the catechesis of children.

First among them are Claudia Petursson, Sr. Maria Joseph Cabiniss-Brown, Mary Mirrione, Kevin Thornton, and Michaela Tudela. Without Claudia's initial push to publish and her skilled editing assistance, my dissertation would have remained on a library shelf in England collecting dust. Sr. Maria Joseph served as my religious community's editor, providing critical feedback as well as needed assistance with Latin translations. Particular thanks goes to Mary Mirrione, who not only funded my CGS library, but also continued to help me navigate its treasures. Mary shared generously of her experience and wisdom gained from many years of being with children in the atrium. I thank the editors at LTP, Kevin Thornton and Michaela Tudela, who carried the book to its final publication. They provided the constant reassurance that a new author needed: "This a good book, Sister." My gratitude extends as well to Sean Garvey, Maggie Radzik, and Emily Barry Sullivan, who read an initial draft of the book and offered both encouragement and suggestions for development.

Several scholars and experts in the field provided important insight into the various aspects of catechesis: Fr. Andrew Hoefer, OP (on the nature of divine revelation), Petroc Willey (on the nature of God's pedagogy), Sr. Maria Teresita Rodkey, OP (on the nature of the child according to Montessori), Sr. Anna Wray, OP (on the nature of knowledge according to Aristotle), Fr. Vivian Boland, OP (on the nature of teaching according to St. Thomas Aquinas), Sr. Anna Christi Solis, OP, Sr. Thomas More Stepnowski (on the nature of the imagination and the role of wonder), and Gerard O'Shea (on the nature of catechesis as an educational activity). Patricia Coulter and Rebekah Rojcewicz also must be recognized for their English translation of Cavalletti and Gobbi's works from Italian. Where this book is concerned, G. K. Chesterton's words couldn't be more true: "We stand on the shoulders of giants."

Thank you to a "cast of thousands" with whom I tested the insights proposed in this book, particularly the *perichoretic* nature of catechesis that I find in the Catechesis of the Good Shepherd approach. Several deserve special recognition for repeated conversations: Sr. Thomas Aquinas Halbmaier, Sr. Mary Brigid Burnham, Sr. Andrea Marie Graham, Sr. Mary Dominic Pitts, Sr. Mary Thomas Huffman, Sr. Jane Dominic Laurel, Sr. Mary Seton Cebrowski, Sr. Anna Christi Solis, Sr. Theresa Anne Knuth, and Sr. Maria Teresita Rodkey. It is no small matter to propose a Copernican change in catechetical practice, and my Dominican Sisters have provided an assurance that in moving forward, I am grounded in the Church's ancient tradition.

My deepest thanks to my religious community of St. Cecilia, especially those in the novitiate and the infirmary, who have carried my research and this book in their prayers for several years. Mother Ann Marie Karlovic, OP, and Mother Anna Grace Neenan, OP, gave me permission and support to write the book. The sisters with whom I have lived at Our Lady Queen of Preachers and Bethany Retreat House carried many of my practical responsibilities so that I could have time to write. Thank you to each one of you for carrying your loads and mine. Here, I must also include my "St. Joe Fellas" who volunteer at Bethany and helped me with all my landscaping projects. You have allowed this Dominican to spend more time at the desk than in the dirt.

I am grateful for my Fox and Huffman family who have supported me in this endeavor to become an author. I am especially grateful to my sister, Chris, who had been my constant cheerleader. Chris succumbed to breast cancer as this book was in its last stages of production, and I believe that her industrious nature and her sufferings contributed to its final push. Chris, may you rest in the peace of the Good Shepherd's love.

Finally, this book would never have come to be without Sofia and Gianna. The Catechesis of the Good Shepherd is the fruit of their gifted intelligence and profound humility. May every catechist follow the Holy Spirit, the Church, and the Child as did they.

APPENDIXES

APPENDIX A

Sample Presentation of the Blue Unity Strip

Title: Blue Unity Strip

Subject: History of the Kingdom of God

Age: 6+ (fairly soon after La Fettuccia)

Liturgical Time: Ordinary Time

Sources:

- Genesis 1:1, 1:27; Luke 2:11, 24:5; 1 Corinthians 15:22 (15:27)
- *Religious Potential of the Child 2* pp. 15–18, 85–87
- *Catechism of the Catholic Church* §282–315, 571–601, 671–674
- Formation Leader

Doctrinal Content: God has a plan for salvation, which has three key moments: Creation, Redemption, and Parousia. In God's great plan he desires to bring all people to the fullness of life in his kingdom. God also has invited people to cooperate in writing the History of the Kingdom of God.

Direct Aim: To enrich the child's knowledge of the most essential moments of the History of the Kingdom of God, its vastness and unity, through their personal work with the materials.

Indirect Aims:

- To encourage independent learning of the history of the Kingdom of God
- To increase appreciation for Sacred Scripture
- To lead to a fuller participation in the liturgy
- To prepare for further work
- To increase interest in the sciences and the natural world

Materials:

1st Moment—blue unity control strip, Bible, cushion, candle, matches, snuffer, weights, title strip (The History of the Kingdom of God)

2nd Moment—blue mute strip; basket that includes the following salvation history images: beginning of universe, galaxy, earth, single-celled creature, trees, flowers, grass, various animals (of sea, land, and air), man, heart and hands, cross with star/comet, blank page, earth with cross; Scripture verses, four word cards: Creation, Redemption, Parousia, current year, and four arrows.

NOTE to CATECHIST: *Leave the blue unity control strip timeline rolled up until it is presented. Then it should be accessible on the wall always so that the children can remove it or work under it.*

Moments of the Presentation: (NOTE: Only the 1st Moment is offered here.)

1st Moment: with the Control Strip:

Overview of this Moment: Recall the theme of the history of the Kingdom of God. Lay the rolled-up Blue Unity Strip on floor, placing weights (such as bean bags) at the beginning to hold it in place. Lay Bible on cushion before the strip. Set the candle by Bible and light the candle, saying, "Jesus said, 'I am the Light of the World.'" Slowly unroll unity strip, from Creation onward, noticing pictures and inviting the children one at a time to help read the text aloud. Discuss pictures and ask questions about them. Point out Creation, Redemption, and Parousia arrows. When the strip is fully rolled out, place weights at end of strip. Lay title "The History of the Kingdom of God" above the strip. Allow children a few moments to meditate. Blue Unity Strip should be displayed on wall in Atrium at eye level of children.

Introduction:

- Invite the children: get the materials with them and name the work.

- Catechist's narrative: (Briefly recall La Fettuccia and what they remember about the History of the Kingdom of God.) "And we said God has a great plan that goes on for thousands of years. It's called Salvation History. And where do we learn of this History? In the Holy Bible. History tells past events and helps us to know who we are and where we come from. Salvation History tells us who we are, where we came from, and what is to come. Do you remember the three moments in the History of the Kingdom of God? (Creation, Redemption, Parousia) I want you to look for those three moments in this work."

[Orient the children to the Blue Unity Strip by unrolling it a little at a time, reading and discussing what they see and hear. Unroll it starting at creation.]

- Catechist's narrative: "In La Fettuccia, each rib of the ribbon was about one thousand years. On this strip each rib is about ten thousand years! We will have things to read and see on this strip. We have the arrow with the word "Creation" and this symbol (comet) is what we use for creation. Did anything exist before the moment of creation?"

[Read text below symbol.]

- Catechist's narrative: "We've read about this in the Holy Bible. This symbol (Scripture book picture) tells us this statement is from the Holy Bible. Who can read the Scripture from this symbol? And, what color is our ribbon? The blue reminds us of the material world. Some think the first life was microscopic organisms. Life and all things were mixed together."

[Read strip below earth symbol.]

- Catechist's narrative: "We know earth, oceans, mountains, valleys, moon, planets, star, clouds, sun. God put everything that was needed in its place. Without the sun we couldn't survive. Water, all living things need water. Just one kind of water? No, there are all kinds: oceans, rivers, streams, ponds, snow, and ice."

[Unroll more to microscopic organism and read. Color of ribbon changes to tan.]

- Catechist narrative: "The tan ribbon stands for life. This was the moment life appeared; scientists think it started with single-celled organisms. And who was guiding that formation? God. This took so much time unfolding. It took tens of thousands of years."

[Unroll to vegetation pictures and read.]

- Catechist's narrative: "Not just one kind of plant, but many kinds: grass, trees, flowers. What are your favorites? Not just any one kind of all those. Plant life even grew in the water."

[Unroll to animals and read animals statement.]

- Catechist's narrative: "Animals live in water, air, and land. Is there just one kind of animal? No, many kinds! What are your favorites?"

[Unroll to next strip, read strip, and Scripture symbol.]

- Catechist's narrative: "The moment in which the first human beings were created. God gave human beings a mind to think with and a heart to love with. He also gave us hands to do good with. And, since then, people have been using their mind and hands to care for themselves and others, especially their children—and to make life better for themselves and others, especially their children. When the first man and woman were created, they looked at everything around them and asked, 'Who has prepared all this for us?'"

[Unroll to yellow portion.]

- Next we see the second moment, the Redemption.
- In the Bible we read, [read text of Scripture symbol].
- The moment of Redemption is when God sends his greatest gift: Jesus. Jesus becomes like a bridge between God and man, making it possible for man to become friends of God.

[Read next strip statement and point to comet star.]

- Catechist narrative: "This is the symbol we use for redemption. The yellow reminds us of the light and life of the risen Christ spreading throughout the world. When did we receive the light? (Baptism)"

[Point to white section and blank page symbol.]

- Catechist narrative: "Now we have a blank page because we don't know what the history of the Kingdom of God will be like in the next hour, week, or year. This is where we are right now. (Point to where yellow and white meet.) We are writing this page with God right now."

[Unroll remainder of strip.]

- Catechist narrative: "And we are waiting for this third moment called the Parousia. This symbol (point to world with yellow cross) is what we use for Parousia."

[Read the Scripture with the moment of Parousia.]

- Catechist narrative: "We see the light of Christ goes on and on. It will never end because we have an immortal soul."

[Read last Scripture card.]

- Catechist narrative: "Perhaps as we go throughout the week we can think, 'How is God inviting me to help write on the blank page? What will the moment of Parousia be like?'"

Reflection: Allow time for the children to ponder, discuss and share about things on the Blue Unity Strip. Possible questions for leading the child's reflection: "In looking back, was there something new you learned? Why did God create all this?"

Prayerful Response: Allow time for silence, song, and prayer.

Restore Materials: If the children do not want to work with the strip right away, you can show them how to put it up on the wall.

Catechist's Observations/Reflections:

APPENDIX B

Blank page free art response to the presentation on The Gifts of God

The direct aim of this presentation is to lift up the history of the Kingdom of God as a history of God's manifold gift-giving, which culminates in the Eucharist. The child will ponder, enjoy, and now personally respond by writing his or her blank page with God. After considering the story of the many gifts of God, the child is invited to ask herself which of the gifts given to her is the greatest, which is most enjoyed. One way of aiding the child's reflection is the free art response such as the sample offered by Rebecca (age 9).

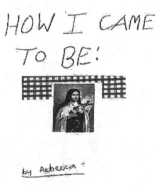

Appendix C

The History of God and My Place in It

Subject: The History of the Kingdom of God
Age: 11+
Liturgical Time: non-specific (usually at the end of child's time in the atrium)
Sources:

- RPC II Ch.1–6 pp. 13–41
- HKG 1 Ch.1–5 pp. 1–15, Ch.41 pp. 136–139
- LV Ch.5, p. 34
- www.cgsusa.org–members only; Level III Materials Manual
- *CCC* 50–53, 54–73
- Notes from Level III Adult Formation: Anna Hurdle June 2021

Doctrinal Content:

- The History of the Kingdom of God: from creation to the covenant with the Jewish people, the Incarnation of Jesus, his death and Resurrection and the birth and growth of the Church, to modern times, is a history of God's gifts and human response to those gifts. Each person has a role in the plan of God, responding to his unique gifts to each of us by building the Kingdom, preparing the Parousia.

Direct Aim:

- To lift up the key moments of the History of the Kingdom of God and ponder my own unique response and contribution to it.

Indirect Aims:

- To foster a sense of personal vocation in the Kingdom of God.
- To educate to hope in the Parousia.

Description of Materials:

- Booklet/Timeline: The History of the Kingdom of God and My Place in It
  - Text for each page of booklet/timeline
  - Patterns for drawings
- Basket or tray for needed supplies (optional)

Moments of the Presentation:

First Moment

Introduction:
- Gather a group of children who are nearing the end of their time in the atrium.

- Linking point: "Ever since you started in the atrium, we've been thinking of the Kingdom of God." Recall with the children the Fettucia, the Plan of God, the Incarnation and Christ's presence today in the Word and the Sacraments: "We've received so many gifts."

- Then say: "We've also seen people's responses to the gifts. Some have been recorded, most have not, but we know people have responded to God's gifts." Recall together some of the responses to God's invitation and gifts, such as Mary's, Moses', the prophets', and so on. Then say: "And think of all the contributions people have made. We don't even know all of them! Perhaps you have already made a contribution to the Kingdom of God. I bet you have. You may not even know it or think about it."

Showing of Material:
- Say: "We're going to make a book. You don't have to show it to anyone, though of course you may. It is a big work and may take a couple of sessions. You can copy the pictures or make your own."

- Unroll the timeline or book to show the children.

Reflection:
- Give children space and time to complete reading and recording the answers to the questions on the timeline in their journals.

- At the end of the time, say: "Would anyone like to share something about this?"

Restoration of the material and invitation to work with the material.
- Reassure the children: "You can continue to think about this."

The Work of the Child:
- Work to make the book.

- Prayer response or prayer art.

Notes for the Catechist:

Observations and Reflections:

GLOSSARY

Atrium: An area usually attached to the church building to allow for easy access to the Church's liturgical life. In the first century, the atrium was the place of religious instruction for the catechumens. The CGS atrium is a sacred space uniquely designed for the spiritual growth of the child. In the atrium, children have the opportunity to interact directly with materials that aid their meditation of divine truths.

Curriculum: The central guide for all educators on what is essential for teaching and learning, so that every student has access to rigorous academic experiences.

Epistemology: The philosophical study of the nature, origin, and limits of human knowledge. The term is derived from the Greek *epistēmē* ("knowledge") and *logos* ("reason"), and accordingly, the field is sometimes referred to as the theory of knowledge.

Existential: Though it has been used to describe a particular school of philosophy or system of ideas that gives no real meaning to the created world, the term *existential* simply refers to existence. The fact that we exist, we are *existential*. Catechesis must be attentive to the lived reality of the people it serves or it will continue on the trajectory of abstraction whereby only facts are offered and not the Person of Jesus Christ.

Exigency: A *life-force* that God has instilled in the human person that enables us to flourish. After studying the life-forces of children, Dr. Maria Montessori created an educational pedagogy that corresponds with the child's exigencies, thereby assisting the child's natural and supernatural development.

Kerygma: The proclamation of the Gospel in its essential form. Though expressed in a variety of ways, the fundamental *kerygma* is: "We are sinners. In His love, Jesus, the Son of God, offered his life to save us from sin. God's grace enables us to live in freedom. Repent and believe in His word."

Liturgical catechesis: In the liturgy, especially in the holy sacrifice of the Eucharist, we participate in God's work of our redemption. Our full participation in the liturgy is augmented when we understand the meaning of its signs and symbols. Liturgical catechesis thus aims to initiate people into the mystery of Christ "by proceeding from the visible to the invisible, from the sign to the signified, from the sacrament to the mysteries" (CCC, 1075).

Modernism/Modernist heresy: A full definition of modernism would be difficult to give. The common desire of modernists is to meet the intellectual, moral, and social needs of a current generation by changing the teachings of Catholicism. It opposes Our Lord's desire that the Church be a leaven in a society that left to its own demise will come to reject God's natural and divine law.

Nouvelle théologie: A theological *ressourcement* (return to the sources). The movement was criticized as a new theology, but in fact, the result was a greater study of the Scriptures, the Church Fathers, and the original writings of St. Thomas Aquinas. The term, meaning "new theology," is in fact a misnomer.

On-going revelation: The theory of *on-going revelation* and *evolution of dogmas* suggests that God continues to give new revelation and, as such, doctrines that held true for one generation could completely change in a subsequent generation. The theories of evolution of dogmas and on-going revelation reject the notion of objective doctrine, suggesting instead that a person's understanding or experience of God can contradict the teachings of the Church.

Parousia: A technical theological term that refers to the Second Coming of Jesus Christ. Drawing from the Our Father prayer, the term is used in the CGS approach to include the establishment of God's Kingdom on earth, as it is in Heaven, and thus refers to a present reality of God in our life and in our world even as we move toward that final coming.

Pedagogy: An educational term, understood as the art or science of teaching. It comprises two words: *paidos*, which means "child," and *agogos*, which means "to lead." A conceptual definition of *pedagogy*, then, would be "to lead the child."

Perichoresis: St. John Damascene used the Greek word *perichore-sis*—"peri" (around) and "choresis" (dance)—to describe the inner life of the Blessed Trinity, as something of an *interpenetrating dance* among the three Divine Persons.

Ressourcement: To "re-source" or return to the sources. In the years prior to the Second Vatican Council, a number of theologians saw the need for theological studies to return to the sources of theology, namely the contemplation of the Scriptures.

Scholasticism: A method of studying theology and philosophy taught in medieval European universities during the sixth through fifteenth centuries. Its "Golden Age" was the thirteenth and fourteenth centuries. Based on Aristotelian logic and the writings of the early Church Fathers, it had a strong emphasis on tradition and dogma.

INDEX

Moran, Gabriel 7, 10, 38ff, 80

Narratio (the) 14, 30ff, 53–54, 58
Nouvelle théologie 15, 26–28, 82

Orthodoxy-orthopraxis 88, 90
O'Shea, Gerard 23n 53 87n 146n

Parenesis 99, 189
Parousia 101
Pedagogy (paideia) 9, 22, 43, 51–52,
    165
    See also curriculum, education
Pedagogy of God (divine pedagogy)
    47ff, 138, 165
Perichoresis / perichoretic xiii, 4, 167,
    177, 195
Pius X
    See also Catechetical movements
Plan of Salvation 47, 100
    See also catechetical content,
    narratio, parousia

Quizzes
    See Assessment, Memory

Religious knowledge / Religious
    experience 3ff, 9, 13, 16–17,
    38, 48, 55–56, 81, 85, 87, 95,
    108, 163

Sacred Scripture 65, 86
Scholasticism 10ff, 23, 28, 91, 192
Silence 24, 48, 50, 77, 123, 129, 171,
    180, 185, 192

Spiral Method (the) 158, 172, 188
Sower Method (the) 20
Stages of (Human) Development 1109,
    113, 128

Tradition (Sacred)
    See deposit of faith
Teaching
    See education, intellect, knowledge
Tests
    See Assessment, Memory
Typology 95ff

Unitive approach 195, 222

Vagaggini, Cipriano 28, 55, 61, 68–69

Wonder 12, 59, 100, 133, 147, 155ff,
    170, 174
    See also child, CGS content,
    education, knowledge

Zakar (zikkaron)
    See memorial
Zolli, Eugenio 61ff

ABOUT THE AUTHOR

Sister Mary Michael Fox, OP, has been a member of the Dominican Sisters of St. Cecilia (Nashville) for over thirty years. During that time, she has been blessed to teach all ages from three to ninety-three. She received a master of arts degree in education from Northwestern State University and a master of arts degree in theology with a specialization in catechetics from Franciscan University. Sister Mary Michael conducted research in the field of catechetics at the Maryvale Institute of Birmingham, England, and holds a PHD through Liverpool-Hope University in Liverpool, England. She has published articles in *The Sower*, *Catechetical Review*, and *Catechist*. Sister Mary Michael serves as a catechetical consultant and is a popular speaker at catechetical conferences.